⊛REI
STAM
AUSTrALIA

GW00707676

Edited by Alan B. Pitt

This comprehensive guide to Australian Stamp Values contains over 2,000 colour photographs, and thousands of valuations.

This book is a must for all collectors, whether you are just beginning or an advanced collector.

Latest information compiled on computer databases ensures up to date accuracy of pricing. Quality reproduction of photos makes it easy to identify items.

Due to renewed collector interest in the early stamps of Australia, those from the six Colonial States have been included in this edition. This addition will make this guide complete. Plus NEW Australia Post issues, and Australian Antarctic Territories through to 30/06/08.

RENNIKS
PUBLICATIONS

Unit 3, 37-39 Green Street
Banksmeadow NSW 2019

ISBN   0 978 0 9752245 88

National Library of Australia Cataloguing-in-Publication entry

Title: Stamps of Australia : the stamp collectors reference guide
                  / editor, Alan B. Pitt

Edition: 11th ed.

ISBN: 9780975224588 (pbk.)

Subjects: Postage stamps--Australia--Catalogues
                  Stamp collecting--Australia--Catalogues

Other Authors
/Contributors: Pitt, Alan B.

Dewey Number: 769. 560994

Printed and bound through Printciple Source, Australia

STAMPS OF AUSTRALIA

11th Edition in full COLOUR

with **AUSTRALIAN ANTARCTIC TERRITORY.**
NOW containing **AUSTRALIAN COLONIAL STATE STAMPS FROM 1850.**
Contains **ALL issues to June 2008**

Includes illustrations and/or values for: (page)

EDITOR:
Alan B Pitt

INTRODUCTION

This publication is a simplified guide showing current values, at date of publication, Australian and Australian Antarctic Territory postage stamps. General information on each issue is given but not specialised details - perforations, watermarks, method of printing etc. For further, more detailed information, please refer to a specialised catalogue such as the Stanley Gibbons British Commonwealth Stamp Catalogue.

Values

In every instance, values quoted are for the most common variety for that particular issue. Every reasonable effort has been made to make values in this catalogue as accurate, realistic and up to date as possible at date of publication. Sources for pricing information are derived from stamp dealers published lists-advertisements-auction realisations and prices solicited from selected dealers.

Minimum Values

The minimum stamp value in this catalogue of .30c represents the cost to a stamp dealer to maintain an inventory and supply to a collector on demand a single copy of even the most common stamp in fault free condition. The comparable minimum for a First Day Cover is $1 which more accurately reflects a dealers cost of doing business than the scarcity of the cover itself.

PreDecimal Values (pre 12/2/66)

MUH MintUnHinged - undamaged, never hinged
MLH MintLightlyHinged - undamaged
FU FineUsed - clear round cancellations with full perforations - heavy cancellations are worth less.

PreDecimal First Day Cover Values :

Values quoted for pre 1935 covers are for plain covers with handwritten or typewritten addresses. Post 1935 cover values are for covers with typewritten addresses (hand addressed worth slightly less). It should be understood that all covers should be in good condition with clear circular cancellations with stamp(s) tied by postmark to cover.

Decimal Values (post 12/2/66)

MUH MintUnHinged - undamaged, never hinged
FU FineUsed - clear round cancellations with full perforations - heavy cancellations are worth less.

Values for Decimal First Day Covers:

Unaddressed covers - addressed covers are generally worth the value of the stamps affixed.

Self Adhesive Type issues

Also referred to as "peel and stick" types. These stamps were first introduced on 23rd August 1989. They differ from the standard stamp as follows: heavier white edging and larger perforations on the self adhesive stamps. Values are similar.

Australian Antarctic Territory Values

All Australian Antarctic Territory mint stamps are listed in MUH and FU condition only.

Condition

Please understand that many early issues were badly centred - values quoted, in each case, are for reasonably centred stamps - the design may be slightly off centre.

Early issues which are well centred are worth a premium - in some cases are as high as 40% off the values shown. This is applicable to **MUH** and **FU** Postmarked stamps with exceptionally fine cancellations but otherwise in a sound condition are worth less than the **FU** values shown.

Listing.

Generally stamps are listed in chronological order. There are exceptions in early definitives issued over a long period - for convenience these have been grouped together.

Officials

Overprinted OS and perforated OS are listed and priced.

Check boxes □

These are shown to the right of the values. Collectors are able to check off stamps already in their possession.

Note

The publisher of this book is NOT a stamp dealer and is unable to identify or value stamps. He will not accept responsibility for stamps sent to him for this purpose. Please mention the catalogue by name when purchasing Australian or AAT stamps from your dealer.

Acknowledgments

Stamps illustrated are reproduced with the permission of Australia Post. The publisher wishes to thank them also for their helpful assistance.

With the inclusion of the Early Colonial State stamps we must thank Richard Juzwin Pty. Limited for provision of scans together with valuations. Seven Seas Stamps Pty. Ltd. must also be thanked for the use of their numbering system for all the Colonial issues

Colonial Stamps of Australia, and their values.

Introductory notes

New South Wales was the first Australian colony to adopt prepayment of postage with adhesive stamps. On 1 January 1850 'Sydney View' stamps were issued featuring the colony's Great Seal, dating from 1792. Locally printed from hand-engraved copper plates, the Sydney View stamps were soon replaced by the 'Laureates', depicting a more conventional image of Queen Victoria's profile. These primitive stamps gave way to stamps produced in England, as a means of having better protection against forgeries; engraved issues by Perkins Bacon in 1854 and eight years later letterpress stamps by De La Rue. New South Wales made a significant departure from tradition in 1888-89 with the issue of the Centennial series. They were the world's first commemorative stamps, although the Centennial issues remained on sale like normal definitive stamps.

NEW SOUTH WALES HISTORY
IMPERFORATED ISSUES

1850 Sydney Views

ASC		Mint	Average Used
		$	$
1	1d Red (No clouds)	7500 ▫	375 ▫
1a	1a Red on blue	7500 ▫	325 ▫
1d	1d Red (Clouds)	7500 ▫	325 ▫
1c	1d Red on blue	7500 ▫	325 ▫
2	2d Blue	5000 ▫	225 ▫
2a	2d Blue on Blue	5000 ▫	225 ▫
3	3d Green	7500 ▫	275 ▫
2a	Green on Blue	7500 ▫	275 ▫

1851 Laureate Issues

4	1d Red	1750 ▫	275 ▫
4a	1d Red on Blue	1750 ▫	50 ▫
4b	1d Orange	450 ▫	50 ▫
5	2d Blue on Blue	300 ▫	35 ▫
5a	2d Blue	300 ▫	20 ▫
6	3d Green on Blue	3000 ▫	175 ▫
6a	3d Green	475 ▫	30 ▫
7	6d Brown	4000 ▫	875 ▫
7a	6d Brown on Blue	4000 ▫	325 ▫
8	8d Orange on Blue	10,000 ▫	625 ▫

1854 Diadem Issues (Large)

9	5d Green	3000 ▫	1500▫
10	6d Grey	1000 ▫	100▫
10a	6d Brown	1250 ▫	75▫
10b	6d Green	1250 ▫	100▫
11	8d Orange	20,000 ▫	2250▫
12	1/- Red	2250 ▫	150▫

ASC		Mint	Average Used
		$	$

1856 Registration Issues

13	6d Red & Blue	2000 ▫	1/5▫
13b	6d Orange & Blue	2000 ▫	225 ▫
13c	6d Orange & Blue On Blue	2250 ▫ / 225 ▫	225 ▫

NEW SOUTH WALES
PERFORATED ISSUES

1856 Diadem Issues (Small)

14	1d Red	325 ▫	30 ▫
14	1d Orange	325 ▫	25 ▫
15	2d Blue	250 ▫	20 ▫
16	3d Green	1250 ▫	125 ▫

1860 Diadem Issues

17	1d Red	175 ▫	25 ▫
17a	1d Orange	275 ▫	40 ▫
18	2d Blue	325 ▫	25 ▫
19	3d Green	20 ▫	5 ▫
20	5d Green	20 ▫	10 ▫
21	6d Brown	750 ▫	100 ▫
21a	6d Violet	275 ▫	20 ▫
21b	6d Grey	750 ▫	175 ▫
22	8d Orange	550 ▫	100 ▫
22a	8d Yellow	275 ▫	30 ▫
23	1/- Red	275 ▫	20 ▫

1860 "Coin" Issue

24	5/- Purple	100 ▫	30 ▫

1860 Registration Issues

25	6d Red on Blue	375 ▫	75 ▫
25a	6d Orange on Blue	475 ▫	150 ▫

ASC catalogue numbers referred to in this colonies listing are numbers published by Seven Seas Stamps and used with their kind permission.

NO.	DESCRIPTION	MUH	FU	NO.	DESCRIPTION	MUH	FU
ASC		Mint Average Used		ASC		Mint	Average Used
		$	$			$	$

1862-84 Various Types

26	1d Red	40 ☐	15 ☐
26a	1d Brown	125 ☐	25 ☐
26b	1d Orange	50 ☐	15 ☐
27	2d Blue	30 ☐	8 ☐
28	4d Brown	90 ☐	20 ☐
29	6d Lilac	100 ☐	20 ☐
30	10d Lilac	25 ☐	20 ☐
31	1/- Black	150 ☐	30 ☐

1885 Overprinted "OS"

-	5/- Green & Violet reprinted (CTO)		750 ☐
47	10/- Red & Violet	5000 ☐	2250 ☐
-	10/- Reprint (CTO) or Specimen	2000 ☐	375 ☐
48	£1 Red & violet	25,000 ☐	12,500☐

1871 Surcharge

32	9d ib 10d Brown	25 ☐	25 ☐
	Double Opt	375 ☐	

1888 Centenary of New South Wales

49	1d Mauve	5 ☐	5 ☐
50	2d Blue	5 ☐	5 ☐
51	4d Brown	15 ☐	6 ☐
52	6d Red	50 ☐	10 ☐
52a	6d Green	50 ☐	25 ☐
52b	6d Yellow	40 ☐	20 ☐
52c	6d Orange	20 ☐	10 ☐
53	8d Magenta	30 ☐	15 ☐
54	1/-Chocolate	25 ☐	15 ☐
55	5/- Violet	375 ☐	100 ☐
56	20/- Blue	375 ☐	150 ☐

1854-71 Overprinted "OS"

In Black or Red

33	1d Red	25☐	10 ☐
33a	1d Brown/Red	25☐	12 ☐
34	2d Blue	20☐	15 ☐
35	3d Green(black)	15 ☐	12 ☐
35a	3d Green (red)	2000☐	750 ☐
36	4d Brown	25 ☐	15 ☐
37	5d Green	30☐	40 ☐
38	6d Lilac	30☐	20 ☐
39	8d Yellow (black)	35☐	30 ☐
39a	8d Yellow (red)	3750☐	750 ☐
40	9d on 10d Brown	1750 ☐	1250 ☐
41	10d Lilac	475☐	275 ☐
42	1/- Black (red)	60☐	35 ☐
43	5/- Purple	430☐	150 ☐

1888 Overprinted "OS"

57	1d Mauve	10 ☐	10 ☐
58	2d Blue	10 ☐	10 ☐
59	4d Brown	20 ☐	15 ☐
60	6d Red	20 ☐	15 ☐
61	8d Magenta	30 ☐	30 ☐
62	1/- Chocolate	35 ☐	20 ☐
63	5/- Violet (black)	350 ☐	200 ☐
63a	5/- Violet (red)	5000 ☐	1250 ☐
64	20/- Blue	4500 ☐	750 ☐

1885 Revenue stamps overprinted "POSTAGE" in black or blue

44	5/- Green & Violet	1250 ☐	375 ☐
45	10/- Red & Violet (blue)	375 ☐	60 ☐
45a	10/- Red & Violet (black)	2250 ☐	425 ☐
46	1 Red & Violet (black)	8500 ☐	7500 ☐
46a	1 Red & Violet (blue)	7500 ☐	5000 ☐

1890

65	2½ Blue	20 ☐	10 ☐

1891 Surcharges

66	½d on 1d Grey	20 ☐	20 ☐
67	7½d on 6d Brown	15 ☐	20 ☐
68	1/0½d on 1/- Red	20 ☐	25 ☐

NO.	DESCRIPTION	MUH	FU
ASC		Mint	Average Used
		$	$

1892-1910

NO.	DESCRIPTION	Mint $	Average Used $
69	½d Grey	10 ☐	10 ☐
69a	½d Grey	5 ☐	5 ☐
70	1d Red	5 ☐	2 ☐
71	2d Blue	5 ☐	4 ☐
72	2½d Violet	30 ☐	15 ☐
72a	2½d Blue	12 ☐	10 ☐
73	2/6d Green	75 ☐	50 ☐

1890-92
Overprinted "OS"

NO.	DESCRIPTION	Mint $	Average Used $
74	½d Grey	15 ☐	20 ☐
75	½d on 1d Grey	125 ☐	125 ☐
76	2½d Blue	20 ☐	25 ☐
77	7½d on 6d Brown	70 ☐	75 ☐
78	1/0½d on 1/- Red	100 ☐	100 ☐

1897
Consumptive Home
– Charity

NO.	DESCRIPTION	Mint $	Average Used $
79	1d (1/-) Green&Brown	40 ☐	40 ☐
80	2½d (2/6d) Red Blue & Gold	250 ☐	200 ☐

1903
"Commonwealth"

NO.	DESCRIPTION	Mint $	Average Used $
81	9d Brown & Blue	20 ☐	15 ☐

NO.	DESCRIPTION	MUH	FU
ASC		Mint	Average Used
		$	$

POSTAGE DUES

NO.	DESCRIPTION	Mint $	Average Used $
D1	½d Green	10 ☐	8 ☐
D2	1d Green	20 ☐	4 ☐
D3	2d Green	25 ☐	5 ☐
D4	3d Green	50 ☐	15 ☐
D5	4d Green	30 ☐	10 ☐
D6	6d Green	50 ☐	15 ☐
D7	8d Green	125 ☐	25 ☐
D8	5/- Green	225 ☐	25 ☐
D9	10/-Green	425 ☐	100 ☐
D10	20/-Green	575 ☐	150 ☐

Queensland was the last Australian colony to issue stamps, this being the result of Queensland's separation from New South Wales in 1859. The following year the first Queensland stamps arrived from England and after being placed on sale, Queensland stamps replaced those of New South Wales. Being named after Queen Victoria, it was appropriate that all of Queensland's stamps featured the Queen's portrait. For many years, the Chalon portrait depicting a very young Queen was used on the stamps. For the most part Queensland's stamps were printed locally using engraved steel plates supplied by the London printers Perkins Bacon. Later, stamps featuring a profile of the Queen were printed letterpress in Brisbane.

QUEENSLAND HISTORY IMPERFORATED ISSUES

1860 Chalons

NO.	DESCRIPTION	Mint $	Average Used $
1	1d Red	5000 ☐	1500 ☐
2	2d Blue	20,000 ☐	4000 ☐
3	6d Green	10,000 ☐	1800 ☐

PERFORATED ISSUES

1860-81 Chalons

NO.	DESCRIPTION	Mint $	Average Used $
4	1d Red	125 ☐	30 ☐
4a	1d Orange	100 ☐	20 ☐
4b	1d Pink	175 ☐	40 ☐
5	2d Blue	50 ☐	5 ☐
6	3d Brown	75 ☐	15 ☐
6a	3d Grey-green	225 ☐	25 ☐
7	4d Lilac	500 ☐	30 ☐
7a	4d Yellow	1500 ☐	50 ☐
8	6d Green	150 ☐	10 ☐
9	1/- Purple	100 ☐	10 ☐
9a	1/- Grey	575 ☐	60 ☐
9b	1/- Olive	750 ☐	150 ☐
10	2/- Blue	200 ☐	50 ☐
11	2/6d Red	325 ☐	150 ☐
12	5/- Rose	750 ☐	250 ☐
12a	5/- Brown	350 ☐	150 ☐
13	10/- Brown	950 ☐	325 ☐
14	20/- Rose	2500 ☐	475 ☐

NO.	DESCRIPTION	MUH	FU
ASC		Mint	Average Used
		$	$

1861
Registration stamp

15	(6d) Yellow	200 ☐	75 ☐

1879-80

16	1d Brown	125 ☐	30 ☐
16a	1d Orange	75 ☐	20 ☐
16b	1d Red	50 ☐	20 ☐
17	2d Blue	90 ☐	20 ☐
18	4d Yellow	350 ☐	35 ☐
19	6d Green	125 ☐	15 ☐
20	1/- Mauve	125 ☐	20 ☐

1880 Surcharge

21	½d on 1d Brown	375 ☐	275 ☐

1882-86
Large Chalon

22	2/- Blue	150 ☐	50 ☐
23	2/6d Vermillion	60 ☐	40 ☐
24	5/- Red	75 ☐	30 ☐
25	10/- Brown	125 ☐	40 ☐
26	£1 Green	225 ☐	75 ☐

1882-95
Various Types

27	½d Green	20 ☐	10 ☐
28	1d Orange	5 ☐	2 ☐
29	2d Blue	15 ☐	2 ☐
30	2½d Red	20 ☐	5 ☐
31	3d Brown	20 ☐	10 ☐
32	4d Yellow	40 ☐	15 ☐
32a	4d Orange	45 ☐	15 ☐
33	6d Green	25 ☐	8 ☐
34	1/- Mauve	30 ☐	10 ☐
35	2/- Brown	100 ☐	75 ☐

NO.	DESCRIPTION	MUH	FU
ASC		Mint	Average Used
		$	$

White background

36	½d Green	10 ☐	10 ☐
37	1d Orange	5 ☐	5 ☐
38	2d Blue	15 ☐	10 ☐
39	2½d Red	20 ☐	15 ☐
40	5d Brown	30 ☐	20 ☐

1896

41	1d Red	30 ☐	10 ☐

1897-1905
Various Types

42	½ Green	15 ☐	15 ☐
43	1d Red	5 ☐	2 ☐
44	2d Blue	10 ☐	2 ☐
45	2½d Red	40 ☐	30 ☐
45a	2½d Purple on Red	15 ☐	10 ☐
46	3d Brown	15 ☐	10 ☐
47	4d Yellow	15 ☐	10 ☐
47a	4d Black	30 ☐	30 ☐
48	5d Brown	5 ☐	10 ☐
49	6d Green	15 ☐	10 ☐
50	1/- Mauve	20 ☐	10 ☐
51	2/- Green	50 ☐	35 ☐

1899-1908

52	½d Green	10 ☐	10 ☐

1900 Charity

53	1d (1/-) Claret	125 ☐	125 ☐
54	2d (2/-) Violet	450 ☐	425 ☐

1903-12

55	9d Brown & Blue	25 ☐	15 ☐

NO.	DESCRIPTION	MUH	FU
ASC		Mint	Average Used
		$	$

POSTAL FISCALS

1866-68
Large Types

F1	1d Blue	100 ☐	50 ☐
F2	6d Violet	175 ☐	150 ☐
F2a	6d Blue	750 ☐	475 ☐
F3	1/- Green	250 ☐	125 ☐
F4	2/- Brown	475 ☐	475 ☐
F5	2/6 Red	575 ☐	275 ☐
F6	5/- Yellow	1250 ☐	500 ☐
F7	10/- Green	1750 ☐	750 ☐
F8	20/- Red	3250 ☐	1500 ☐

1871-72 Small Type

F9	1d Mauve	30 ☐	25 ☐
F10	6d Brown	150 ☐	75 ☐
F10a	6d Mauve	375 ☐	275 ☐
F11	1/- Green	150 ☐	100 ☐
F12	2/- Blue	225 ☐	125 ☐
F13	2/6d Red	275 ☐	200 ☐
F14	5/- Brown	750 ☐	225 ☐
F15	10/ Brown	1000 ☐	325 ☐
F16	20/- Red	2500 ☐	1250 ☐

1878-79

F17	1d Violet	200 ☐	100 ☐

1892

F18	6d Green	225 ☐	225 ☐
F19	5/- Red	1250 ☐	750 ☐
F20	10/- Brown	1750 ☐	1250 ☐

NO.	DESCRIPTION	MUH	FU
ASC		Mint	Average Used
		$	$

South Australia was the last colony (except for Queensland) to issue stamps in 1855. The usual course was followed of ordering an initial supply of stamps from Perkins Bacon in London, with the printing plates being forwarded to Adelaide for further supplies to be produced locally. The stamps featured the royal portrait in a conventional format until 1886 when the first series of 'Long' stamps were issued. These stamps were twice the size of normal stamps and they appeared in higher denominations (2s.6d and over) for both postal and fiscal use. After Federation, the Long stamp format was adopted for postage stamps from 3d upwards. Another interesting variation was the solitary halfpenny stamp of 1898 which depicted the Adelaide GPO.

SOUTH AUSTRALIA HISTORY
IMPERFORATED ISSUES

1855-68

1	1d Green	6500 ☐	675 ☐
2	2d Red	1250 ☐	125 ☐
3	6d Blue	5000 ☐	225 ☐
4	1/- Orange	10,000 ☐	675 ☐

PERFORATED ISSUES

1858-1902

5	1d Green	120 ☐	30 ☐
6	2d Red	120 ☐	20 ☐
6a	2d Orange	120 ☐	20 ☐
7	6d Blue	120 ☐	15 ☐
8	1/- Orange	2750 ☐	100 ☐
8a	1/- Yellow	1250 ☐	125 ☐
8b	1/- Brown	35 ☐	10 ☐

1874
Overprinted "OS"

9	1d Green	2750 ☐	1000 ☐
10	6d 6d Blue	150 ☐	25 ☐
11	1/- Brown	100 ☐	20 ☐

1860-1902

12	4d Violet	75 ☐	10 ☐
13	9d Purple	20 ☐	15 ☐
13a	9d Grey	225 ☐	20 ☐
14	2/- Red	75 ☐	15 ☐

NO.	DESCRIPTION	MUH	FU	NO.	DESCRIPTION	MUH	FU
ASC		Mint	Average Used	ASC		Mint	Average Used
		$	$			$	$

SOUTH AUSTRALIA PERFORATED ISSUES

1874 Overprinted "OS"

15	4d Violet	125 ☐	15 ☐
16	9d Purple	5000 ☐	2250 ☐
17	2/- Red	225 ☐	30 ☐

Surcharges Perf & Imperforated

18	3d on 4d Blue (Black opt)	175 ☐	25 ☐
18a	3d on 4d Blue (Red opt)	1250 ☐	375 ☐
19	8d on 9d Brown	300 ☐	25 ☐
20	10d on 9d Orange (Blue opt)	475 ☐	75 ☐
20a	10d on 9d Yellow (Blue opt)	625 ☐	75 ☐
20b	10d on 9d Yellow (Black opt)	4500 ☐	200 ☐

1874 Overprinted "OS"

21	3d on 4d Blue	7500 ☐	3500 ☐
22	8d on 9d Brown	6000 ☐	3000 ☐

1868-1911 Various Types

23	1d Green	5 ☐	5 ☐
23a	1d Red	5 ☐	5 ☐
24	2d Orange	25 ☐	5 ☐
24a	2d Yellow	25 ☐	10 ☐
24b	2d Violet	10 ☐	5 ☐

1874 Overprinted "OS"

25	1d Green	30 ☐	2 ☐
25a	1d Red	30 ☐	2 ☐
26	2d Orange	40 ☐	2 ☐
26a	2d Yellow	40 ☐	10 ☐
26b	2d Violet	40 ☐	10 ☐

1882 Surcharge

27	½d on 1d Green	25 ☐	20 ☐

1882 Overprinted "OS"

28	½d on 1d Green	250 ☐	50 ☐

1883-99

29	½d Brown	8 ☐	8 ☐
30	3d Green	12 ☐	8 ☐
31	4d Violet	15 ☐	8 ☐
32	6d Blue	25 ☐	8 ☐

1883-99 Overprinted "OS"

33	½d Brown	40 ☐	10 ☐
34	4d Violet	80 ☐	10 ☐
35	6d Blue	40 ☐	10 ☐

1886-1896 Long Types

36	2/6d Mauve	60 ☐	20 ☐
37	5/- Pink	75 ☐	40 ☐
38	10/- Green	225 ☐	125 ☐
39	15/- Brown	550 ☐	275 ☐
40	£1 Blue	375 ☐	175 ☐
41	£2 Red	4000 ☐	750 ☐
42	50/- Pink	6250 ☐	1000 ☐
43	£3 Green	6250 ☐	1000 ☐
44	£4 Yellow	7500 ☐	1500 ☐
45	£5 Grey	7500 ☐	1500 ☐
45a	£5 Brown	5500 ☐	1500 ☐
46	£10 Bronze	6500 ☐	2250 ☐
47	£15 Silver	25,000 ☐	3000 ☐
48	£20 Claret	30,000 ☐	3500 ☐

Note: Specimen set (14) also issued

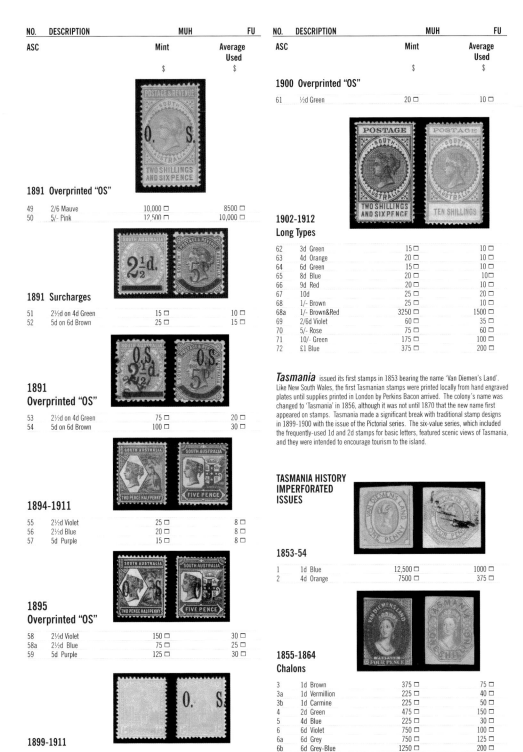

1891 Overprinted "OS"

| 49 | 2/6 Mauve | 10,000 □ | 8500 □ |
| 50 | 5/- Pink | 12,500 □ | 10,000 □ |

1891 Surcharges

| 51 | 2½d on 4d Green | 15 □ | 10 □ |
| 52 | 5d on 6d Brown | 25 □ | 15 □ |

1891 Overprinted "OS"

| 53 | 2½d on 4d Green | 75 □ | 20 □ |
| 54 | 5d on 6d Brown | 100 □ | 30 □ |

1894-1911

55	2½d Violet	25 □	8 □
56	2½d Blue	20 □	8 □
57	5d Purple	15 □	8 □

1895 Overprinted "OS"

58	2½d Violet	150 □	30 □
58a	2½d Blue	75 □	25 □
59	5d Purple	125 □	30 □

1899-1911

| 60 | ½D Green | 5 □ | 8 □ |

1900 Overprinted "OS"

| 61 | ½d Green | 20 □ | 10 □ |

1902-1912 Long Types

62	3d Green	15 □	10 □
63	4d Orange	20 □	10 □
64	6d Green	15 □	10 □
65	8d Blue	20 □	10 □
66	9d Red	20 □	10 □
67	10d	25 □	20 □
68	1/- Brown	25 □	10 □
68a	1/- Brown&Red	3250 □	1500 □
69	2/6d Violet	60 □	35 □
70	5/- Rose	75 □	60 □
71	10/- Green	175 □	100 □
72	£1 Blue	375 □	200 □

Tasmania issued its first stamps in 1853 bearing the name 'Van Diemen's Land'. Like New South Wales, the first Tasmanian stamps were printed locally from hand engraved plates until supplies printed in London by Perkins Bacon arrived. The colony's name was changed to 'Tasmania' in 1856, although it was not until 1870 that the new name first appeared on stamps. Tasmania made a significant break with traditional stamp designs in 1899-1900 with the issue of the Pictorial series. The six-value series, which included the frequently-used 1d and 2d stamps for basic letters, featured scenic views of Tasmania, and they were intended to encourage tourism to the island.

TASMANIA HISTORY IMPERFORATED ISSUES

1853-54

| 1 | 1d Blue | 12,500 □ | 1000 □ |
| 2 | 4d Orange | 7500 □ | 375 □ |

1855-1864 Chalons

3	1d Brown	375 □	75 □
3a	1d Vermillion	225 □	40 □
3b	1d Carmine	225 □	50 □
4	2d Green	475 □	150 □
5	4d Blue	225 □	30 □
6	6d Violet	750 □	100 □
6a	6d Grey	750 □	125 □
6b	6d Grey-Blue	1250 □	200 □
7	1/- Orange	1250 □	250 □

NO.	DESCRIPTION	MUH	FU	NO.	DESCRIPTION	MUH	FU
ASC		Mint	Average Used	ASC		Mint	Average Used
		$	$			$	$

PERFORATED ISSUES

1864-1880
Chalons

8	1d Vermillion	175 ☐	40 ☐
8a	1d Carmine	125 ☐	25 ☐
9	2d Green	750 ☐	200 ☐
10	4d Blue	175 ☐	40 ☐
11	6d Violet	475 ☐	100 ☐
11a	6d Claret	750 ☐	25 ☐
11b	6d Grey-Blue	575 ☐	150 ☐
12	1/- Orange	275 ☐	50 ☐

1870-1913
Sidefaces

13	½d Orange	10 ☐	10 ☐
14	1d Rose	10 ☐	5 ☐
14a	1d Pink	15 ☐	10 ☐
15	2d Green	15 ☐	5 ☐
16	3d Brown	15 ☐	10 ☐
17	4d Blue	1750 ☐	675 ☐
17a	4d Yellow	100 ☐	40 ☐
17b	4d Buff	25 ☐	20 ☐
18	8d Purple	20 ☐	20 ☐
19	9d Blue	20 ☐	15 ☐
20	10d Blue	30 ☐	30 ☐
21	5/- Mauve	375 ☐	175 ☐

1889-1891
Surcharges

22	½d on 1d Red	25 ☐	25 ☐
23	2½d on 9d Blue	15 ☐	10 ☐

1892-1913
Tablets

24	½d Orange & Mauve	5 ☐	5 ☐
25	2½d Purple	10 ☐	10 ☐
26	5d Blue & Brown	10 ☐	12 ☐
27	6d Violet & Black	20 ☐	15 ☐
28	10d Lake & Green	25 ☐	30 ☐
29	1/- Red & Green	20 ☐	20 ☐
30	2/6d Brown & Blue	50 ☐	40 ☐
31	5/- Purple & Red	75 ☐	70 ☐
32	10/- Mauve & Brown	125 ☐	100 ☐
33	£1 Green & Yellow	625 ☐	425 ☐

1899-1912
Pictorials

34	½d Green	10 ☐	8 ☐
35	1d Red	10 ☐	2 ☐
36	2d Violet	10 ☐	2 ☐
37	2½d Blue	25 ☐	15 ☐
38	3d Brown	15 ☐	10 ☐
39	4d Orange	25 ☐	15 ☐
40	5d Blue	40 ☐	20 ☐
41	6d Lake	25 ☐	15 ☐

1904
Surcharge

42	1½d on 5d Blue & Brown	5 ☐	5 ☐

1912 Surcharge

43	1d on 2d Violet	5 ☐	5 ☐

TASMANIA POSTAL FISCALS

1863
Imperf

F1	3d Green	875	475
F2	2/6d Green	625	375
F3	5/- Green	750	425
F3a	5/- Brown	1000	525
F4	10/- Orange	875	575

1864
Perforated

F5	3d Green	625 ☐	325 ☐
F6	2/6d Green	150 ☐	100 ☐
F7	5/- Green	475 ☐	250 ☐
F7a	5/- Brown	575 ☐	425 ☐
F8	10/- Orange	425 ☐	275 ☐

1880

F9	1d Slade	30 ☐	15 ☐
F10	3d Slade	30 ☐	10 ☐
F11	6d Mauve	125 ☐	15 ☐
F12	1/- Pink	175 ☐	30 ☐

1900 Revenue Overprints

F13	1d Blue	30 ☐	30 ☐
F14	2d Brown	40 ☐	40 ☐
F15	3d Brown	40 ☐	40 ☐
F16	6d Mauve	200 ☐	100 ☐
F17	1/- Pink	350 ☐	175 ☐
F18	2/6d Red (imperf)	750 ☐	750 ☐
F18a	2/6d Red (perf)	575 ☐	475 ☐
F19	10/- Orange	750 ☐	750 ☐
F20	£1 Green & Yellow	250 ☐	200 ☐

Victoria was the second Australian colony to issue stamps; its first issue being the 'Half-Length' stamps featuring a seated portrait of Queen Victoria. The stamps were issued on 3 January 1850 in anticipation of Victoria's separation from New South Wales, an event that occurred 18 months later. Victoria was distinctive among the six colonies, in that, with the exception of two stamps, all its stamps were wholly produced in Melbourne. Also, with very few exceptions, all of Victoria's stamps portrayed Queen Victoria's portrait. One of the exceptions involved two high denomination stamps issued in 1901-02 featuring King Edward VII – the only Australian stamps to feature the King.

VICTORIA HISTORY IMPERFORATE ISSUES

1850-1856
Half Lengths

1	1d Orange	5500 ☐	575 ☐
1a	1d Brown	3500 ☐	225 ☐
1b	1d Red	2250 ☐	100 ☐
2	2d Violet	7500 ☐	750 ☐
2a	2d Grey	3500 ☐	275 ☐
2b	2d Brown	2250 ☐	175 ☐
3	3d Blue	1250 ☐	75 ☐
3a	Blue-Green	1500 ☐	125 ☐

1852-1864
Queen on Throne

4	2d Brown	475 ☐	40 ☐
4a	2d Grey	575 ☐	40 ☐
4b	2d Purple	475 ☐	40 ☐

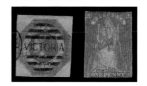

1854
Octagonal

5	1/- Blue	1500 ☐	125 ☐

1856
Queen on Throne

6	1d Green	175 ☐	25 ☐

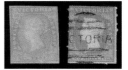

1854
Woodblocks

7	6d Orange	475 ☐	40 ☐
8	2/- Green	5750 ☐	375 ☐

1854
Registration Stamp

9	1/- Red & Blue	5000 ☐	275 ☐

1855
"Too Late" Stamp

10	6d Lilac & Group	5000 ☐	325 ☐

1857
Emblems

11	1d Green	275 ☐	30 ☐
12	2d Lilac	325 ☐	30 ☐
13	4d Orange	575 ☐	40 ☐
13a	4d Red	475 ☐	30 ☐

PERFORATED ISSUES

A few of the early stamps that were perforated also come rouletted and may on occasions be supplied in this form. Others were actually issued only in rouletted form.

NO. ASC	DESCRIPTION	MUH Mint $	FU Average Used $

1857-59

| 14 | 3d Half Length | 3000 ☐ | 175 ☐ |
| 15 | 1/- Blue (Octangonal) | 375 ☐ | 50 ☐ |

1858 - Queen on Throne

| 16 | 6d Blue | 275 ☐ | 20 ☐ |

1857-1864
Woodblocks

17	6d Orange	475 ☐	150 ☐
17a	6d Black	475 ☐	75 ☐
18	2/- Green	525 ☐	100 ☐
18a	2/- Blue on Green	475 ☐	25 ☐

1859 Emblems

19	1d Green	175 ☐	25 ☐
20	2d Violet	325 ☐	25 ☐
20a	2d Grey	325 ☐	25 ☐
20b	2d Brown	375☐	25 ☐
21	4d Orange	375 ☐	175 ☐
21a	4d Orange	275 ☐	20 ☐

VICTORIA HISTORY PERFORATED ISSUES

1860-1862
Beaded Ovals

22	3d Blue	475 ☐	40 ☐
22a	3d Claret	475 ☐	150 ☐
23	4d Red	377 ☐	10 ☐
24	6d Orange	10,000 ☐	675 ☐
24a	6d Black	475 ☐	25 ☐

1861-63

| 25 | 1d Green | 275 ☐ | 20 ☐ |

1862-64

| 26 | 6d Black | 275 ☐ | 20 ☐ |

1863-1884
Various Types

27	1d Green	125 ☐	10 ☐
28	2d Violet	150 ☐	10 ☐
28a	2d Grey	275 ☐	10 ☐
29	3d Lilac	475 ☐	50 ☐
29a	3d Orange	30 ☐	15 ☐
29b	3d Yellow	150 ☐	25 ☐
30	4d Red	100 ☐	10 ☐
30a	4d Pink	275 ☐	10 ☐
31	6d Blue	75 ☐	10 ☐
31a	6d Green	50 ☐	25 ☐
32	8d Orange	675 ☐	125 ☐
32a	8d Brown on Pink	275 ☐	20 ☐
33	10d Grey	1000 ☐	125 ☐
33a	10d Brown on Pink	325 ☐	50 ☐
34	1/- Blue on Blue	275 ☐	12 ☐
35	5/- Blue on Yellow	3000 ☐	750 ☐
35a	5/- Blue and Red	675 ☐	50 ☐
35b	5/- Red and Blue	475 ☐	75 ☐

1871-73
Surcharges

| 36 | ½d on 1d Green | 125☐ | 35 |
| 37 | 9d on 10d Brown | 875☐ | 40 |

1870

| 38 | 2d Lilac | 150☐ | 10 |

1873-1884 Various Types

39	½d Red	5 ☐	5 ☐
39a	½d Red on Pink	60 ☐	30 ☐
39b	½d Green	5 ☐	5 ☐
40	1d Green	40 ☐	5 ☐
40a	1d Green on Yellow	275 ☐	50 ☐
40b	1d Green on Grey	375 ☐	175 ☐
41	2d Mauve	30 ☐	5 ☐
41a	2d Mauve on Green	375 ☐	50 ☐
41b	2d Mauve on Lilac	6500 ☐	3000 ☐
41c	2d Mauve on Brown	425 ☐	75 ☐
42	9d Brown on Pink	325 ☐	25 ☐
42a	9d Brown	25 ☐	20 ☐
42b	9d Red	20 ☐	15 ☐
43	1/- Blue on Blue	125 ☐	15 ☐
43a	1/- Yellow	40 ☐	35 ☐

1876 Surcharge

44	8d on 9d Brown on Pink	475 ☐	100 ☐

1880-84

45	1d Green	30 ☐	15 ☐
46	2d Brown	25 ☐	10 ☐
46a	2d Mauve	10 ☐	8 ☐
47	4d Red	125 ☐	30 ☐
47a	4d Yellow	50 ☐	35 ☐
48	2/- Blue on Yellow	325 ☐	40 ☐
48a	2/- Blue on Pink	90 ☐	60 ☐

1885 Stamp Duty Overprints

49	3d Yellow	125 ☐	75 ☐
50	4d Red	125 ☐	100 ☐
51	1/- Blue on Blue (black opt)	150 ☐	75 ☐
51a	1/- Blue on Blue (black opt)	5000 ☐	3000 ☐
52	2/- Blue on Blue	225 ☐	100 ☐

1884-1900 Stamp Duty Series

53	½d Red	20 ☐	5 ☐
54	1d Green	20 ☐	5 ☐
55	2d Mauve	10 ☐	5 ☐
56	3d Yellow	15 ☐	5 ☐
56	3d Brown	25 ☐	15 ☐
56b	3d Green	20 ☐	30 ☐
57	4d Magenta	75 ☐	25 ☐
57a	4d Lilac (error of colour)	10,000 ☐	4000 ☐
58	6d Blue	100 ☐	20 ☐
59	8d Red on Pink	30 ☐	20 ☐
60	1/- Blue on Yellow	225 ☐	40 ☐
61	2/- Green on Green	50 ☐	30 ☐
61a	2/- Turquoise	30 ☐	25 ☐
61b	2/- Apple-Green	30 ☐	25 ☐
62	2/6d Orange	275 ☐	60 ☐
62a	2/6d Yellow	250 ☐	50 ☐

1886-1900 Stamp Duty Series

63	½d Lilac	40 ☐	25 ☐
63a	½d Red	5 ☐	10 ☐
63b	½d Pink	5 ☐	5 ☐
63c	½d Green	15 ☐	10 ☐
64	1d Green	25 ☐	10 ☐
65	2d Green	10 ☐	5 ☐
66	4d Red	20 ☐	10 ☐
67	6d Blue	25 ☐	5 ☐
68	1/- Chocolate	125 ☐	20 ☐
68a	1/- Red	40 ☐	20 ☐
69	1/6d Blue	275 ☐	175 ☐
69a	1/6d Orange	50 ☐	25 ☐
70	£5 Blue & Maroon	6000 ☐	250 ☐
71	£6 Yellow & Blue	7500 ☐	250 ☐
72	£7 Red & Black	7500 ☐	250 ☐
73	£8 Mauve & Orange	8000 ☐	250 ☐
74	£9 Green & Red	9000 ☐	250 ☐

NO. ASC	DESCRIPTION	MUH Mint $	FU Average Used $

1899-1900

NO.	DESCRIPTION	MUH	FU
75	1d Brown on Pink	25 ☐	20 ☐
75a	1d Brown	5 ☐	8 ☐
75b	1d Yellow	600 ☐	375 ☐
75c	1d Red	20 ☐	8 ☐
75d	1d Olive	40 ☐	35 ☐
76	1½d Green	10 ☐	8 ☐
76a	1½d Red on Yellow	15 ☐	10 ☐
77	2½d Red on Yellow	20 ☐	10 ☐
77a	2½d Blue	25 ☐	12 ☐
78	5d Brown	30 ☐	10 ☐

1897 Charity

NO.	DESCRIPTION	MUH	FU
79	1d(1/-) Blue	40 ☐	40 ☐
80	2½d (2/6d) Brown	200 ☐	200 ☐

1900 Patriotic Fund

NO.	DESCRIPTION	MUH	FU
81	1d (1/-) Brown	125 ☐	125 ☐
82	2d (2/-) Green	250 ☐	250 ☐

1901 Postage Issues

NO.	DESCRIPTION	MUH	FU
83	½d Green	5 ☐	5 ☐
84	1d Red	5 ☐	2 ☐
85	1½d Red on Yellow	10 ☐	5 ☐
86	2d Mauve	15 ☐	5 ☐
87	2½d Blue	15 ☐	5 ☐
88	3d Brown	15 ☐	5 ☐
88a	3d Yellow	20 ☐	15 ☐
89	4d Yellow	0 ☐	15 ☐
89a	4d Olive	25 ☐	15 ☐
90	5d Brown	20 ☐	12 ☐
91	6d Green	15 ☐	8 ☐
92	9d Red	20 ☐	15 ☐
93	1/- Orange	25 ☐	20 ☐
93a	1/- Yellow	50 ☐	30 ☐
94	2/- Blue on Pink	35 ☐	20 ☐
95	5/- Red & Blue	125 ☐	15 ☐
93	1/- Orange	25 ☐	20 ☐
93a	1/- Yellow	50 ☐	30 ☐
94	2/- Blue on Pink	35 ☐	20 ☐
95	5/- Red & Blue	125 ☐	35 ☐
96	£1 Red	425 ☐	275 ☐
97	£2 Blue	1250 ☐	575 ☐

1912 Surcharge

NO.	DESCRIPTION	MUH	FU
98	1d on 2d Mauve	5 ☐	8 ☐

VICTORIA POSTAL FISCALS

1870-1883 Statute Issue

NO.	DESCRIPTION	MUH	FU
F1	½d on 1d Green	375 ☐	275 ☐
F2	1d Green	250 ☐	175 ☐
F3	3d Violet	1750 ☐	1250 ☐
F4	4d Red	1500 ☐	1000 ☐
F5	6d Blue	300 ☐	125 ☐
F6	1/- Blue on Blue	275 ☐	75 ☐
D7	2/- Blue on Green	375 ☐	200 ☐
F8	2/6d Orange	750 ☐	375 ☐
F8a	2/6d Yellow	750 ☐	375 ☐

NO. ASC	DESCRIPTION	MUH Mint $	FU Average Used $
F9	5/- Blue on Yellow	750 ☐	325 ☐
F10	10/- Brown on Pink	2750 ☐	675 ☐
F11	£1 Violet on Yellow	2250 ☐	675 ☐
F12	£5 Black & Green	10,000 ☐	1250 ☐

1879-1900 Stamp Duty

F13	1d Green	150 ☐	100 ☐
F14	1d Brown	100 ☐	30 ☐
F15	6d Blue	375 ☐	75 ☐
F16	1/- Blue on Blue	375 ☐	30 ☐
F16a	1/- Blue on Yellow	450 ☐	50 ☐
F17	1/6d Red	425 ☐	50 ☐
F18	2/- Blue on Green	375 ☐	100 ☐
F19	3/- Purple on Blue	1000 ☐	150 ☐
F19a	3/- Grey	200 ☐	30 ☐
F19b	3/- Green	275 ☐	125 ☐
F20	4/- Orange	175 ☐	40 ☐
F21	5/- Purple on Yellow	175 ☐	40 ☐
F21a	5/- Red	375 ☐	40 ☐
F22	6/- Green	450 ☐	50 ☐
F23	10/- Brown on Pink	1500 ☐	200 ☐
F23a	10/- Green	750 ☐	75 ☐
F24	15/- Mauve	3750 ☐	675 ☐
F24a	15/-Brown	2000 ☐	275 ☐
F25	£1 Orange	1500 ☐	125 ☐
F26	25/- Pink	4000 ☐	750 ☐
F27	30/- Green (Fiscal)	4000 ☐	375 ☐
F28	35/- Violet (Fiscal)	15,000 ☐	500 ☐
F29	£2 Blue	2500 ☐	275 ☐
F30	45/- Violet	7500 ☐	275 ☐
F31	£5 Red (Fiscal)	12,500 ☐	175 ☐
F32	£6 Blue on Pink (Fiscal)	175 ☐	
F33	£7 Violet on Blue (Fiscal)	175 ☐	
F34	£8 Red on Yellow		225 ☐
F35	£9 Green on Green (Fiscal)		225 ☐
F36	£10 Violet (CTO)	10,000 ☐	125 ☐
F37	£25 Green (CTO)	–	425 ☐
F38	£50 Violet (CTO)	–	475 ☐
F39	£100 Red (CTO)	–	525 ☐

Used prices are for postally used or cancelled to order examples. Stamps with (Fiscal) appearing after description are prices as "Fiscally used". This applies to F12, F28 and F35. These values are seldom if ever available in any other form.

Other values are also available fiscally used.

1890-94

D1	½d Blue & Red	15 ☐	15 ☐
D2	1d Blue & Red	15 ☐	15 ☐
D3	2d Blue & Red	30 ☐	15 ☐
D4	4d Blue & Red	40 ☐	25 ☐
D5	5d Blue & Red	25 ☐	25 ☐
D6	6d Blue & Red	30 ☐	25 ☐
D7	10d Blue & Red	150 ☐	100 ☐
D8	1/- Blue & Red	100 ☐	40 ☐
D9	2/- Blue & Red	225 ☐	150 ☐
D10	5/- Blue & Red	375 ☐	225 ☐

1895-1908

D11	½d Red & Green	15 ☐	10 ☐
D12	1d Red & Green	15 ☐	5 ☐
D13	2d Red & Green	15 ☐	5 ☐
D14	4d Red & Green	25 ☐	10 ☐
D15	5d Red & Green	30 ☐	20 ☐
D16	6d Red & Green	40 ☐	25 ☐
D17	10d Red & Green	75 ☐	50 ☐
D18	1/- Red & Green	50 ☐	20 ☐
D19	2/- Red & Green	225 ☐	125 ☐
D20	5/- Red & Green	325 ☐	150 ☐

Catalogue numbers referred to in this colonies listing are numbers published by Seven Seas Stamps and used with their kind permission.

Western Australia issued its first stamp in 1854. Being one penny and printed in black the stamp imitated Great Britain's first stamp, but it did not depict Queen Victoria. Instead, Western Australia's first stamp featured the colony's emblem of the black swan. Throughout the years up to Federation the colony's stamps continued to feature the black swan – an unusual exception to the convention of royal portraits. It was only following Federation that Western Australian stamps appeared with a royal portrait, these being printed in Melbourne and being derivations of Victoria's stamp designs. Notably, Western Australia has produced Australia's most valuable stamp error: the 4d Blue 'Inverted Frame' of 1854, of which about 14 examples are known to exist.

WESTERN AUSTRALIA HISTORY IMPERFORATE ISSUES

1854-60			
1	1d Black	1500 ☐	325 ☐
2	2d Orange	150 ☐	125 ☐
3	4d Blue (Octagonal)	425 ☐	275 ☐
4	4d Blue	350 ☐	3000 ☐
5	6d Green	3750 ☐	575 ☐
6	1/- Brown	850 ☐	425 ☐

NO.	DESCRIPTION	MUH	FU
ASC		Mint	Average Used
		$	$

NO.	DESCRIPTION	MUH	FU
ASC		Mint	Average Used
		$	$
22	4d Brown	25 ☐	8 ☐
23	5d Yellow	25 ☐	10 ☐
23a	5d Green	35 ☐	20 ☐
24	6d Violet	30 ☐	10 ☐
25	1/- Green	40 ☐	15 ☐

1857

7	2d Brown on Red	6500 ☐	750 ☐
8	6d Black	7500 ☐	750 ☐

PERFORATED ISSUES
1861-90

9	1d Carmine	100 ☐	10 ☐
9a	1d Yellow	40 ☐	10 ☐
9b	1d Pink	30 ☐	12 ☐
10	2d Blue	100 ☐	25 ☐
10a	2d Yellow	40 ☐	10 ☐
10b	2d Grey	50 ☐	10 ☐
11	4d Vermillion	575 ☐	275 ☐
11a	4d Carmine	100 ☐	20 ☐
11b	4d Brown	100 ☐	30 ☐
12	6d Brown	375 ☐	75 ☐
12a	6d Purple on Blue	5750 ☐	675 ☐
12b	6d Violet	120 ☐	15 ☐
13	1/- Green	150 ☐	25 ☐

1893
Surcharges

26	½d on 3d Brown	20 ☐	25 ☐
26a	½d on 3d Brown	275 ☐	
27	1d on 3d Brown	25 ☐	25 ☐

1875
Surcharges

14	1d on 2d Yellow	875 ☐	150 ☐

1900

28	2½d Blue	20 ☐	20 ☐

1872

15	3d Brown	20 ☐	15 ☐

1884-1885
Surcharges

16	½d on 1d Yellow	40 ☐	30 ☐
17	1d on 3d Brown	30 ☐	25 ☐

1902-12

29	1d Red	10 ☐	2 ☐
30	2d Yellow	10 ☐	2 ☐
31	4d Brown	15 ☐	5 ☐
32	8d Green	25 ☐	12 ☐
33	9d Orange	30 ☐	15 ☐
34	10d Red	40 ☐	15 ☐
34a	10d Orange	45 ☐	35 ☐
35	2/- Red on Yellow	50 ☐	20 ☐
36	2/6d Blue on Yellow	5 ☐	25 ☐
37	5/- Green	100 ☐	50 ☐
38	10/- Mauve	225 ☐	125 ☐
39	£1 Orange-Brown	575 ☐	315 ☐

1885-1912

18	½d Green	10 ☐	10 ☐
19	1d Red	10 ☐	5 ☐
20	2d Grey	25 ☐	8 ☐
20a	2d Yellow	25 ☐	5 ☐
21	2½d Blue	25 ☐	10 ☐

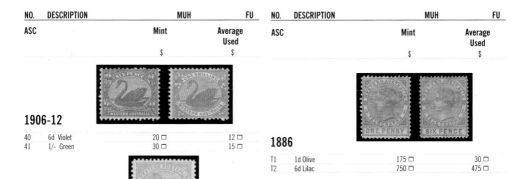

1906-12

| 40 | 6d Violet | 20 ☐ | 12 ☐ |
| 41 | 1/- Green | 30 ☐ | 15 ☐ |

1886

| T1 | 1d Olive | 175 ☐ | 30 ☐ |
| T2 | 6d Lilac | 750 ☐ | 475 ☐ |

1912 Surcharges

| 42 | 1d on Yellow | 15 ☐ | 10 ☐ |

WESTERN AUSTRALIA HISTORY POSTAL FISCALS

1893

F1	1d Purple	40 ☐	20 ☐
F2	2d Purple	250 ☐	150 ☐
F3	3d Purple	150 ☐	20 ☐
F4	6d Purple	200 ☐	30 ☐
F5	1/- Purple	230 ☐	35 ☐
F6	2/6 Purple	500 ☐	350 ☐
F7	3/- Purple	675 ☐	525 ☐
F8	5/- Purple	1,250 ☐	650 ☐

1893 IR Overprint in Green

| F8a | 1d Ochre | 550 ☐ | 425 ☐ |

1893 IR Overprint in black

F9	1d on 3d Lilac	2000 ☐	2000 ☐
F10	2d on 3d Lilac	50 ☐	30 ☐
F11	3d on 3d Lilac	150 ☐	90 ☐
F12	6d on 3d Lilac	550 ☐	300 ☐
F13	1/- on 3d Lilac	1600 ☐	1600 ☐

THE AUSTRALIAN KANGAROO and KING GEORGE V SERIES of STAMPS

On 1st March 1901 control of all the postal services within Australia was taken control by the newly constituted Government however the various State stamps which had been on issue for many years continued to be used throughout the Commonwealth till 2nd January 1913 when the first stamps, inscribed "Australia" became the legal entity for postage.

The first stamps to be issued inscribed "Australia" were, firstly, those of the Kangaroo series commencing 2nd January 1913 shortly followed 1914 by the series featuring the then reigning monarch King George V. Both these issues were printed with various watermarks (inverted/sideways) – printing paper qualities-variations in colour-perforation variations-dies with a host of varieties were created due to printing techniques of the time particularly during period of World War 1. During this period several printers were used which added a further range of varieties with both series.

Whilst the last of the kangaroo series was printed 1931-36 these, together with the King George V series, remained legal postage till the advent of decimal currency in 1996.

As the scope of "Stamps of Australia" is to provide a simplified listing of Australian stamps the complex and complete range of both the kangaroo and King George V series are not listed. For those collectors requiring this more detailed information on both series reference should be made to the Australian specialist stamp catalogues as published by Stanley Gibbons Publications Ltd.

The colour variations of the two series, alone, provides much interest for collectors and for information purposes only we are including the major types but without values and catalogue numbers for obvious reasons.

Stamps of Australia, and their values.

PreDecimal Stamps
1913-1966

Values for PreDecimal stamps are expressed as **M**int **U**n **H**inged (in undamaged condtion), **M**int **L**ightly **H**inged (in undamaged condtion) and **F**ine **U**sed (clear round cancellations with full perforations - heavy cancellations are worth less).

PreDecimal First Day Covers
Values quoted for pre 1935 covers are for plain covers with handwritten or typewritten addresses. Post 1935 cover values are for covers with typewritten addresses (hand addressed worth slightly less). It should be understood that all covers should be in good condition with clear cancellations with stamp(s) tied by postmark to cover.

NO.	DESCRIPTION	MUH	MLH	FU

1. Kangaroo

19. Kangaroo

14. Kangaroo

15. Kangaroo

Kangaroo Definitive issues

1	½d Green	18.00☐	12.00☐	10.00☐
2	1d Red	25.00☐	15.00☐	2.00☐
3	2d Grey	60.00☐	30.00☐	15.00☐
4	2½d Indigo	40.00☐	20.00☐	15.00☐
5	3dOlive	80.00☐	40.00☐	15.00☐
6	4dOrange	750.00☐	150.00☐	40.00☐
7	5d Brown	350.00☐	140.00☐	48.00☐
8	6d Ultramarine	500.00☐	125.00☐	20.00☐
9	6d Brown	50.00☐	20.00☐	10.00☐
10	9d Violet	125.00☐	50.00☐	10.00☐
11	1/- Green	175.00☐	75.00☐	20.00☐
12	2/- Brown	2,000.00☐	400.00☐	35.00☐
13	2/- Maroon	15.00☐	5.00☐	5.00☐
14	5/- Grey & Yellow	950.00☐	350.00☐	30.00☐
15	10/- Grey & Pink	2,250.00☐	750.00☐	225.00☐
16	£1 Brown & Blue	15,000.00☐	3,500.00☐	2,500.00☐
17	£1 Grey	2,500.00☐	900.00☐	400.00☐
18	£2 Black & Red	12,500.00☐	5,000.00☐	750.00☐

OS Overprinted 1932
19	6d Brown	42.00☐	32.00☐	28.00☐

16. Kangaroo

18. Kangaroo

20. Geo. V (engraved)

21. Geo. V (typographed)

George V Definitive Issue (engraved) 1913
20	1d Red (engraved)	8.00☐	6.00☐	6.00☐

George V Definitive Issue 1913-36
21	½d Green	13.00☐	6.00☐	2.00☐
22	½d Orange	12.00☐	5.00☐	1.00☐
23	1d Red	15.00☐	7.00☐	3.00☐
24	1d Violet	15.00☐	7.00☐	3.00☐
25	1d Green	10.00☐	4.00☐	2.00☐
26	1½d Black-Brown	18.00☐	9.00☐	3.00☐
27	1½d Brown	20.00☐	11.00☐	4.00☐
28	1½d Green	15.00☐	7.00☐	4.00☐
29	1½d Red	20.00☐	11.00☐	3.00☐
30	2d Orange	38.00☐	20.00☐	5.00☐
31	2d Red	5.00☐	16.00☐	4.00☐
32	2d Brown	20.00☐	24.00☐	10.00☐
33	3d Blue	70.00☐	40.00☐	5.00☐
34	4d Orange	100.00☐	40.00☐	20.00☐
35	4d Lemon	1,250.00☐	250.00☐	40.00☐
36	4d Violet	45.00☐	20.00☐	25.00☐
37	4d Blue	170.00☐	90.00☐	25.00☐
38	4d Olive	75.00☐	40.00☐	15.00☐
39	4½d Violet	75.00☐	40.00☐	15.00☐
40	5d Brown	150.00☐	40.00☐	10.00☐
41	1/4d Blue	500.00☐	175.00☐	15.00☐

42. OS

48. Kookaburra

OS Overprinted 1932-33
42	½d Orange	20.00☐	10.00☐	5.00☐
43	1d Green	15.00☐	8.00☐	2.00☐
44	2d red	25.00☐	15.00☐	10.00☐
45	3d Blue	25.00☐	15.00☐	10.00☐
46	4d Olive	40.00☐	20.00☐	20.00☐
47	5d Brown	75.00☐	48.00☐	45.00☐

Issues of OS stamps ceased in Feb 1933

Kookaburra 1914 28 Aug
48	6d Claret	250.00☐	125.00☐	75.00☐

NO.	DESCRIPTION	MUH	MLH	FU
NO.	DESCRIPTION	MUH	MLH	FU

49. Parliament House, Canberra

50. Kookaburra

51. Miniature Sheet - Kookaburra

52. Aeroplane over sheep

Parliament House Canberra   **1927 9 May**

49	1½d Lake	2.00□	1.00□	1.00□
	First Day Cover			100.00□

Australian Philatelic Exhibition (Melb)   **1928 29 Oct**

*Issued as a single stamp and a block of 4 in a miniature sheet format

50	3d Blue - Kookaburra	10.00□	5.00□	5.00□
	First Day Cover			125.00□
51	3d Blue - Kookaburra - Australian Philatelic Exhibition (Melb)			
Miniature sheet in a block of four		325□	225.00□	350.00□
	First Day Cover	.		1,250.00□
Exhibition cancels on 50 & 51 are worth considerably more				

Airmail   **1929 20 May**

52	3d Green:	15.00□	8.00□	7.00□
	First Day Cover			175.00□

53. Swan

54. Charles Sturt

West Australian Centenary   **1929 28 Sep**

53	1½d Red Swan	2.00□	0.75□	1.00□
	First Day Cover			100.00□

Charles Sturt Centenary   **1930 02 Jun**

54	1½d Red Charles Sturt	2.00□	0.75□	1.00□
55	3d Blue Charles Sturt	8.00□	3.00□	4.00□
	First Day Cover (2)			225.00□

56. Surcharge

57. Surcharge

George V Surcharges   **1930 01 Aug**

56	2d on 1½d Red	4.00□	2.00□	1.00□
57	5d on 4½d Violet	12.00□	6.00□	6.00□

58. The Southern Cross

61. The Southern Cross - OS Overprint

Commemorating flights by Charles Kingsford Smith

1931 19 Mar

58	2d Red - Plane across globe	2.00□	1.00□	0.50□
59	3d Blue - Plane across globe	5.00□	3.00□	3.00□
60	6d Violet - Plane across globe	12.00□	7.00□	6.00□
	First Day Cover (3)			225.00□

Commemorating flights by Charles Kingsford Smith

1931 04 May

OS Overprinted

No.	Description	MUH	MLH	FU
61	2d Red - Plane across globe	300.00	125.00	40.00
62	3d Blue - Plane across globe	750.00	350.00	80.00

63. Air Mail Service

64. Air Mail Service - OS Overprint

Commemorating flights by Charles Kingsford Smith

1931 04 Nov

Inscribed 'Air Mail Service'

No.	Description	MUH	MLH	FU
63	6d Sepia -Plane across globe	40.00	20.00	20.00
	First Day Cover			750.00

Commemorating flights by Charles Kingsford Smith

1931 17 Nov

OS Overprinted but was on general sale through Post Offices.
Inscribed 'Air Mail Service'

No.	Description	MUH	MLH	FU
64	6d Sepia -Plane across globe	45.00	30.00	25.00
	First Day Cover			1,500.00

65. Kookaburra

66. Lyre Bird

67. Lyre Bird - OS Overprint

Australian Birds

1932 15 Feb

6d issued Jun 1st 1932. 1/- issued 15th Feb 1932

No.	Description	MUH	MLH	FU
65	6d Brown Kookaburra	30.00	15.00	2.00
	First Day Cover (6d only)			400.00
66	1/- Green Lyre Bird	90.00	40.00	7.00
	First Day Cover (1/- only)			375.00

Australian Birds

1932 15 Feb

OS Overprinted

No.	Description	MUH	MLH	FU
67	1/- Green Lyre Bird OS overprint	120.00	70.00	50.00
	First Day Cover			1,750.00

68. Sydney Harbour Bridge

Opening of the Sydney Harbour Bridge

1932 14 Mar

No.	Description	MUH	MLH	FU
68	2d Red Sydney Harbour Bridge	4.00	2.00	2.00
69	2d Red (engraved)	4.00	2.00	2.00
	First Day Cover			50.00
70	3d Blue Sydney Harbour Bridge	6.00	4.00	3.50
	First Day Cover			65.00
71	5/- Green	1,500.00	500.00	350.00
	First Day Cover (3)			5000.00

72. Sydney Harbour Bridge
OS Overprint

Opening of the Sydney Harbour Bridge

1932 14 Mar

OS Overprinted

No.	Description	MUH	MLH	FU
72	2d Red (engraved)	7.00	4.00	4.00
73	3d Blue	30.00	20.00	18.00
	First Day Cover (2)			750.00

74. Yarra River & Melbourne
View with an Aborigine.

77. Merino Sheep

Victorian Centenary

1934 02 Jul

Yarra River & Melbourne View with an Aboriginal Australian.

No.	Description	MUH	MLH	FU
74	2d Red	5.00	2.00	2.00
75	3d Blue	8.00	4.00	3.00
76	1/- Black	100.00	50.00	37.00
	First Day Cover			425.00

Centenary of John Macarthur

1934 01 Nov

No.	Description	MUH	MLH	FU
77	2d Red Merino Sheep	5.00	3.00	1.00
78	3d Blue	20.00	12.00	11.00
79	9d Bright Purple	75.00	45.00	35.00
	First Day Cover (3)			450.00

80. Hermes God of Speed

Air Mail   **1934 01 Jan**

| 80 | 1/6 Purple Hermes God of Speed | 10.00 | 5.00 | 3.00 |

81. Cenotaph London

83. King George on Horse

86. Amphitrite

20th Anniversary of Gallipoli Landing   **1935 18 Mar**

ANZAC

81	2d Red Cenotaph London	3.00	2.00	0.50
82	1/- Black Cenotaph London	85.00	50.00	40.00
	First Day Cover (2)			400.00

Silver Jubilee of George V   **1935 02 May**

83	2d Red King George on Horse	3.00	2.00	0.50
84	3d Blue	8.00	5.00	3.00
85	2/- Violet	85.00	50.00	40.00
	First Day Cover (3)			425.00

Opening of submarine cable between mainland and Tasmania **1936 01 Apr**

86	2d Red - Amphitrite	3.00	1.00	0.50
87	3d Blue	8.00	4.50	3.00
	First Day Cover (2)			125.00

88. Proclamation Tree Adelaide

91. Capt Philip at Sydney Cove,
Jan 26 1788

Centenary of South Australia   **1936 03 Aug**

88	2d RedProclamation Tree Adelaide	3.00	0.75	0.50
89	3d Blue	8.00	5.00	3.50
90	1/- Green	30.00	18.00	12.00
	First Day Cover (3)			225.00

150th Anniversary of the founding of New South Wales

          1937 01 Oct

91	2d Red Capt Philip at Sydney	3.00	2.00	1.00
92	3d Blue	7.00	3.50	3.50
93	9d Purple	30.00	15.00	15.00
	First Day Cover (3)			30.00

94. Elizabeth

96. George VI

100. George VI

George VI Definitive Issue   **1937/38**

94	1d Green Elizabeth 1937 Die I	2.50	1.00	0.50
	First Day Cover			10.00
94a	1d Green Elizabeth 1938 Die II	2.50	1.00	0.50
	First Day Cover			50.00
95	1d Maroon Elizabeth	2.00	1.00	0.30
	First Day Cover			750.00
96	1½d Maroon George VI	6.00	4.00	4.00
	First Day Cover			75.00
97	1½d Green George VI	2.00	1.00	0.30
	First Day Cover			600.00
98	2d Red George 1937 Die I	2.50	1.00	0.50
	First Day Cover			25.00
98a	2d Red George 1938 Die II	3.00	1.00	0.50
	First Day Cover			25.00
99	2d Purple George VI	2.00	1.00	0.30
	First Day Cover			300.00
100	3d Blue George VI	45.00	25.00	3.00
	First Day Cover			
101	3d Brown George VI	1.00	0.50	0.30
	First Day Cover			375.00
102	1/4d Magenta George VI	4.00	2.00	1.00
	First Day Cover			50.00

First Day Covers: Values quoted for pre 1935 covers are for plain covers with handwritten
or typewritten addresses. Post 1935 cover values are for covers with typewritten addresses
(hand addressed worth slightly less). It should be understood that all covers should be in good
condition with clear cancellations with stamp(s) tied by postmark to cover.
Decimal First Day Covers refer to page 21.

103. Kangaroo 104. Koala 105. Sheep

106. Kookaburra 107. Platypus 108. Lyre bird

Australian Animals and Birds 1937/59

No.	Description	MUH	MLH	FU
103	½d Orange Kangaroo	1.00☐	0.50☐	0.30☐
	First Day Cover			30.00☐
104	4d Green Koala	1.00☐	0.50☐	0.30☐
	First Day Cover			50.00☐
105	5d Purple Sheep	2.00☐	0.60☐	0.30☐
	First Day Cover			50.00☐
106	6d Brown Kookaburra	2.00☐	1.00☐	0.30☐
	First Day Cover			75.00☐
107	9d Brown Platypus	3.00☐	1.50☐	0.30☐
	First Day Cover			50.00☐
108	1/- Green Lyrebird	3.00☐	1.20☐	0.30☐
	First Day Cover			50.00☐

109. Queen Elizabeth 110. King George VI

111. King George VI & Queen Elizabeth

George VI Definitive Issue High Values 1938 01 Apr
1st Apr 5/- & 10/-, £1 1st Nov

No.	Description	MUH	MLH	FU
109	5/- Claret Queen Elizabeth	20.00☐	8.00☐	5.00☐
	First Day Cover			275.00☐
110	10/- Purple King George VI	40.00☐	25.00☐	18.00☐
	First Day Cover			750.00☐
111	£1 Dull Blue King & Queen	120.00☐	75.00☐	42.00☐
	First Day Cover (3)			1,500.00☐

112. Sailor, Soldier, Airman & Nurse

Australian Armed Services 1940 15 Jul
Sailor, Soldier, Airman and Nurse

No.	Description	MUH	MLH	FU
112	1d Green	3.50☐	2.00☐	1.00☐
113	2d Red	4.00☐	1.25☐	1.00☐
114	3d Blue	10.00☐	4.50☐	3.00☐
115	6d Purple	28.00☐	15.00☐	11.00☐
	First Day Cover (4)			40.00☐

116. 2½d. Surcharge George VI 117. 3½d. Surcharge George VI 118. 5½d. Surcharge Sheep

Surcharges on George VI Issues 1941 10 Dec

No.	Description	MUH	MLH	FU
116	2½d on 2d Red George VI	2.00☐	0.50☐	0.30☐
117	3½d on 3d Blue George VI	2.00☐	0.50☐	0.30☐
118	5½d on 5d Purple Sheep	7.00☐	4.00☐	4.00☐
	First Day Cover (3)			325.00☐

119. Queen Elizabeth 120. Queen Elizabeth 121. King George VI

122. King George VI 123. King George VI 124. Emu

George VI Definitive Issue 1942-1944

No.	Description	MUH	MLH	FU
119	1d Dull Purple Elizabeth	1.50☐	0.50☐	0.30☐
	First Day Cover			100.00☐
120	1½d Green Elizabeth	1.50☐	0.50☐	0.30☐
	First Day Cover			100.00☐
121	2d Purple George VI	1.50☐	1.00☐	0.30☐
	First Day Cover			125.00☐
122	2½d Red George VI	1.50☐	1.00☐	0.30☐
	First Day Cover			100.00☐
123	3½d Blue George VI	2.00☐	1.00☐	0.30☐
	First Day Cover			125.00☐
124	5½d Blue Emu	2.00☐	1.00☐	0.30☐
	First Day Cover			1,250.00☐

125. Duke & Duchess of Gloucester

Duke & Duchess of Gloucester   **1945 19 Feb**

No.	Description	MUH	MLH	FU
125	2½d Red	0.50	0.35	0.30
126	3½d Blue	0.50	0.35	0.30
127	5½d Dark Blue	0.50	0.35	0.30
	First Day Cover (3)			15.00

128. Star & Olive Wreath

129. Australian Flag & Dove of Peace

130. Peace, Motherhood & Industry

Peace and Victory   **1946 18 Feb**

No.	Description	MUH	MLH	FU
128	2½d Red Star & Olive Wreath	0.50	0.35	0.30
129	3½d Blue Australian Flag & Dove	0.50	0.35	0.30
130	5½d Green Peace, Motherhood, Industry	0.50	0.35	0.30
	First Day Cover (3)			15.00

131. Sir Thomas Mitchell & Map of Queensland

Centenary of Mitchell's Exploration   **1946 14 Oct**
Sir Thomas Mitchell and Map of Queensland

No.	Description	MUH	MLH	FU
131	2½d Red	0.60	0.35	0.30
132	3½d Blue	0.60	0.35	0.30
133	1/- Green	0.60	0.35	0.30
	First Day Cover (3)			25.00

134. Lt Shortland

135. Steel Foundry

136. Coal Crane

150th Anniversary of Newcastle   **194708Sep**

No.	Description	MUH	MLH	FU
134	2½d Red Lt Shortland	0.50	0.35	0.30
135	3½d Blue Steel Foundry	0.50	0.35	0.30
136	5½d Green Coal Crane	0.50	0.35	0.30
	First Day Cover			15.00

137. Princess Elizabeth

Marriage of Princess Elizabeth   **1947 20 Nov**

No.	Description	MUH	MLH	FU
137	1d Purple Princess Elizabeth	0.50	0.30	0.30
	First Day Cover			5.00

138. Bull

139. Rock Carving

Australian Animals   **1948 16 Feb**

No.	Description	MUH	MLH	FU
138	1/3 Brown Bull	3.00	1.10	0.60
	First Day Cover			20.00
139	2/- Brown Rock Carving	3.00	1.10	0.60
	First Day Cover			225.00

140. William Farrer

William Farrer   **1948 12 Jul**

No.	Description	MUH	MLH	FU
140	2½d Red William Farrer	0.50	0.35	0.30
	First Day Cover			2.75

141. Von Mueller

Sir Ferdinand von Mueller   1948 13 Sep
141   2½d Red Von Mueller   0.50☐   0.35☐   0.30☐
     First Day Cover   2.50☐

Stamp with similar design issued in 1952 with a higher denomination

142. Boy Scout

Pan Pacific Scout Jamboree   1948 15 Nov
142   2½d Red Boy Scout   0.50☐   0.35☐   0.30☐
     First Day Cover   2.50☐

143. Henry Lawson

HenryLawson   1949 17 Jun
143   2½d Red Henry Lawson   0.50☐   0.35☐   0.30☐
     First Day Cover   2.50☐

144. Outback Mail Carrier

75th Anniversary of Universal Postal Union   1949 10 Oct
144   3½d Blue Outback Mail Carrier   0.50☐   0.35☐   0.30☐
     First Day Cover   2.50☐

145. Lord Forrest

Lord Forrest of Bunbury   1949 28 Nov
145   2½d Red Lord Forrest   0.50☐   0.35☐   0.30☐
     First Day Cover   2.50☐

146. Hermes & Globe

Air Mail   1949 01 Sep
146   1/6 Black Hermes & Globe   3.00☐   1.20☐   0.50☐
     First Day Cover   20.00☐

147. Commonwealth Coat of Arms

George VI High Value Definitive - Coat of Arms   1949 11 Apr
5/- 3/10/49. 10/- 28/11/49. £1 x 18,279 £2
147   5/- Red Coat of Arms   5.00☐   2.00☐   1.00☐
     First Day Cover   50.00☐
148   10/- Purple Coat of Arms   30.00☐   15.00☐   2.00☐
     First Day Cover   375.00☐
149   £1 Blue Coat of Arms   60.00☐   28.00☐   9.00☐
     First Day Cover   650.00☐
150   £2 Green Coat of Arms   190.00☐   100.00☐   25.00☐
     First Day Cover (3)   1,750.00☐

151. Queen Elizabeth   153. King George VI   157. King George VI

161. King George VI   162. Aborigine

163. King George VI   164. Aborigine

NO.	DESCRIPTION	MUH	MLH	FU

George VI Definitives | | | | 1950-51

NO.	DESCRIPTION	MUH	MLH	FU
151	1½d Green Elizabeth	1.00☐	0.35☐	0.30☐
	First Day Cover			25.00☐
152	2d Dull Green Elizabeth	1.00☐	0.35☐	0.30☐
	First Day Cover			25.00☐
153	2½d Red George VI	1.00☐	0.35☐	0.30☐
	First Day Cover			30.00☐
154	2½d Brown George VI	1.00☐	0.35☐	0.30☐
	First Day Cover			30.00☐
155	3d Red George VI	1.00☐	0.35☐	0.30☐
	First Day Cover			30.00☐
156	3d Green George VI	1.00☐	0.35☐	0.30☐
	First Day Cover			30.00☐
157	3½d Brown/Purple George VI	1.00☐	0.35☐	0.30☐
	First Day Cover			30.00☐
158	4½d Red George VI	1.00☐	0.35☐	0.30☐
	First Day Cover			4.00☐
159	6½d Brown	1.00☐	0.35☐	0.30☐
	First Day Cover			50.00☐
160	6½d Green George VI	1.00☐	0.35☐	0.30☐
	First Day Cover			60.00☐
161	7½d Blue George VI	1.00☐	0.35☐	0.30☐
	First Day Cover			60.00☐
162	8½d Brown Aborigine	1.00☐	0.35☐	0.30☐
	First Day Cover			80.00☐
163	1/0 ½d George VI	2.50☐	1.50☐	0.35☐
	First Day Cover			80.00☐
164	2/6 Brown Aborigine	6.00☐	2.50☐	0.40☐
	First Day Cover			90.00☐

165. NSW Seal   166. Queen Victoria

Centenary of First Adhesive Postage Stamps in Australia | 1950 27 Sep

NO.	DESCRIPTION	MUH	MLH	FU
165	2½d Brown NSW Seal	1.00☐	0.50☐	0.30☐
166	2½d Brown Queen Victoria	1.00☐	0.50☐	0.30☐
167	Joined pair (165/166)	2.00☐	1.00☐	0.70☐
	First Day Cover (pair)			4.00☐

168. Sir Edmund Barton   169. Sir Henry Parkes

171. Duke of York
opening first Federal Parliament

172. Parliament House

Golden Jubilee of Commonwealth of Australia | | 1951 01 May

NO.	DESCRIPTION	MUH	MLH	FU
168	3d Red Sir Edmund Barton	1.00☐	0.35☐	0.30☐
169	3d Red Sir Henry Parkes	1.00☐	0.35☐	0.30☐
170	Joined pair (168/169)	2.00☐	0.75☐	0.70☐
171	5½d Blue Opening of Parliament	1.50☐	0.50☐	0.50☐
172	1/6 Brown Parliament House	2.00☐	0.80☐	0.80☐
	First Day Cover (4)			7.50☐

173. Edward Hargraves   174. Charles Latrobe

Centenary of the discovery of gold in | | 1951 02 Jul
Australia and Centenary of responsible government in Victoria

NO.	DESCRIPTION	MUH	MLH	FU
173	3d Red Edward Hargraves	1.00☐	0.35☐	0.30☐
174	3d Red Charles Latrobe	1.00☐	0.35☐	0.30☐
175	Joined pair (173/174)	2.00☐	0.75☐	0.70☐
	First Day Cover (Pair)			4.00☐

176. Boy Scout

Pan Pacific Scout Jamboree | | 1952 19 Nov

NO.	DESCRIPTION	MUH	MLH	FU
176	3½d Red Boy Scout	1.00☐	0.35☐	0.30☐
	First Day Cover			2.75☐

179. Butter   177. Wheat   178. Beef

184. Butter   182. Wheat   183. Beef

Food Production   1953 11 Feb

No.	Description	MUH	MLH	FU
177	3d Green Wheat	1.80	1.00	0.30
178	3d Green Beef	1.80	1.00	0.30
179	3d Green Butter	1.80	1.00	0.30
180	Joined strip of 3 (177/8/9)	8.00	4.00	4.00
181	Block of nine	40.00	25.00	40.00
	First Day Cover (strip of 3)			30.00
182	3½d Red Wheat	1.60	0.90	0.30
183	3½d Red Beef	1.60	0.90	0.30
184	3½d Red Butter	1.60	4.50	0.30
	Joined strip of 3 (182/3/4)	8.00	3.50	3.50
	Block of nine	30.00	20.00	30.00
	First Day Cover (strip of 3)			30.00

187. Queen Elizabeth II

190. Queen Elizabeth II

Coronation of Queen Elizabeth II   1953 25 May

No.	Description	MUH	MLH	FU
187	3½d Scarlet	0.50	0.35	0.30
188	7½d Purple	1.00	0.50	0.50
189	2/- Dull Blue Green	1.50	1.00	1.20
	First Day Cover (3)			10.00

Queen Elizabeth Definitive Issue

No.	Description	MUH	MLH	FU
190	1d Purple	0.50	0.35	0.30
	First Day Cover			10.00
191	2½d Blue	0.50	0.35	0.30
	First Day Cover			15.00
192	3d Green	0.50	0.35	0.30
	First Day Cover			15.00
193	3½d Red	1.00	0.35	0.30
	First Day Cover			15.00
194	6½d Orange	1.50	0.70	0.30
	First Day Cover			20.00

NO.	DESCRIPTION	MUH	MLH	FU

195. Young Farmers Clubs

25th Anniversary Australian Young Farmers Clubs

1953 03 Sep

195	3½d Brown/Green YoungFarmers Clubs	0.50☐	0.35☐	0.30☐
	First Day Cover			4.00☐

196. Lt Gov Collins   197. Lt Gov Paterson

199. HMT Ocean at anchor in Sullivan Cove, Hobart 1804

150th Anniversary settlement of Tasmania

1953 23 Sep

196	3½d Brown Lt Gov Collins	0.50☐	0.35☐	0.30☐
197	3½d Brown Lt Gov Paterson	0.50☐	0.35☐	0.30☐
198	Joined pair (196/197)	2.00☐	2.00☐	2.00☐
199	2/- Green HMT Ocean in Hobart	5.00☐	3.00☐	3.00☐
	First Day Cover (3)			20.00☐

200. Tasmanian Stamp of 1853

Centenary of First Tasmanian Postage Stamp

1953 11 Nov

200	3d Red Tasmanian Stamp of 1853	0.50☐	0.35☐	0.30☐
	First Day Cover			5.00☐

201. Queen Elizabeth II & Duke of Edinburgh

NO.	DESCRIPTION	MUH	MLH	FU

202. Queen Elizabeth II

Royal Visit

1954 02 Feb

201	3½d Scarlet Queen & Duke	0.80☐	0.35☐	0.30☐
202	7½d Purple Queen Elizabeth	1.00☐	0.50☐	0.50☐
203	2/- Green Queen & Duke	2.00☐	1.00☐	1.20☐
	First Day Cover (3)			8.00☐

204. Telegraph Pole & Morse Key

Centenary of Australian Telegraph

1954 07 Apr

204	3½d Red Telegraph Pole	0.80☐	0.35☐	0.30☐
	First Day Cover			4.00☐

205. Red Cross & Globe

40th Anniversary of Australian Red Cross

1954 09 Jun

205	3½d Red & Blue - Red Cross & Globe	0.80☐	0.35☐	0.30☐
	First Day Cover			4.00☐

206. Black Swan

Centenary First Western Australia Postage Stamp

1954 02 Aug

206	3½d Black - Black Swan	0.80☐	0.35☐	0.30☐
	First Day Cover			4.00☐

207. Locomotives 1854-1954

Centenary Australian Railways — 1954 13 Sep

No.	Description	MUH	MLH	FU
207	3½d Maroon Locomotives	0.80☐	0.35☐	0.30☐
	First Day Cover			4.00☐

208. Emblem of Antarctic Division of Australian Department of External Affairs

Australian Antarctic Research — 1954 17 Nov

No.	Description	MUH	MLH	FU
208	3½d Black Antarctic Emblem	0.80☐	0.35☐	0.30☐
	First Day Cover			4.00☐

210. 1956 Olympic Games Symbol

Melbourne Olympic Games — 1954 01 Dec

No.	Description	MUH	MLH	FU
209	2/- Blue Olympic Games symbol	7.00☐	3.50☐	3.50☐
	First Day Cover			10.00☐
210	2/- Green Olympic Games symbol	4.00☐	3.00☐	3.50☐
	First Day Cover			10.00☐

211. Rotary Symbol

50th Anniversary Rotary — 1955 23 Feb

No.	Description	MUH	MLH	FU
211	3½d Red Rotary Symbol	0.80☐	0.35☐	0.30☐
	First Day Cover			4.00☐

212. US Memorial Canberra

Australian American Friendship — 1955 04 May

No.	Description	MUH	MLH	FU
212	3½d Blue US Memorial Canberra	0.80☐	0.35☐	0.30☐
	First Day Cover			4.00☐

213. Queen Elizabeth II   217. Queen Elizabeth II

Queen Elizabeth II Definitive issue — 1955

No.	Description	MUH	MLH	FU
213	4d Lake Elizabeth	1.00☐	0.50☐	0.30☐
	First Day Cover			5.00☐
214	7½d Violet Elizabeth	1.50☐	0.70☐	0.70☐
	First Day Cover			10.00☐
215	10d Blue Elizabeth	1.50☐	0.80☐	0.55☐
	First Day Cover			15.00☐
216	1/0 ½d Blue Elizabeth	4.00☐	2.50☐	0.60☐
	First Day Cover			15.00☐
217	1/7 Brown Elizabeth	6.50☐	4.00☐	0.60☐
	First Day Cover			20.00☐

218. Cobb & Co Coach

Mail Coach Pioneers — 1955 06 Jul

No.	Description	MUH	MLH	FU
218	3½d Sepia Cobb & Co Coach	0.80☐	0.35☐	0.30☐
219	2/- Brown Cobb & Co Coach	4.00☐	2.50☐	2.00☐
	First Day Cover			10.00☐

220. YMCA Emblem

World Centenary YMCA — 1955 10 Aug

No.	Description	MUH	MLH	FU
220	3½d Green & Red YMCA Emblem	0.80☐	0.35☐	0.30☐
	First Day Cover			3.00☐

NO.	DESCRIPTION	MUH	MLH	FU

221. Florence Nightingale

Centenary of Nursing　　　　　　**1955 21 Sep**

| 221 | 3½d Purple Florence Nightingale | 0.80☐ | 0.35☐ | 0.30☐ |
| | First Day Cover | | | 3.00☐ |

222. Queen Victoria

Centenary of First South Australian Postage Stamp

　　　　　　　　　　　　　　1955 17 Oct

| 222 | 3½d Green Queen Victoria | 0.80☐ | 0.35☐ | 0.30☐ |
| | First Day Cover | | | 3.00☐ |

223. Badges of NSW, Vic, Tas

Centenary of Responsible Government in New South Wales, Victoria and Tasmania.　　**1955 26 Sep**

| 223 | 3½d Red Badges of States | 0.80☐ | 0.35☐ | 0.30☐ |
| | First Day Cover | | | 3.00☐ |

224. Coat of Arms of Melbourne

225. Olympic Torch

NO.	DESCRIPTION	MUH	MLH	FU

226. Collins St Melbourne

227. Melbourne across the Yarra

XVIth Melbourne Olympic Games　　**1956 31 Oct**

224	4d Carmine Red Arms of Melb.	0.80☐	0.35☐	0.30☐
225	7½d Bright Blue Olympic Torch	1.00☐	0.50☐	0.40☐
226	1/- Multi Collins St Melbourne	2.00☐	0.60☐	0.60☐
227	2/- Multi Yarra & Melbourne	2.00☐	1.50☐	0.95☐
	First Day Cover (4)			20.00☐

228. Coat of Arms of South Australia

Centenary of responsible government in South Australia

　　　　　　　　　　　　　　1957 17 Apr

| 228 | 4d Red Brown South Australia Arms | 0.80☐ | 0.35☐ | 0.30☐ |
| | First Day Cover | | | 3.00☐ |

229. Map of Australia & Caduceus

Flying Doctor Service　　　　　　**1957 21 Aug**

| 229 | 7d Ultramarine Map & Caduceus | 0.80☐ | 0.35☐ | 0.30☐ |
| | First Day Cover | | | 5.00☐ |

230. "The Child Samuel of Prayer" painting by Sir Joshua Reynolds

Christmas Issue　　　　　　　　**1957 06 Nov**

230	3½d Scarlet Child Praying	0.80☐	0.35☐	0.30☐
231	4d Purple Child Praying	0.80☐	0.35☐	0.30☐
	First Day Cover (2)			3.00☐

232. Super Constellation

Inauguration of Qantas Round the World Air Service

1958 06 Jan

		MUH	MLH	FU
232	2/- Deep Blue Super Constellation	3.00□	1.60□	2.50□
	First Day Cover			7.00□

233. Sailor, Airman

234. Soldier, Nurse

Australian War Memorial, Canberra

1958 10 Feb

		MUH	MLH	FU
233	5½d Brown/Red Sailor, Airman	1.50□	0.70□	0.50□
234	5½d Brown/Red Soldier, Nurse	1.50□	0.70□	0.50□
235	Joined pair (233/234)	5.00□	2.60□	3.80□
	First Day Cover (2)			10.00□

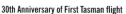

236. Kingsford Smith

30th Anniversary of First Tasman flight

1958 27 Aug

		MUH	MLH	FU
236	8d Deep Blue Kingsford Smith	2.00□	1.00□	0.90□

237. Silver Mines Broken Hill

238. Scarlet Nativity Scene

75th Anniversary of Broken Hill

1958 10 Sep

		MUH	MLH	FU
237	4d Brown Silver Mines Broken Hill	0.80□	0.35□	0.30□
	First Day Cover			3.00□

Christmas Issue

1958 05 Nov

		MUH	MLH	FU
238	3½d Scarlet Nativity Scene	0.80□	0.35□	0.30□
239	4d Violet Nativity Scene	0.80□	0.35□	0.30□
	First Day Cover (2)			5.00□

240. Queen Elizabeth II

241. Queen Elizabeth II

242. Queen Elizabeth II

243. Queen Elizabeth II

244. Queen Elizabeth II

245. Queen Elizabeth II

Queen Elizabeth II Definitive Issue

1959-1962

		MUH	MLH	FU
240	1d Slate Purple Elizabeth	0.50□	0.35□	0.30□
	First Day Cover			5.00□
241	2d Brown Elizabeth	0.50□	0.35□	0.30□
	First Day Cover			5.00□
242	3d Blue Green Elizabeth	0.50□	0.35□	0.30□
	First Day Cover			10.00□
243	3½d Deep Green Elizabeth	0.50□	0.35□	0.30□
	First Day Cover			10.00□
244	4d Lake Elizabeth	0.50□	0.35□	0.30□
	First Day Cover			10.00□
245	5d Deep Blue Elizabeth	0.50□	0.35□	0.30□
	First Day Cover			10.00□

246. Isaac Nichols: Postmaster

150th Anniversary Australian Post Office

1959 22 Apr

		MUH	MLH	FU
246	4d Slate Isaac Nichols Postmaster	0.80□	0.35□	0.30□
	First Day Cover			3.00□

247. Christmas Bells

248. Flannel Flowers

249. Wattle

251. Banksia

252. Waratah

Native Flower Definitives — 1959-1964

No.	Description	MUH	MLH	FU
247	1/6 Red Yellow Christmas Bells	2.50	1.50	0.30
	First Day Cover			5.00
248	2/- Grey Blue Flannel Flowers	2.00	0.70	0.30
	First Day Cover			6.00
249	2/3 Green Yellow Wattle	4.00	1.50	0.50
	First Day Cover			10.00
250	2/3 Green Wattle	6.00	3.75	2.00
	First Day Cover			15.00
251	2/5 Brown Yellow Banksia	9.00	4.00	0.45
	First Day Cover			15.00
252	3/- Red Waratah	4.00	2.20	0.35
	First Day Cover			15.00

253. Parliament House, Brisbane

254. Magi guided by Star

Centenary self government in Queensland — 1959 05 Jun

No.	Description	MUH	MLH	FU
253	4d Green Lilac Parliament Brisbane	0.80	0.35	0.30
	First Day Cover			3.00

Christmas Issue — 1959 04 Nov

No.	Description	MUH	MLH	FU
254	5d Red/Violet Magi & Star	0.80	0.35	0.30
	First Day Cover			3.00

255. Banded Anteater

256. Tiger Cat

257. Kangaroos

258. Rabbit Bandicoot

259. Platypus

260. Tasmanian Tiger

Australian Animals — 1959-1962

No.	Description	MUH	MLH	FU
255	6d Brown Banded Anteater	1.50	0.35	0.30
	First Day Cover			10.00
256	8d Red Brown Tiger Cat	1.50	0.35	0.30
	First Day Cover			15.00
257	9d Sepia Kangaroos	2.00	0.70	0.35
	First Day Cover			15.00
258	11d Blue Rabbit Bandicoot	2.00	0.70	0.35
	First Day Cover			15.00
259	1/- Green Platypus	5.00	2.50	0.40
	First Day Cover			15.00
260	1/2d Deep Purple Tasmanian Tiger	2.00	0.70	0.35
	First Day Cover			20.00

261. Guide & Baden Powell

50th Anniversary Girl Guides — 1960 18 Aug

No.	Description	MUH	MLH	FU
261	5d Deep Blue Guide & Baden Powell	0.80	0.35	0.30
	First Day Cover			3.00

262. "Overlanders" by Sir Daryl Lindsay

Centenary Northern Territory Exploration — 1960 21 Sep

No.	Description	MUH	MLH	FU
262	5d Magenta Overlanders by Lindsay	0.80	0.35	0.30
	First Day Cover			3.00

263. Archer

Centenary of Melbourne Cup   1960 12 Oct
263   5d Sepia Archer   0.80☐   0.35☐   0.30☐
    First Day Cover   3.00☐

264. Queen Victoria

Centenary First Queensland Postage Stamp   1960 02 Nov
264   5d Green Queen Victoria   0.80☐   0.35☐   0.30☐
    First Day Cover   3.00☐

265. Bible

Christmas Issue   1960 09 Nov
265   5d Carmine Red Bible   0.80☐   0.35☐   0.30☐
    First Day Cover   3.00☐

266. Colombo Plan Emblem

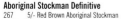

267. Aboriginal Stockman

10th Anniversary Colombo Plan   1961 30 Jun
266   1/- Red Brown Colombo Plan Emblem   2.00☐   0.70☐ · 0.30☐
    First Day Cover   3.00☐

Aboriginal Stockman Definitive   1961 26 Jul
267   5/- Red Brown Aboriginal Stockman   30.00☐   15.00☐   2.00☐
267a   5/- Red Brown Aboriginal Stockman   140.00☐   100.00☐   20.00☐
    white paper
    First Day Cover   30.00☐

268. Dame Nellie Melba   269. Prayer Book & Text

Centenary Birth of Dame Nellie Melba   1961 20 Sep
268   5d Blue Dame Nellie Melba   0.80☐   0.35☐   0.30☐
    First Day Cover   3.00☐

Christmas Issue   1961 08 Nov
269   5d Brown Prayer Book & Text   0.80☐   0.35☐   0.30☐
    First Day Cover   3.00☐

270. John McDouall Stuart   271. Flynn's Grave at Alice Springs

Centenary Stuart's Overland Crossing   1962 25 Jul
270   5d Red John McDouall Stuart   0.80☐   0.35☐   0.30☐
    First Day Cover   3.00☐

50th Anniversary Australian Inland Mission   1962 05 Sep
271   5d Multi Flynn's Grave at Alice Springs   0.80☐   0.35☐   0.30☐
    First Day Cover   3.00☐

272. CWA Allegory   273. Madonna & Child

Conference of Country Women of the World   1962 26 Sep
272   5d Deep Green CWA Allegory   0.80☐   0.35☐   0.30☐
    First Day Cover   3.00☐

Christmas Issue   1962 17 Oct
273   5d Purple Madonna & Child   0.80☐   0.35☐   0.30☐
    First Day Cover   3.00☐

274. Kangaroo Paw Flowers 275. Perth Coat of Arms

281. Export theme

British Empire & Commonwealth Games 1962 01 Nov

274	5d Multi Kangaroo Paw Flowers	1.00☐	0.35☐	0.30☐
275	2/3 Multi Perth Coat of Arms	5.00☐	3.00☐	3.00☐
	First Day Cover (2)			15.00☐

Export Campaign 1963 28 Aug

| 281 | 5d Red Export theme | 0.80☐ | 0.35☐ | 0.30☐ |
| | First Day Cover | | | 3.00☐ |

276. Queen Elizabeth II 277. Queen Elizabeth II & Prince Philllip

282. Queen Elizabeth II

283. Queen Elizabeth II

Royal Visit 1963 18 Feb

276	5d Green Elizabeth	0.80☐	0.35☐	0.30☐
277	2/3 Brown/Lake Elizabeth/Phillip	5.00☐	2.30☐	3.00☐
	First Day Cover (2)			15.00☐

282a. Queen Elizabeth II

278. Walter Burley Griffin

282b. Queen Elizabeth II

50th Anniversary of Canberra 1963 08 Mar

| 278 | 5d Deep Green Walter Burley Griffin | 0.80☐ | 0.35☐ | 0.30☐ |
| | First Day Cover | | | 3.00☐ |

282c. Queen Elizabeth II

282a, 282b, 282c are from sheets of uncut booklet pages

279. Red Cross 280. Blaxland, Lawson & Wentworth on Mount York

Centenary of Red Cross 1963 08 May

| 279 | 5d Blue/Red/Grey Red Cross | 0.80☐ | 0.35☐ | 0.30☐ |
| | First Day Cover | | | 3.00☐ |

150th Anniversary Blue Mountain Crossing 1963 28 May

| 280 | 5d Blue Blaxland, Lawson & Wentworth on Mount York | 0.80☐ | 0.35☐ | 0.30☐ |
| | First Day Cover (2) | | | 8.00☐ |

Queen Elizabeth II Definitive 1963-1965

282	5d Green Queen Elizabeth II	1.00☐	0.35☐	0.30☐
	First Day Cover			5.00☐
282a	5d Green pair imperforate between	4.00☐	1.30☐	2.00☐
282b	5d Green imperforate at right	15.00☐	8.00☐	13.00☐
282c	5d Green imperforate at left	15.00☐	8.00☐	13.00☐
283	5d Red Queen Elizabeth II	1.00☐	0.35☐	0.30☐
	First Day Cover			5.00☐

284. Abel Tasman

285. William Dampier

292. Yellow Tailed thornbill

293. Black Backed Magpie

286. James Cook

287. Mathew Flinders

294. Galah

295. Golden Whistler

288. George Bass

289. Phillip Parker King

296. Blue Wren

297. Scarlet Robin

Early Navigators of Australia   1963-1964

No.	Description	MUH	MLH	FU
284	4/- Ultramarine Abel Tasman	4.00☐	3.00☐	0.75☐
	First Day Cover			10.00☐
285	5/- Red Brown William Dampier	8.00☐	3.00☐	2.20☐
	First Day Cover			10.00☐
286	7/6 Olive James Cook	15.00☐	11.00☐	11.00☐
	First Day Cover			30.00☐
287	10/- Maroon Mathew Flinders	35.00☐	22.00☐	8.00☐
	First Day Cover			40.00☐
288	£1 Purple George Bass	80.00☐	36.00☐	30.00☐
	First Day Cover			75.00☐
289	£2 Sepia Phillip Parker King	95.00☐	85.00☐	85.00☐
	First Day Cover			175.00☐

298. Straw Necked Ibis

290. Christmas Star

291. Cable encircling globe

Christmas Issue   1963 25 Oct

No.	Description	MUH	MLH	FU
290	5d Blue Christmas Star	0.80☐	0.35☐	0.30☐
	First Day Cover			3.00☐

Opening of COMPAC Commonwealth Pacific Cable   1963 03 Dec

No.	Description	MUH	MLH	FU
291	2/3 Multi Cable encircling globe	5.50☐	3.00☐	3.00☐
	First Day Cover			8.00☐
	First Day Cover			12.00☐

Bird Definitives   1964-65

No.	Description	MUH	MLH	FU
292	6d Multi Yellow Tailed Thornbill	1.50☐	0.35☐	0.30☐
	First Day Cover			5.00☐
293	9d Multi Black Backed Magpie	2.00☐	0.80☐	1.00☐
	First Day Cover			10.00☐
294	1/6 Multi Galah	2.00☐	0.80☐	1.00☐
	First Day Cover			15.00☐
295	2/- Multi Golden Whistler	2.00☐	0.65☐	0.50☐
	First Day Cover			15.00☐
296	2/5 Multi Blue Wren	7.00☐	3.20☐	3.00☐
297	2/6 Multi Scarlet Robin	5.00☐	3.00☐	2.00☐
	First Day Cover			25.00☐
298	3/- Multi Straw Necked Ibis	3.00☐	3.00☐	1.00☐
	First Day Cover			20.00☐

NO.	DESCRIPTION	MUH	MLH	FU

299. Bleriot XI Monoplane

50th Anniversary of First Airmail — **1964 01 Jul**

NO.	DESCRIPTION	MUH	MLH	FU
299	5d Green Bleriot XI Monoplane	0.80	0.35	0.30
300	2/3 Red Bleriot XI Monoplane	4.00	3.00	3.50
	First Day Cover (2)			10.00

301. Child & Nativity Scene

Christmas Issue — **1964 21 Oct**

301	5d Multi Child & Nativity Scene	0.80	0.35	0.30

302. Simpson & Donkey

50th Anniversary of Gallipoli Landing — **1965 14 Apr**

302	5d Khaki Simpson & Donkey	0.80	0.35	0.30
303	8d Blue Simpson & Donkey	1.00	0.75	0.75
304	2/3 Maroon Simpson & Donkey	3.50	2.00	3.00
	First Day Cover (3)			15.00

305. Globe, Mast & Satellite

Centenary International Telecommunications — **1965 10 May**

305	5d Multi Globe, Mast & Satellite	0.80	0.35	0.30
	First Day Cover			3.00

306. Sir Winston Churchill

Sir Winston Churchill — **1965 24 May**

306	5d Black/Grey/Pale Blue Churchill	0.80	0.35	0.30
	First Day Cover			3.00

307. Sir John Monash

Centenary Birth General Sir John Monash — **1965 23 Jun**

307	5d Multi Sir John Monash	0.80	0.35	0.30
	First Day Cover			3.00

308. Hargrave

309. ICY Symbol

310. Nativity

Anniversary of Death of Aviation Pioneer — **1965 04 Aug**

308	5d Multi Hargrave	0.80	0.35	0.30
	First Day Cover			3.00

International Co-operation Year — **1965 01 Sep**

309	2/3 Blue & Green ICY Symbol	3.00	1.80	2.50
	First Day Cover			10.00

Christmas Issue — **1965 20 Oct**

310	5d Multi Nativity	0.80	0.35	0.30
	First Day Cover			3.00

Perforated O S Issues

OS   O S   OS

Large OS (-OSL)   Small OS (-OSS)   Medium OS (-OSM)

This catalogue only lists, on a simplified basis, official stamps issued within Commonwealth government departments.
The first Kangaroo stamps were perforated (punctured) with Large O S (A) – this size perforation weakened the stamps so that within a short period of time they were replaced with Small O S (B) – other issues were perforated with different size O S (C) –a point to remember is that many O S perforated stamps were from stock which were badly centred.
Prices quoted are for stamps, which are reasonably centred – perfectly centred stamps are rarely available and are worth, in most instances, a considerable premium. Badly centred stamps are worth less.

This is a simplified listing of the cheapest copy available of each value from ½d to £2 in the Kangaroo series

01-OSL. Kangaroo

Kangaroo Issue Definitives perforated with large O S
(-OSL suffix on standard issue stamp catalogue number)

No.	Description	MUH	MLH	FU
01-OSL	½d Green	30.00	18.00	15.00
02-OSL	1d Red	45.00	15.00	6.00
03-OSL	2d Grey	190.00	45.00	15.00
04-OSL	2½d Indigo	800.00	350.00	225.00
05-OSL	3d Olive	550.00	250.00	50.00
06-OSL	4d Orange	800.00	350.00	25.00
07-OSL	5d Brown	750.00	325.00	50.00
08-OSL	6d Ultramarine	700.00	275.00	30.00
10-OSL	9d Violet	700.00	275.00	90.00
11-OSL	1/- Green	1,250.00	350.00	35.00
12-OSL	2/- Brown	3,250.00	750.00	200.00
14-OSL	5/- Grey & Yellow	4,750.00	1,500.00	750.00
15-OSL	10/- Grey & Pink	8,000.00	4,000.00	2,300.00
16-OSL	£1 Brown & Blue	25,000.00	7,500.00	4,500.00
18-OSL	£2 Black & Rose	60,000.00	15,000.00	6,000.00

01-OSS. Kangaroo

Kangaroo Definitive Issues O S Perforated with Small O S

(-OSS suffix on standard issue stamp catalogue number)

No.	Description	MUH	MLH	FU
01-OSS	½d Green	45.00	20.00	15.00
02-OSS	1d Red	50.00	30.00	15.00
03-OSS	2d Grey	125.00	60.00	12.00
04-OSS	2½d Indigo	380.00	150.00	25.00
05-OSS	3d Olive	275.00	60.00	15.00
06-OSS	4d Orange	1,250.00	600.00	150.00
07-OSS	5d Brown	950.00	425.00	65.00
08-OSS	6d Ultramarine	700.00	100.00	10.00
09-OSS	6d Brown	75.00	40.00	50.00
10-OSS	9d Violet	325.00	150.00	100.00
11-OSS	1/- Green	125.00	60.00	30.00
12-OSS	2/- Brown	2,500.00	750.00	30.00
13-OSS	2/- Maroon	500.00	300.00	40.00
14-OSS	5/- Grey & Yellow	2,250.00	1,250.00	125.00
15-OSS	10/- Grey & Pink	2,750.00	1,000.00	125.00
16-OSS	£1 Brown & Blue	27,500.00	6,000.00	7,500.00
17-OSS	£1 Grey	4,000.00	1,800.00	1,750.00
18-OSS	£2 Black & Rose	17,500.00	9,000.00	5,000.00

George V Definitive Issue perforated small O S

31-OSS. KGV

(-OSS suffix on standard issue stamp catalogue number)

No.	Description	MUH	MLH	FU
20-OSS	½d Green	30.00	15.00	10.00
21-OSS	½d Orange	35.00	8.00	4.00
23-OSS	1d Red	30.00	15.00	2.00
24-OSS	1d Violet	130.00	50.00	20.00
25-OSS	1d Green	30.00	10.00	2.00
26-OSS	1½d Black-Brown	110.00	50.00	10.00
27-OSS	1½d Brown	110.00	60.00	10.00
28-OSS	1½d Green	135.00	70.00	20.00
29-OSS	1½d Red	30.00	15.00	8.00
30-OSS	2d Orange	130.00	70.00	8.00
31-OSS	2d Red	40.00	18.00	5.00
32-OSS	2d Brown	135.00	60.00	30.00
33-OSS	3d Blue	200.00	125.00	5.00
34-OSS	4d Orange	325.00	150.00	10.00
35-OSS	4d Lemon	2,750.00	1,200.00	125.00
36-OSS	4d Violet	450.00	175.00	35.00
37-OSS	4d Blue	400.00	150.00	25.00
38-OSS	4d Olive	180.00	60.00	15.00
39-OSS	4½d Violet	550.00	250.00	40.00
40-OSS	5d Brown	350.00	200.00	30.00
41-OSS	1/4d Blue	300.00	150.00	35.00

49-OSM. Parliament House Canberra

Parliament House Canberra, Medium O S   **1927 09 May**

(-OSM suffix on standard issue stamp catalogue number)
49-OSM 1½d Parliament House Canberra   25.00☐   12.00☐   10.00☐

50-OSM. Kookaburra

Kookaburra, Medium O S   **1928 29 Oct**

(-OSM suffix on standard issue stamp catalogue number)
50-OSM 3d Blue Kookaburra   40.00☐   20.00☐   15.00☐

52-OSM. Aeroplane over flock of sheep

53-OSM. Swan

Airmail, Medium O S   **1929 20 May**

(-OSM suffix on standard issue stamp catalogue number)
52-OSM 3d Green, Aeroplane   45.00☐   25.00☐   20.00☐

Western Australia Centenary, Medium O S   **1929 28 Sep**

(-OSM suffix on standard issue stamp catalogue number)
53-OSM 1½d Red, Swan   25.00☐   15.00☐   15.00☐

54-OSM. Charles Sturt

Sturt Centenary, Medium O S   **1930 02 Jun**

(-OSM suffix on standard issue stamp catalogue number)
54-OSM 1½d Red, Charles Sturt   15.00☐   10.00☐   5.00☐
55-OSM 3d Blue, Charles Sturt   40.00☐   20.00☐   20.00☐

Decimal Stamps
1966-1999

DECIMAL CURRENCY
No. 310 was the last stamp issued with the designation in £sd currency. At the close of trading on Saturday, Feb 12, 1966, all current £sd issues were withdrawn from sale at Australian Post Offices.
Values for Decimal Stamps are expressed as **M**int **U**n **H**inged (in undamaged condition), and **F**ine **U**sed (clear round cancellations with full perforations - heavy cancellations are worth less).
Values for Decimal first day covers are for unaddressed covers - addressed covers are generally worth the value of the stamps affixed.

311. Queen Elizabeth II

319. Thornbill

321. Honeyeater.

322. Humbug Fish

324. Coral Fish

325. Hermit Crab

326. Anemone Fish

327. Avocet

328. Galah

329. Whistler

330. Kingfisher

331. Scarlet Robin

332. Ibis

333. Abel Tasman

334. William Dampier

335. James Cook

336. Mathew Flinders

337. George Bass

338. Phillip Parker King

NO.	DESCRIPTION	MUH	FU

Decimal Definitive Issue — 1966 14Feb

NO.	DESCRIPTION	MUH	FU
311	1c Red Brown Elizabeth	0.30▢	0.30▢
312	2c Olive Green Elizabeth	0.75▢	0.30▢
313	3c Grey Green Elizabeth	0.75▢	0.30▢
314	3c Multi (coil) Elizabeth	0.50▢	0.30▢
315	4c Red Elizabeth	0.30▢	0.30▢
316	4c Multi (coil) Elizabeth.	0.75▢	0.30▢
317	5c Blue Elizabeth.	0.85▢	0.30▢
318	5c Multi (coil) Elizabeth	0.80▢	0.30▢
319	5c Thornbill	0.30▢	0.30▢
320	6c Orange Elizabeth	0.35▢	0.30▢
321	6c Multi Honeyeater	0.55▢	0.30▢
322	7c Multi Humbug Fish	1.25▢	0.30▢
323	7c Purple Elizabeth	0.30▢	0.30▢
324	8c Coral Fish	1.25▢	0.30▢
325	9c Hermit Crab	1.25▢	0.30▢
326	10c Anemone Fish	1.25▢	0.30▢
327	13c Avocet	2.00▢	0.30▢
328	15c Galah	2.00▢	0.50▢
329	20c Whistler	5.50▢	0.30▢
330	24c Kingfisher	1.00▢	0.85▢
331	25c Scarlet Robin	5.00▢	0.55▢
332	30c Ibis	17.00▢	0.55▢
333	40c Ultramarine Abel Tasman	11.00▢	0.30▢
334	50c Red/Brown William Dampier	16.00▢	0.30▢
335	75c Olive Green James Cook	1.00▢	1.00▢
336	$1 Maroon Mathew Flinders	2.50▢	0.40▢
337	$2 Purple George Bass	9.00▢	1.40▢
338	$4 Sepia Phillip Parker King	7.00▢	4.00▢
	First Day Cover Original set of 24		150.00▢

341. Dutch Ship

342. Hands & Bible

Anniversary of Dirk Hartog's Landing — 1966 24 Oct

341	4c Multi Dutch Ship	0.30▢	0.30▢
	First Day Cover		2.00▢

150th Anniversary British & Foreign Bible Society — 1967 07 Mar

342	4c Multi Hands & Bible	0.30▢	0.30▢
	First Day Cover		2.00▢

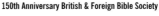

343. Lock & Keys

150th Anniversary Banking in Australia — 1967 05 Apr

343	4c Green Blue Lock & Keys	0.30▢	0.30▢
	First Day Cover		2.00▢

344. Lions Emblem

50th Anniversary Lions International — 1967 07 Jun

344	4c Blue Gold Lions Emblem	0.30▢	0.30▢
	First Day Cover		2.00▢

339. Life Saver

75th Anniversary Royal Life Saving Society — 1966 06 Jul

339	4c Black Blue Life Saver	0.30▢	0.30▢
	First Day Cover		2.00▢

345. YWCA Emblem

340. Adoration of the Shepherds

Christmas Issue — 1966 19 Oct

340	4c Olive Black - Adoration of the Shepherds	0.30▢	0.30▢
	First Day Cover		2.00▢

World YWCA Meeting — 196721 Aug

345	4c Multi YWCA Emblem	0.30▢	0.30▢
	First Day Cover		2.00▢

346. Medical Symbols

World Congress of Gynaecology and Obstetrics		1967 20 Sep
346	4c Multi Medical Symbols	0.30☐	0.30☐
	First Day Cover		2.00☐

347. Queen Elizabeth II

Definitive 5c surcharged on 4c Red		1967 29 Sep
347	5c on 4c Red Elizabeth	0.75☐	0.30☐
347a	Booklet pane 5 stamps & label	5.00☐	7.00☐
	First Day Cover		3.00☐

348. Bells & Arches

349. Decorative Cross

Christmas Issue		1967 18 Oct
348	5c Multi Bells & Arches	0.30☐	0.30☐
349	25c Multi Decorative Cross	2.50☐	2.00☐
	First Day Cover (2)		4.00☐

350. Satellite

351. Weather Map

World Weather Watch		1968 20 Mar
350	5c Multi Satellite	0.30☐	0.30☐
351	20c Multi Weather Map	3.00☐	3.00☐
	First Day Cover		6.00☐

352. Antenna

World Satellite Communications		1968 20 Mar
352	25c Antenna	2.50☐	3.00☐
	First Day Cover		4.50☐

353. Kangaroo Paw

354. Heath

355. Blue Gum

356. Desert Pea

357. Orchid

358. Waratah

State Floral Emblems		1968 10 Jul
353	6c Kangaroo Paw	0.40☐	0.30☐
354	13c Pink Heath	0.50☐	0.30☐
355	15c Blue Gum	2.00☐	0.30☐
356	20c Desert Pea	5.00☐	0.30☐
357	25c Orchid	4.00☐	0.30☐
358	30c Waratah	1.50☐	0.30☐
	First Day Cover (6)		13.00☐

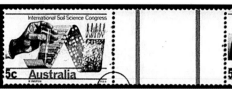

359. Soil Sample

360. Medical Design

362. Torchbearer
& Aztec Calender Stone

363. Aztec Calendar Stone
& Mexican Flag

International Soil Congress & World Medical Assembly

			1968 06 Aug
359	5c Soil Sample	0.40☐	0.30☐
360	5c Medical Design	0.40☐	0.30☐
361	Joined gutter pair (359/360)	12.00☐	11.00☐
	First Day Cover (gutter pair) unfolded		24.00☐

365. Bethlehem Scene

Christmas Issue

			1968 23 Oct
365	5c Bethlehem Scene	0.30☐	0.30☐
	First Day Cover		2.00☐

366. Banjo Paterson

367. Caroline Chisholm

368. William Edgeworth David

369. Albert Namatjira

Famous Australians

			1968 06 Nov
366	5c Blue Black Banjo Paterson	1.40☐	0.30☐
	5c Booklet pane 5 stamps & label	8.00☐	6.00☐
367	5c Purple Caroline Chisholm	1.40☐	0.30☐
	5c Booklet pane 5 stamps & label	8.00☐	6.00☐
368	5c Green William Edgeworth David	1.40☐	0.30☐
	Booklet pane 5 stamps & label	8.00☐	6.00☐
369	5c Brown Albert Namatjira	1.40☐	0.30☐
	Booklet pane 5 stamps & label	8.00☐	6.00☐
	First Day Cover (1 each value)		7.00☐

Olympic Games Mexico

			1968 02 Oct
362	5c Torchbearer & Aztec calendar	0.30☐	0.30☐
363	25c Aztec Calendar Stone & Mexican Flag	2.50☐	2.00☐
	First Day Cover		4.00☐

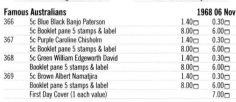

370. Macquarie Lighthouse

364. House & dollar symbols

Building & Savings Societies Congress

			1968 16 Oct
364	5c House & dollar symbols	0.30☐	0.30☐
	First Day Cover		2.00☐

Anniversary Macquarie Lighthouse

			1968 27 Nov
370	5c Black Pale Yellow Macquarie Lighthouse	0.30☐	0.30☐
	First Day Cover		2.00☐

371. Survey Team & Darwin View

Centenary Northern Territory Settlement — 1969 05 Feb

| 371 | 5c Survey Team & Darwin View | 0.30 | 0.30 |
| | First Day Cover | | 2.00 |

372. Harbour Scene

International Ports & Harbours Conference — 1969 26 Feb

| 372 | 5c Harbour Scene | 0.30 | 0.30 |
| | First Day Cover | | 2.00 |

373. ILO Symbol

50th Anniversary International Labour Organisation

1969 04 Jun

| 373 | 5c ILO Symbol | 0.30 | 0.30 |
| | First Day Cover | | 2.00 |

374. Sugar

375. Timber

376. Wheat

377. Wool

Primary Industries — 1969 17 Sep

374	7c Sugar	1.00	1.00
375	15c Timber	4.00	3.00
376	20c Wheat	2.00	1.00
377	25c Wool	3.00	1.00
	First Day Cover (4)		10.00

378. Stained Glass Window

379. Tree of Life

Christmas Issue — 1969 15 Oct

378	5c Stained Glass Window	0.30	0.30
379	25c Tree of Life	3.00	2.50
	First Day Cover		6.00

380. Sir Edmund Barton

381. Alfred Deakin

382. J C Watson

383. Sir George Reid

Prime Ministers — 1969 22 Oct

380	5c Sir Edmund Barton	1.50	0.30
380a	Booklet pane 5 stamps & 1 label	8.00	6.50
381	5c Alfred Deakin	1.50	0.30
381a	Booklet pane 5 stamps & 1 label	8.00	6.50
382	5c J C Watson	1.50	0.30
382a	Booklet pane 5 stamps & 1 label	8.00	6.50
383	5c Sir George Reid	1.50	0.30
383a	Booklet pane 5 stamps & 1 label	8.00	6.50
	First Day Cover (1 each value)		7.00

385. BE-2E Aircraft

386. Vickers Vimy Aircraft

384. Ford Truck

50th Anniversary First Flight England to Australia

			1969 12 Nov
384	5c Ford Truck	0.70	0.30
385	5c BE-2E Aircraft	0.70	0.30
386	5c Vickers Vimy Aircraft	0.70	0.30
	Joined strip 3 (horizontal)	5.00	3.75
	Block of nine 3 x 3	15.00	13.00
	First Day Cover (3)		9.50

388. Diesel Locomotive

Standard G Auge Railway Link Sydney - Perth   **1970 11 Feb**

388	5c Diesel Locomotive	0.30	0.30
	First Day Cover		2.00

389. Australian Pavilion

Values for First Day Covers from the
1970 World Expo are for official Australia
Post illustrated, unaddressed covers.
Generally, other covers are worth less

390. Southern Cross
& Japanese characters

World EXPO '70 at Osaka Japan   **1970 16 Mar**

389	5c Australian Pavilion	0.30	0.30
390	20c Red Southern Cross & Japanese characters	1.00	0.75
	First Day Cover (2) AP		8.50

391. Queen Elizabeth II & Prince Phillip

392. Australian Flag & Queen Elizabeth II

Royal Visit   **1970 31 Mar**

391	5c Queen & Prince Phillip	0.30	0.30
392	30c Australian Flag & Queen	1.50	1.50
	First Day Cover		70.00
392A	Se-tenant block x 4 of both issues included		
	in Royal Visits to Australia Prestige Booklet issued		
	March 2006. As a se-tenant pair	5.00	5.00

393. Cow & Cotton

International Grasslands Conference   **1970 13 Apr**

393	5c Cow & Cotton	0.30	0.30
	First Day Cover		65.00

| 394. Cook | 395. Landing | 396. Discovery | 397. The Team | 398. Possession |

400. Cook - montage

Bicentenary of Captain Cook's Discovery of Australia

			1970 20 Apr	
394	5c Cook		0.40 ☐	0.30 ☐
395	5c Landing		0.40 ☐	0.30 ☐
396	5c Discovery		0.40 ☐	0.30 ☐
397	5c The Team		0.40 ☐	0.30 ☐
398	5c Possession		0.40 ☐	0.30 ☐
399	Joined Strip of 5		2.00 ☐	2.00 ☐
400	30c Cook - montage		2.50 ☐	2.00 ☐
	First Day Cover (6) AP Large			40.00 ☐
401	Miniature Sheet 30c &			
	strip of 5c stamps imperforate		16.00 ☐	13.00 ☐
	First Day Cover (1/30c) AP Small size			250.00 ☐

Captain Cook Bicentenary

DISCOVERY OF EAST COAST OF AUSTRALIA IN 1770

| Cook, giant among navigators, enters the Pacific ... | and fixes the position of the eastern part of Australia ... | where he finds new people and strange animals. | He and his scientists chart the shores and sketch the flora ... | and sovereignty is proclaimed over the land discovered. |

401. Miniature Sheet 30c & strip of 5c stamps imperforate

402. Desert Rose   403. Wattle   404. Desert Rose

Coil Stamps Flowers 1970
4c & 5c issued 27/4/70, 6c issued 28/09/70

402	4c Multi Desert Rose	0.30	0.30
403	5c Multi Wattle	0.30	0.30
	First Day Cover (4c & 5c) AP		30.00
404	6c Desert Rose	1.10	0.45
	First Day Cover AP		6.00

405. Snowy Mountains Scheme   406. Ord River Scheme

407. Bauxite to Aluminium   408. Oil & Natural Gas

National Development 1970 31 Aug

405	7c Snowy Mountains Scheme	0.70	0.50
406	8c Ord River Scheme	0.40	0.30
407	9c Bauxite to Aluminium	0.40	0.30
408	10c Oil & Natural Gas	0.80	0.30
	First Day Cover AP		15.00

409. Rising Flame   410. Illawara Shorthorns

Commonwealth Parliamentary Conference 1970 02 Oct

| 409 | 6c Rising Flame | 0.30 | 0.30 |
| | First Day Cover AP | | 5.00 |

18th International Dairy Congress 1970 07 Oct

410	6c Illawara Shorthorns	0.30	0.30
	First Day Cover AP		5.00
	Booklet pane 5 stamps & label	8.00	8.00

411. Nativity   412. 25th Anniversary UN

Christmas Issue 1970 14 Oct

| 411 | 6c Nativity | 0.30 | 0.30 |
| | First Day Cover AP | | 4.00 |

25th Anniversary United Nations 1970 19 Oct

| 412 | 6c Symbols | 0.30 | 0.30 |
| | First Day Cover AP | | 3.00 |

413. Boeing 707 & Avro 504K   414. Sunbeam Dyak & Boeing 707

50th Anniversary Qantas 1970 02 Nov

413	6c Boeing 707 & Avro 504K	0.30	0.30
414	30c Sunbeam Dyak & Boeing 707	0.90	1.10
	First Day Cover AP		4.00

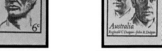

415. Adam Lindsay Gordon   416. Reginald & John Duigan

417. John Eyre   418. Lachlan Macquarie

Famous Australians Series 2 1970 16 Nov

415	6c Mauve Adam Lindsay Gordon	1.60	0.30
	Booklet pane 5 stamps & label	8.00	8.00
416	6c Blue Reginald & John Duigan	1.60	0.30
417	6c Brown Red John Eyre	1.60	0.30
	Booklet pane 5 stamps & label	8.00	8.00
418	6c Black Buff Lachlan Macquarie	1.60	0.30
	Booklet pane 5 stamps & label	8.00	8.00
	First Day Cover (4), Australia Post Booklets only AP		3.50

419. Theatrical Characters

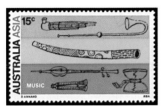

420. Musical Instruments

421. Sea Craft

Australia - Asian Issue   **197106 Jan**
419	7c Theatrical Characters	0.65☐	0.30☐
420	15c Musical Instruments	1.50☐	1.00☐
421	20c Sea Craft	1.00☐	0.55☐
	First Day Cover AP		7.50☐

422. Symbolic Design

423. Symbolic Design

Centenary Natives Association   **197121 Apr**
422	6c Multi Symbolic Design	0.30☐	0.30☐
	First Day Cover AP		4.00☐

Centenary Sydney Stock Exchange   **197105 May**
423	6c Red Blue Symbolic Design	0.30☐	0.30☐
	First Day Cover AP		4.00☐

424. Rotary Emblem

50th Anniversary of Australian Rotary   **1971 17 May**
424	6c Rotary Emblem	0.30☐	0.30☐
	First Day Cover AP		4.00☐

425. Mirage Jets

50th Anniversary R.A.A.F   **197109 Jun**
425	6c Mirage Jets	0.30☐	0.30☐
	First Day Cover AP		2.75☐

426. Horse Cat & Dog

427. Scientist & Lamb

428. Kangaroo

429. Guide Dog

RSPCA Centenary   **1971 05 Jul**
426	6c Horse Cat & Dog	0.30☐	0.30☐
427	12c Scientist & Lamb	0.50☐	0.30☐
428	18c Kangaroo	0.70☐	0.30☐
429	24c Guide Dog	1.00☐	0.65☐
	First Day Cover (4) AP		6.00☐

430. Bark Painting

431. Body Decoration

434. Desert Rose

432. Cave Painting

433. Grave Posts

435. Sturt's Desert Pea

Aboriginal Art
1971 29 Sep

430	20c Bark Painting	0.50	0.30
431	25c Body Decoration	0.50	0.40
432	30c Cave Painting	1.00	0.40
433	35c Grave Posts	1.50	0.40
	First Day Cover (4) AP		17.00
	First Day Cover (3) AP including 7c purple		3.80

Coil Issues Flowers
197101 Oct

| 434 | 2c Desert Rose | 0.40 | 0.30 |
| 435 | 7c Sturt's Desert Pea | 0.40 | 0.30 |

Christmas Issue
197113 Oct

436	7c Pink Star on Pink	3.00	0.30
437	7c Pink Star on Red	3.00	0.30
438	7c Pink Star on Green	12.00	0.60
439	7c Red Star on Red	3.00	0.30
440	7c Green Star on White	3.00	0.30
441	7c Blue Star on Green	4.00	2.00
442	7c Blue Star on Pink	13.00	3.00
443	Block Showing all 7 Stamps *Cream paper	45.00	30.00
443A	Pane of 25 Stamps *Cream paper	115.00	100.00
	First Day Cover (Block 7) AP		42.00

*Issued on both cream and white paper. White paper valued 20% higher.

442. Blue Star on Pink

440. Green Star on White

441. Blue Star on Green

439. Red Star on Red

436. Pink Star on Pink

437. Pink Star on Red

438. Pink Star on Green

at left: diagram showing positions of the 7 different colour combinations.

444. Andrew Fisher

445. Joseph Cook

451. Fish

446. W M Hughes

447. S M Bruce

452. Beef

Prime Ministers (2)   1972 08 Mar

444	7c Blue Andrew Fisher	0.80	0.30
444A	Booklet pane 5 stamps & label	8.00	5.00
445	7c Red Joseph Cook	0.80	0.30
445A	Booklet pane 5 stamps & label	8.00	5.00
446	7c Blue W M Hughes	0.80	0.30
446A	Booklet pane 5 stamps & label	8.00	5.00
447	7c Red S M Bruce	0.80	0.30
447A	Booklet pane 5 stamps & label	8.00	5.00
	First Day Cover (4) AP		3.00

Primary Industries   1972 14 Jun

449	20c Fruit	2.00	1.20
450	25c Rice	2.50	1.60
451	30c Fish	1.50	2.20
452	35c Beef	4.00	4.80
	First Day Cover (4) AP		15.00

453. Worker in Wheelchair

448. CWA Emblem

50th Anniversary Country Women Association   1972 18 Apr

448	7c CWA Emblem	0.30	0.30
	First Day Cover AP		3.00
	Only issued in Post Office Booklets		

454. Occupational Therapy

449. Fruit

450. Rice

455. Boy in Toronto Splint

Rehabilitation of the Disabled   1972 02 Aug

453	12c Worker in Wheelchair	0.40	0.40
454	18c Occupational Therapy	1.00	0.55
455	24c Boy in Toronto Splint	0.75	0.40
	First Day Cover (3) AP		3.00

456. Overland Telegraph Line

Centenary of Overland Telegraph 1972 22 May

456	7c Overland Telegraph Line	0.30□	0.30□
	First Day Cover AP		3.00□

462. Pioneer Family Portrait

463. Water Pump

457. Rowing

458. Athletics

464. Wheat Harvest

465. Pioneer Homestead

466. Stage Coach & Horse

459. Swimming

460. Equestrian

Olympic Games Munich 1972 28 Aug

457	7c Rowing	0.40□	0.30□
458	7c Athletics	0.40□	0.30□
459	7c Swimming	0.40□	0.30□
460	35c Equestrian	2.50□	2.00□
	First Day Cover (4) AP		6.50□

467. Communications -Morse Key

461. Abacus & Computer Circuit

468. Commerce-Paddle Steamer

International Congress of Accountants 1972 16 Oct

461	7c Abacus & Computer Circuit	0.30□	0.30□
	First Day Cover AP		4.25□

Pioneer Life Issue 1972 15 Nov

462	5c Pioneer Family Portrait	0.30□	0.30□
463	10c Water Pump	0.30□	0.30□
464	15c19th Century Wheat Harvest	0.30□	0.30□
465	40c Pioneer Homestead	0.60□	0.30□
466	50c Stage Coach & Horse	1.00□	0.30□
467	60c Communications - Morse Key	1.50□	0.50□
468	80c Commerce - Paddle Steamer	1.50□	0.65□
	First Day Cover (7) AP		14.00□

Note: Issued on both cream and white paper.

469. Jesus & Children

470. Dove in Flight

Christmas Issue | | **1972 20 Nov**
469	7c Jesus & Children	0.30☐	0.30☐
470	35c Dove in Flight	8.50☐	8.50☐
	First Day Cover (2) AP		16.00☐

471. Metric Conversion: Length

472. Metric Conversion: Mass

473. Metric Conversion: Volume

474. Metric Conversion: Temperature

Metric Conversion | | **1973 07 Mar**
471	7c Metric Conversion: Length	0.60☐	0.30☐
472	7c Metric Conversion: Mass	0.60☐	0.30☐
473	7c Metric Conversion: Volume	0.60☐	0.30☐
474	7c Metric Conversion: Temperature	0.60☐	0.30☐
	First Day Cover (4) AP		3.00☐

475. WHO Emblem

25th Anniversary World Health Organisation | | **1973 04 Apr**
| 475 | 7c Green Pink WHO Emblem | 0.30☐ | 0.30☐ |
| | First Day Cover AP | | 3.00 1 |

(left) 476. Dame Mary Gilmore

(right) 477. Marcus Clarke

(left) 478. William Charles Wentworth

(right) 479. Sir Isaac Isaacs

Famous Australians | | **1973 16 May**
476	7c Dame Mary Gilmore	0.70☐	0.30☐
477	7c Marcus Clarke	0.70☐	0.30☐
478	7c William Charles Wentworth	0.70☐	0.30☐
479	7c Sir Isaac Isaacs	0.70☐	0.30☐
480	Block of four se-tenant	4.00☐	4.00☐
	First Day Cover (Block 4) AP		6.00☐

481. Shipping

482. Iron Ore & Steel

483. Beef Roads

484. Mapping

NationalDevelopment | | **1973 06 Jun**
481	20c Shipping	1.00☐	0.50☐
482	25c Iron Ore & Steel	1.00☐	1.00☐
483	30c Beef Roads	2.50☐	1.50☐
484	35c Mapping	2.00☐	2.00☐
	First Day Cover (4) AP		14.00☐

NO.	DESCRIPTION	MUH	FU	NO.	DESCRIPTION	MUH	FU

485. Banded Coral Shrimp

486. Fiddler Crab

487. Reticulated Coral Crab

488. Mauve Stinger

489. Green Gem Chysoprase

490. Red Green Gem Agate

491. Opal

492. Pink Gem Rhodomite

Marine & Gemstone Definitive Issue — 1973 11 Jul

No.	Description	MUH	FU
485	1c Banded Coral Shrimp	0.30☐	0.30☐
486	2c Fiddler Crab	0.30☐	0.30☐
487	3c Reticulated Coral Crab	0.30☐	0.30☐
488	4c Mauve Stinger	0.30☐	0.30☐
	First Day Cover (Marine 4 values above) AP		2.00☐
489	6c Green Gem Chysoprase	0.30☐	0.30☐
490	7c Red Green Gem Agate	0.30☐	0.30☐
491	8c Opal	0.30☐	0.30☐
492	9c Pink Gem Rhodomite	0.30☐	0.30☐
	First Day Cover (Gemstones 4 values above) AP		4.00☐

494. Baptism of Christ

495. Good Shepherd

Christmas Issue — 1973 03 Oct

No.	Description	MUH	FU
494	7c Green Gold Baptism of Christ	0.30☐	0.30☐
495	30c Purple Gold Good Shepherd	2.50☐	2.00☐
	First Day Cover (2) AP		6.00☐

496. Opera House Sydney

497. Buchan's Hotel, Townsville

498. Como Melbourne

499. St James Church Sydney

Architecture Issues — 1973 17 Oct

No.	Description	MUH	FU
496	7c Opera House Sydney	0.30☐	0.30☐
497	10c Buchan's Hotel, Townsville	0.30☐	0.30☐
498	40c Como Melbourne	0.80☐	0.80☐
499	50c St James Church Sydney	2.00☐	1.10☐
	First Day Cover (4) AP		3.50☐

493. Legacy 50th Anniversary

Legacy 50th Anniversary — 1973 05 Sep

No.	Description	MUH	FU
493	7c Brown Children at Play	0.30☐	0.30☐
	First Day Cover AP		3.00☐

500. Valve Radio & Speaker

50th Anniversary of Radio Broadcasting in Australia — 1973 21 Nov

No.	Description	MUH	FU
500	7c 2 Valve Radio & Speaker	0.30☐	0.30☐
	First Day Cover AP		3.00☐

501. Wombat

502. Spiny Anteater

503. Bushtail Possum

504. Feather Tailed Glider

Animal Definitive Issues 1974 13 Feb

No.	Description	MUH	FU
501	20c Wombat	0.30	0.30
502	25c Spiny Anteater	0.80	0.50
503	30c Bushtail Possum	0.50	0.50
504	75c Feather Tailed Glider	1.50	0.75
	First Day Cover (4) AP		7.00

505. Sergeant of Light Horse (Lambert)

506. Red Gums of Far North (H Heysen)

507. Shearing the Rams (Roberts)

Painting Definitives 1974 24 Apr

No.	Description	MUH	FU
505	$1 Sergeant of Light Horse (Lambert)	2.00	0.30
506	$2 Red Gums of Far North (H Heysen)	3.50	0.30
507	$4 Shearing the Rams (Roberts)	6.50	2.00
	First Day Cover (3) AP		40.00

508. Supreme Court Judge

150th Anniversary Charter of Justice 1974 15 May

No.	Description	MUH	FU
508	7c Supreme Court Judge	0.30	0.30
	First Day Cover AP		3.00

509. Football

510. Golf

516. Stylised Pigeon

517. Stylised Pigeon

Universal Postal Union — 1974 09 Oct

		MUH	FU
516	7c Stylised Pigeon	0.40	0.30
517	30c Stylised Pigeon	1.00	1.00
	First Day Cover AP		3.00

511. Cricket

512. Surfing

518. William C Wentworth

519. Opal Stamp

520. Star Sapphire

150th Anniversary Independent Newspapers — 1974 09 Oct

		MUH	FU
518	7c Black on Buff -William C Wentworth	0.30	0.30
	First Day Cover AP		2.00

Surcharge & New Definitive Issue — 1974 16 Oct

		MUH	FU
519	9c Surcharge on 8c Opal Stamp	0.30	0.30
520	10c Star Sapphire	0.30	0.30
	First Day Cover (2) AP		1.80

513. Australian Rules Football

514. Tennis

515. Bowls

Non Olympic Sports — 1974 24 Jul

		MUH	FU
509	7c Football	0.40	0.40
510	7c Golf	0.40	0.40
511	7c Cricket	0.40	0.40
512	7c Surfing	0.40	0.40
513	7c Australian Rules Football	0.40	0.40
514	7c Tennis	0.40	0.40
515	7c Bowls	0.40	0.40
	First Day Cover (7) AP		4.00

521. Adoration of the Magi

522. Flight into Egypt

Christmas Issue — 1974 13 Nov

		MUH	FU
521	10c Black on Yellow - Adoration of the Magi	0.30	0.30
522	35c Black on Yellow - Flight into Egypt	0.80	0.80
	First Day Cover (2) AP		3.00

NO.	DESCRIPTION	MUH	FU

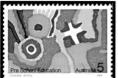

523. Pre School Painting

524. Correspondence Schools

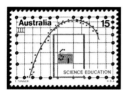

525. Science Education

526. Advanced Education

Educational Definitive Issue — 1974 20 Nov

NO.	DESCRIPTION	MUH	FU
523	5c Pre School Painting	0.30 ☐	0.30 ☐
524	11c Correspondence Schools	0.40 ☐	0.30 ☐
525	15c Science Education	0.50 ☐	0.40 ☐
526	60c Advanced Education	1.20 ☐	1.20 ☐
	First Day Cover (4) AP		4.00 ☐

527. Desert Pea

Coil Issue Flowers — 1975 15 Jan

NO.	DESCRIPTION	MUH	FU
527	10c Desert Pea	0.30 ☐	0.30 ☐
	First Day Cover AP		1.50 ☐

528. Road Safety

529. Pollution

530. Bushfire Dangers

Environment Dangers — 1975 29 Jan

NO.	DESCRIPTION	MUH	FU
528	10c Road Safety	0.40 ☐	0.30 ☐
529	10c Pollution	0.40 ☐	0.30 ☐
530	10c Bushfire Dangers	0.40 ☐	0.30 ☐
	First Day Cover (3) AP		3.00 ☐

531. IWY Graphic

International Women's Year — 1975 12 Mar

NO.	DESCRIPTION	MUH	FU
531	10c Dark Blue/Green IWY Graphic	0.30 ☐	0.30 ☐
	First Day Cover AP		2.00 ☐

532. Earl Page

533. J B Chifley

534. J A Lyons

535. J J Scullin

536. Arthur Fadden

537. John Curtin

Australian Prime Ministers — 1975 26 Mar

NO.	DESCRIPTION	MUH	FU
532	10c Earl Page	0.30 ☐	0.30 ☐
533	10c J B Chifley	0.30 ☐	0.30 ☐
534	10c J A Lyons	0.30 ☐	0.30 ☐
535	10c J J Scullin	0.30 ☐	0.30 ☐
536	10c Arthur Fadden	0.30 ☐	0.30 ☐
537	10c John Curtin	0.30 ☐	0.30 ☐
	First Day Cover (6) AP		4.00 ☐

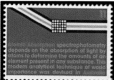

538. Atomic Absorption

539. Radio Astronomy

540. Immunology

541. Oceanography

Scientific Development — 1975 14 May

538	11c Atomic Absorption	0.35	0.30
539	24c Radio Astronomy	0.50	0.40
540	33c Immunology	0.80	0.70
541	48c Oceanography	1.00	0.90
	First Day Cover (4) AP		3.50

542. Australian Postal Commission

543. Aus Telecom Commission

New Postal & Telecommunication Commission — 1975 01 Jul

542	10c Australian Postal Commission	0.40	0.30
543	10c Australian Telecom Commission	0.40	0.30
	Joined pair 542/543	1.50	1.00
	First Day Cover (Joined pair) AP		2.00

Whole set-

545. Edith Cowan

547. Henry Handel
Richardson

546. Louisa Lawson

548. Catherine Spence   549. Truganini   550. Constance Stone

Famous Australian Women — 1975 06 Aug

545	10c Edith Cowan	0.40	0.30
546	10c Louisa Lawson	0.40	0.30
547	10c Henry Handel Richardson	0.40	0.30
548	10c Catherine Spence	0.40	0.30
549	10c Truganini	0.40	0.30
550	10c Constance Stone	0.40	0.30
	First Day Cover (6) AP		5.00

551. Helichrysum Thomsonii

552. Callistemon Teretifolius

Wildflower definitive Issue — 1975 27 Aug

551	18c Helichrysum Thomsonii	0.30	0.30
552	45c Callistemon Teretifolius	0.65	0.30
	First Day Cover (2) AP		1.00

553. Opera House,
Tambaran (Spirit House)

554. Stylized Bird

Commemorating the Independence of Papua New Guinea on 16th Sep 1975 — 1975 16 Sep

553	18c Opera House, Tambaran (Spirit House)	0.45	0.30
554	25c Stylized Bird	0.80	0.60
	First Day Cover (2) AP		2.00

555. Three Wise Men Mary & Crib
556. Star & Rays of Light

Christmas · 1975 29 Oct

555	15c Three Wise Men Mary & Crib	0.40	0.30
556	45c Star & Rays of Light	1.50	1.00
	First Day Cover (2) AP		3.00

557. Australian Coat of Arms
558. 1878 Bell Telephone

75th Anniversary of Nationhood · 1976 05 Jan

| 557 | 18c Australian Coat of Arms | 0.40 | 0.30 |
| | First Day Cover AP | | 2.00 |

100th Anniversary First Telephone Transmission · 1976 10 Mar

| 558 | 18c 1878 Bell Telephone | 0.40 | 0.30 |
| | First Day Cover AP | | 2.00 |

Whole set

559. John Forrest
560. Ernest Giles

561. William Gosse
562. Hume & Hovell

563. John Oxley
564. Peter Warburton

19th Century Explorers of Australia · 1976 09 Jun

559	18c John Forrest	0.40	0.40
560	18c Ernest Giles	0.40	0.40
561	18c William Gosse	0.40	0.40
562	18c Hume & Hovell	0.40	0.40
563	18c John Oxley	0.40	0.40
564	18c Peter Warburton	0.40	0.40
	First Day Cover (6) AP		5.00

565. Measuring Stick

50th Anniversary Commonwealth Scientific &Industrial Research Organisation - CSIRO · 1976 15 Jun

| 565 | 18c Measuring Stick | 0.40 | 0.30 |
| | First Day Cover AP | | 2.00 |

Whole set

566. Soccer

567. Gymnastics
568. Diving

569. Cycling

Olympic Games - Montreal · 1976 14 Jul

566	18c Soccer	0.40	0.30
567	18c Gymnastics	0.40	0.30
568	25c Diving	0.60	0.60
569	40c Cycling	0.80	0.80
	First Day Cover (4) AP		2.00

RENNIKS

NO.	DESCRIPTION	MUH	FU	NO.	DESCRIPTION	MUH	FU

570. Richmond Bridge

571. Broken Bay

574. Barrier Reef

575. Ayers Rock

572. Wittenoom Gorge

573. Mount Buffalo

Australian Scenes Definitive Issue — 1976 25 Aug

No.	Description	MUH	FU
570	5c Richmond Bridge	0.30	0.30
571	25c Broken Bay	0.50	0.30
572	35c Wittenoom Gorge	0.60	0.30
573	50c Mount Buffalo	1.00	0.60
574	70c Barrier Reef	1.20	0.70
575	85c Ayers Rock	1.40	1.00
	First Day Cover (6) AP		6.00

576. William Blamire Young

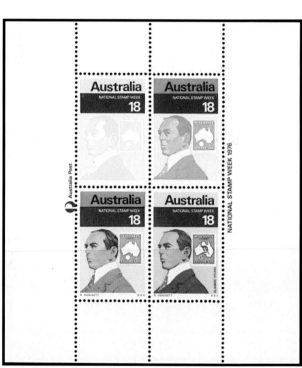
577. Stamp in mini sheet (4)

National Stamp Week — 1976 27 Sep

No.	Description	MUH	FU
576	18c William Blamire Young	0.45	0.30
	First Day Cover AP		1.00
577	18c Stamp in Miniature Sheet (4)	1.25	2.00
	First Day Cover (Miniature Sheet) AP		6.00

578. Light Blue Madonna & Child

579. Holly, Toy Koala Tree & bird

Christmas

578	15c Light Blue Madonna & Child		
579	45c Holly, Toy Koala Tree & Bird		
	First Day Cover (2) AP		

1976 01 Nov

	MUH	FU
578	0.30☐	0.30☐
579	0.90☐	0.75☐
		2.00☐

580. John Gould

581. Thomas Laby

582. Sir Baldwin Spencer

583. Griffith Taylor

Famous Australians

1976 10 Nov

		MUH	FU
580	18c John Gould	0.40☐	0.40☐
581	18c Thomas Laby	0.40☐	0.40☐
582	18c Sir Baldwin Spencer	0.40☐	0.40☐
583	18c Griffith Taylor	0.40☐	0.40☐
	First Day Cover (4) AP		3.00☐

584. Music

585. Drama

586. Dance

587. Opera

Performing Arts

1977 19 Jan

		MUH	FU
584	20c Music	0.45☐	0.30☐
585	30c Drama	0.50☐	0.30☐
586	40c Dance	0.70☐	0.40☐
587	60c Opera	1.00☐	0.60☐
	First Day Cover (4) AP		3.00☐

588. Queen Elizabeth II

589. The Queen & Prince Phillip

Silver Jubilee Queen Elizabeth II

1977 02 Feb

		MUH	FU
588	18c Queen Elizabeth II	0.45☐	0.30☐
589	45c The Queen & Prince Phillip	1.00☐	0.75☐
	First Day Cover (2) AP		2.00☐

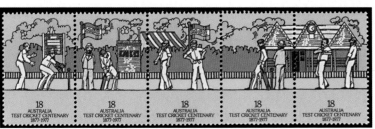

590. Wicket Keeper   591. Batsman   592. MCC Flag   593. Batsman   594. Bowler

596. Batsman's End of Pitch

Centenary Test Cricket		1977 09 Mar	
590	18c Wicket Keeper	0.40☐	0.30☐
591	18c Batsman	0.40☐	0.30☐
592	18c MCC Flag	0.40☐	0.30☐
593	18c Batsman	0.40☐	0.30☐
594	18c Bowler	0.40☐	0.30☐
595	Joined strip of 5	3.00☐	2.25☐
596	45c Batsman's End of Pitch	1.00☐	0.70☐
	First Day Cover (6) AP		5.00☐

597. Parliament House Canberra   598. Australian Workers

50th Anniversary Opening Parliament House — 1977 03 Apr
597	18c Parliament House Canberra	0.40☐	0.30☐
	First Day Cover AP		2.00☐

50th Anniversary ACTU — 1977 09 May
598	10c Australian Workers	0.40☐	0.30☐
	First Day Cover AP		2.00☐

600. Surfing Santa

601. Madonna & Child

Christmas — 1977 31 Oct
600	15c Surfing Santa	0.45☐	0.30☐
601	45c Madonna & Child	0.70☐	0.70☐
	First Day Cover (2) AP		2.00☐

599. Coming South (T Roberts)

602. Australian Flag

Painting Definitive — 1977 19 Oct
599	$10 Coming South Painting (T Roberts)	17.00☐	3.50☐
	First Day Cover AP		18.00☐

Australia Day — 1978 26 Jan
602	18c Australian Flag	0.40☐	0.30☐
	First Day Cover AP		2.00☐

603. Harry Hawker

604. Bert Hinkler

605. Charles Kingsford Smith

606. Charles Ulm

607. Miniature Sheet imperforate (4)

Australian Aviators 1978 19 Apr

No.	Description	MUH	FU
603	18c Harry Hawker	0.45☐	0.30☐
604	18c Bert Hinkler	0.45☐	0.30☐
605	18c Charles Kingsford Smith	0.45☐	0.30☐
606	18c Charles Ulm	0.45☐	0.30☐
	First Day Cover (4) AP		2.00☐
607	Miniature Sheet imperforate (4)	2.50☐	2.50☐
	First Day Cover Miniature Sheet AP		5.00☐

608. Flying Doctor Service

50th Anniversary Royal Flying Doctor Service 1978 15 May

No.	Description	MUH	FU
608	18c Flying Doctor Service	0.45☐	0.30☐
	First Day Cover AP		2.00☐

609. Flame Tree

610. Ghost Gum Tree

611. Grass Tree

612. Cootamundra Wattle

Australian Trees
1978 01 Jun

No.	Description	MUH	FU
609	18c Flame Tree	0.45	0.30
610	25c Ghost Gum Tree	0.50	0.50
611	40c Grass Tree	0.70	0.60
612	45c Cootamundra Wattle	0.90	0.60
	First Day Cover AP		3.00

613. Rose & Map of Australia

Establishment of Government in the Northern Territory
1978 19 Jun

No.	Description	MUH	FU
613	18c Rose & Map of Australia	0.45	0.30
	First Day Cover AP		1.00

614. Hooded Dotterel

615. Little Grebe

616. Spur wing Plover

617. Pied Oystercatcher

618. Lotus Bird

Australian Birds Definitive Issues
1978

(20c & 55c) 3 Jul - (5c, 25c & 30c) 17 Jul

No.	Description	MUH	FU
614	5c Hooded Dotterel	0.30	0.30
615	20c Little Grebe	0.40	0.30
616	25c Spur wing Plover	0.45	0.30
617	30c Pied Oystercatcher	0.55	0.30
618	55c Lotus Bird	1.20	0.50
	First Day Cover (20c & 55c) AP 3 Jul		1.20
	First Day Cover (5c, 25c & 30c) AP 17 Jul		1.20

619. Repro. 1928 Kookaburra

National Stamp Week   **1978 25 Sep**
619	20c Repro. 1928 Kookaburra	0.45☐	0.30☐
620	Miniature Sheet (4)	1.50☐	1.50☐
	First Day Cover		1.00☐
	First Day Cover Miniature Sheet		5.00☐

621. Madonna & Child (Van Eyck)   622. Virgin & Child (Marmion)

620. Miniature Sheet Repro. 1928 Kookaburra

623. Holy Family (del Vaga)

624. Tulloch

625. Bernborough

626. Phar Lap

627. Peter Pan

Christmas Issue   **1978**
(25c) 03 Oct - (15c, 55c) 01 Nov
621	15c Madonna & Child (Van Eyck)	0.40☐	0.30☐
622	25c Virgin & Child (Marmion)	0.45☐	0.35☐
623	55c Holy Family (del Vaga)	1.00☐	0.70☐
	First Day Cover (25c) AP		1.00☐
	First Day Cover (15c, 55c) AP		2.00☐

Australian Racehorses   **1978 18 Oct**
624	20c Tulloch	0.45☐	0.30☐
625	35c Bernborough	0.70☐	0.30☐
626	50c Phar Lap	0.80☐	0.70☐
627	55c Peter Pan	0.90☐	0.70☐
	First Day Cover (4) AP		4.00☐

RENNIKS

NO.	DESCRIPTION	MUH	FU	NO.	DESCRIPTION	MUH	FU

628. Flag Raising Sydney Cove

633. McMahon's Point (A Streeton)

Australia Day

		1979 26 Jan	
628	20c Flag Raising Sydney Cove	0.45□	0.30□
	First Day Cover AP		1.00□

Additional Australian Painting Definitive

McMahon's Point by Sir Arthur Streeton

		1979 14 Mar	
633	$5 McMahon's Point - (A Streeton)	8.50□	2.50□
	First Day Cover AP		8.00□

629. PS Canberra

630. MV Lady Denman

631. PS Murray River Queen

632. HV Curl Curl

Australian Ferries & Steamers

		1979 14 Feb	
629	20c PS Canberra	0.45□	0.30□
630	35c MV Lady Denman	0.70□	0.30□
631	50c PS Murray River Queen	0.90□	0.70□
632	55c HV Curl Curl	0.90□	0.80□
	First Day Cover (4) AP		4.00□

National Parks

		1979 09 Apr	
634	20c Port Campbell, Victoria	0.45□	0.30□
635	20c Uluru, Northern Territory	0.45□	0.30□
636	20c Royal National Park, NSW	0.45□	0.30□
637	20c Flinders Range, SA	0.45□	0.30□
638	20c Nambung, WA	0.45□	0.30□
639	Joined Strip of five	1.80□	1.50□
640	20c Mount Field, Tasmania	0.45□	0.30□
641	20c Girraween, Queensland	0.45□	0.30□
642	Joined pair (640/641)	0.90□	0.80□
642A	Gutter Pair (493/494)	2.10□	2.10□
	First Day Cover (7) AP		4.00□

634. Port Campbell, Victoria   635. Uluru, Northern Territory   636. Royal National Park, NSW

637. Flinders Range, SA   638. Nambung, WA

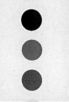

640. Mount Field, Tasmania   641. Girraween, Queensland

643. Double Fairlie   644. Puffing Billy   649. Zebra Finch   650. Crimson Finch

645. Pichi Richi

651. Forest Kingfisher

646. Zig Zag

652. Eastern Yellow Robin

Australian Steam Locomotives   1979 16 May

		MUH	FU
643	20c Double Fairlie	0.45☐	0.30☐
644	35c Puffing Billy	0.70☐	0.50☐
645	50c Pichi Richi	0.90☐	0.60☐
646	55c Zig Zag	0.90☐	0.70☐
	First Day Cover (4) AP		3.00☐

653. Lovely Wren

647. WA 150th Ann. Swan

150th Anniversary Western Australia   1979 06 Jun

		MUH	FU
647	20c Swan	0.45☐	0.30☐
	First Day Cover AP		1.00☐

654. Flame Robin

648. Children Playing

International Year of the Child   1979 13 Aug

		MUH	FU
648	20c Children Playing	0.45☐	0.30☐
	First Day Cover AP		1.00☐

Australian Birds Definitive Issue   1979 17 Sep

		MUH	FU
649	1c Zebra Finch	0.30☐	0.30☐
650	2c Crimson Finch	0.30☐	0.30☐
651	15c Forest Kingfisher	0.30☐	0.30☐
652	20c Eastern Yellow Robin	0.40☐	0.30☐
653	40c Lovely Wren	0.90☐	0.30☐
654	50c Flame Robin	1.00☐	0.40☐
	First Day Cover (6) AP		8.00☐

NO.	DESCRIPTION	MUH	FU	NO.	DESCRIPTION	MUH	FU

655. Christ's Nativity

656. Parcels wrapped in flags

662. Mathew Flinders

Australia Day   **1980 23 Jan**

662	20c Mathew Flinders	0.45	0.30
	First Day Cover AP		1.00

657. Madonna & Child

Christmas Issue   **(25c) 24 Sept, (15c, 55c) 01 Nov, 1979**

655	15c Christ's Nativity	0.40	0.30
656	25c Parcels wrapped in flags	0.60	0.40
657	55c Madonna & Child	0.80	0.40
	First Day Cover (15c & 55c) AP		1.60
	First Day Cover (25c) AP		3.00

663. Dingo   664. Border Collie

665. Australian Terrier   666. Australian Cattle Dog

667. Australian Kelpie

Australian Dogs   **1980 20 Feb**

663	20c Dingo	0.45	0.30
664	25c Border Collie	0.50	0.40
665	35c Australian Terrier	0.60	0.60
666	50c Australian Cattle Dog	0.80	0.60
667	55c Australian Kelpie	0.90	0.70
	First Day Cover (5) AP		3.50

658. Trout Fishing

659. Pleasure Fishing

668. White Tailed Kingfisher   669. Rainbow Bird

670. King Parrot

660. Deep Sea Fishing

661. Surf Fishing

Fishing in Australia   **1979 24 Oct**

658	20c Trout Fishing	0.45	0.30
659	35c Pleasure Fishing	0.70	0.30
660	50c Deep Sea Fishing	0.80	0.50
661	55c Surf Fishing	0.80	0.50
	First Day Cover (4) AP		3.00

Australian Birds Definitive Issue   **1980 31 Mar**

668	22c White Tailed Kingfisher	0.45	0.30
669	28c Rainbow Bird	0.55	0.40
670	60c King Parrot	1.20	0.60
	First Day Cover AP		2.50

Queen Elizabeth II Birthday — 1980 21 Apr

| 671 | 22c Queen Elizabeth II | 0.45☐ | 0.30☐ |
| | First Day Cover AP | | 1.00☐ |

671. Queen Elizabeth II

| 672. Swagman | 673. Swagman & Sheep | 674. Squatter | 675. Policeman | 676. Swagman's Ghost |

Australian Folklore — 1980 07 May

672	22c Swagman	0.45☐	0.30☐
673	22c Swagman & Sheep	0.45☐	0.30☐
674	22c Squatter	0.45☐	0.30☐
675	22c Policeman	0.45☐	0.30☐
676	22c Swagman's Ghost	0.45☐	0.30☐
677	Joined Strip of 5	2.00☐	2.00☐
	First Day Cover (strip 5) AP		2.60☐

678. High Court Building, Canberra

Opening of High Court Building Canberra — 1980 19 May

| 678 | 22c High Court Building | 0.45☐ | 0.30☐ |
| | First Day Cover AP | | 1.00☐ |

Australian Birds Definitive Issues — 1980 01 Jul

(10c, 35c, 45c, 80c, $1) 01 July - (18c) 17 Nov

679	10c Golden Shouldered Parrot	0.30☐	0.30☐
680	18c Spotted Catbird	0.35☐	0.30☐
681	35c Regent Bower Bird	0.60☐	0.40☐
682	45c Masked Woodswallow	0.90☐	0.50☐
683	80c Rainbow Pitta	1.50☐	0.80☐
684	$1 Western Magpie	1.80☐	0.50☐
	First Day Cover 10c, 35c, 45c, 80c, $1 (5) AP		10.00☐
	First Day Cover 18c (1) AP		1.00☐

679. Golden Shouldered Parrot

680. Spotted Catbird

681. Regent Bower Bird

682. Masked Woodswallow

683. Rainbow Pitta

684. Western Magpie

685. Salvation Army

686. St Vincent de Paul

687. Meals on Wheels

688. Life, Be In It

689. Post Box   690. Postman   691. Delivery Van   692. Postman & Postbox   693. Postman Delivering

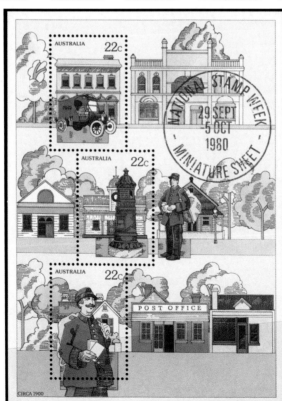

695. Miniature Sheet (3)

Community Welfare — 1980 11 Aug

NO.	DESCRIPTION	MUH	FU
685	22c Salvation Army	0.45	0.30
686	22c St Vincent de Paul	0.45	0.30
687	22c Meals on Wheels	0.45	0.30
688	22c Life, Be In It (cyclists)	0.45	0.30
	First Day Cover AP		2.50

National Stamp Week — 1980 29 Sep

NO.	DESCRIPTION	MUH	FU
689	22c Post Box	0.45	0.30
690	22c Postman	0.45	0.30
691	22c Delivery Van	0.45	0.30
692	22c Postman & Postbox	0.45	0.30
693	22c Postman Delivering	0.45	0.30
694	Joined strip of 5	2.25	2.25
695	Miniature Sheet (3)	1.25	1.50
	First Day Cover (strip 5) AP		3.00
	First Day Cover (m/s) AP		3.00

696. Virgin Enthroned

697. Holy Family

698. Madonna & Child

Christmas — (28c) 01 Oct, (15c, 60c) 03 Nov, 1980

NO.	DESCRIPTION	MUH	FU
696	15c Virgin Enthroned	0.40	0.30
697	28c Holy Family	0.50	0.30
698	60c Madonna & Child	0.90	0.30
	First Day Cover (28c) AP		1.00
	First Day Cover (15c, 60c) AP		1.50

699. Wackett

700. Winjeel

701. Boomerang

702. Nomad

Australian Aircraft — 1980 19 Nov

NO.	DESCRIPTION	MUH	FU
699	22c Wackett	0.45	0.30
700	40c Winjeel	0.70	0.50
701	45c Boomerang	0.80	0.60
702	60c Nomad	1.00	0.70
	First Day Cover (4) AP		3.00

703. Australian Flag & Australia

Australia Day — 1981 21 Jan

NO.	DESCRIPTION	MUH	FU
703	22c Australian Flag & Australia	0.45	0.30
	First Day Cover AP		1.00

704. Darby Munro - Jockey

705. Victor Trumper - Cricket

706. Norman Brookes - Tennis

707. Walter Lindrum - Snooker

Australian Sporting Personalities — 1981 18 Feb

NO.	DESCRIPTION	MUH	FU
704	22c Darby Munro - Jockey	0.45	0.30
705	35c Victor Trumper - Cricket	0.70	0.60
706	55c Norman Brookes - Tennis	0.80	0.80
707	60c Walter Lindrum - Snooker	1.00	0.85
	First Day Cover (4) AP		3.00

708. Kingsford Smith World Flight

709. Kingsford Smith World Flight

50th Anniversary of First Australian U.K Air Mail Flight — 1981 25 Mar

NO.	DESCRIPTION	MUH	FU
708	22c Kingsford Smith World Flight	0.45	0.30
709	60c Kingsford Smith World Flight	1.00	0.70
	First Day Cover (2) AP		1.50

NO.	DESCRIPTION	MUH	FU	NO.	DESCRIPTION	MUH	FU

710. Apex Symbol & Australia

711. Queen Elizabeth Australian Flag

Anniversary Founding of APEX

1981 06 Apr

710	22c Apex Symbol & Australia	0.45☐	0.30☐
	First Day Cover AP		1.00☐

Queen Elizabeth II Birthday

1981 21 Apr

711	22c Queen Elizabeth Australian Flag	0.45☐	0.30☐
	First Day Cover AP		1.00☐

712. Quality of Washing Stuff

713. Puddling

714. Licence Inspected

715. On Route to Gold Fields

Gold Rush Era

1981 20 May

712	22c Quality of Washing Stuff	0.45☐	0.30☐
713	22c Puddling	0.45☐	0.30☐
714	22c Licence Inspected	0.45☐	0.30☐
715	22c On Route to Gold Fields	0.45☐	0.30☐
	First Day Cover (4) AP		2.00☐

716. 'On The Wallaby Track' (Fred McCubbin)

Painting Definitive

1981 17 Jun

716	$2 'On The Wallaby Track' (Fred McCubbin)	3.50☐	0.55☐
	First Day Cover AP		5.00☐

717. Wombat

718. Tasmanian Tiger Thylacine

719. Greater Bilby

721. Possum

720. Bridled Nail-Tailed Wallaby

722. Stick-nest Rat

Australian Animals Definitive Issue: Endangered species

1981 01 Jul

717	5c Wombat	0.30☐	0.30☐
718	24c Tasmanian Tiger Thylacine	0.45☐	0.30☐
719	25c Greater Bilby	0.45☐	0.30☐
720	30c Bridled Nail-Tailed Wallaby	0.55☐	0.30☐
721	50c Possum	0.80☐	0.40☐
722	55c Stick-nest Rat	0.90☐	0.40☐
	First Day Cover (24c) AP		1.00☐
	First Day Cover (5) AP		3.00☐

723. Royal Couple White Background

724. Royal Couple Red Background

Royal Wedding

1981 29 Jul

723	24c Royal Couple White Background	0.45☐	0.30☐
724	60c Royal Couple Red Background	1.30☐	0.85☐
	First Day Cover (2) AP		2.00☐

725. Cortinarius cinnabarinus

726. Coprinus comatus

732. Christmas Bush

733. Silvers Stars

727. Armillaria luteobubalina

728. Cortinarius austro-venetus

734. Noel Time

Australian Fungi — 1981 19 Aug

725	24c Cortinarius cinnabarinus	0.50	0.30
726	35c Coprinus comatus	0.70	0.60
727	55c Armillaria luteobubalina	1.00	0.60
728	60c Cortinarius austro-venetus	1.00	0.70
	First Day Cover (4) AP		3.00

Christmas — (30c) 28 Sep - (18c, 60c) 02 Nov, 1981

732	18c Christmas Bush	0.40	0.30
733	30c Silvers Stars	0.50	0.50
734	60c Noel Time	1.00	0.60
	First Day Cover (30c) AP		0.70
	First Day Cover (18c & 60c) AP		1.80

729. Paraplegic Basketballers

International Year Disabled Persons — 1981 16 Sep

729	24c Paraplegic Basketballers	0.45	0.30
	First Day Cover AP		1.00

735. Ocean Racer

736. Lightweight Sharpie

730. Gold CHOGM Design

731. Silver CHOGM Design

737. 12 Metre Yacht

738. Sabot

Commonwealth Heads of Government Meeting Melbourne — 1981 30 Sep

730	24c Gold CHOGM Design	0.50	0.30
731	60c Silver CHOGM Design	1.00	0.85
	First Day Cover (2) AP		1.50

Australian Yachts — 1981 14 Oct

735	24c Ocean Racer	0.50	0.30
736	35c Lightweight Sharpie	0.70	0.60
737	55c 12 Metre Yacht	0.80	0.60
738	60c Sabot	1.00	0.70
	First Day Cover (4) AP		4.00

739. Immigrants

Australia Day Issue: Immigrants   1982 20 Jan

| 739 | 24c Immigrants | 0.50 | 0.30 |
| | First Day Cover AP | | 1.00 |

740. Sperm Whale

741. Southern Right Whale

742. Blue Whale

743. Humpback Whale

Whales   1982 17 Feb

740	24c Sperm Whale	0.50	0.30
741	35c Southern Right Whale	0.70	0.60
742	55c Blue Whale	0.90	0.70
743	60c Humpback Whale	1.00	0.70
	First Day Cover (4) AP		4.00

744. Corroboree Frog

745. Snake Necked Tortoise

746. Blue Mountain Tree Frog

747. Knob Tailed Gecko

748. Yellow Faced Whip Snake

749. Water Dragon Lizard

750. Freshwater Crocodile

Australian Animals definitive issue   1982
19th Apr 3c, 27c, 65c, 75c, 16th Jun 15c, 40c, 90c

744	3c Corroboree Frog	0.30	0.30
745	15c Snake Necked Tortoise	0.30	0.30
746	27c Blue Mountain Tree Frog	0.50	0.30
747	40c Knob Tailed Gecko	0.65	0.40
748	65c Yellow Faced Whip Snake	1.20	0.55
749	75c Water Dragon Lizard	1.30	0.60
750	90c Freshwater Crocodile	1.60	0.80
	First Day Cover (3c, 27c, 65c, 75c) AP		3.00
	First Day Cover (15c, 40c, 90c) AP		3.00

751. Queen Elizabeth II Portrait

Queen Elizabeth II Birthday   1982 21 Apr

| 751 | 27c Queen Elizabeth II Portrait | 0.50 | 0.30 |
| | First Day Cover AP | | 1.00 |

752. Marjorie Atherton Rose

753. Imp Rose

754. Minni Watson Rose

755. Satellite Rose1

Australian Roses   1982 19 May

No.	Description	MUH	FU
752	27c Marjorie Atherton Rose	0.50☐	0.30☐
753	40c Imp Rose	0.60☐	0.55☐
754	65c Minni Watson Rose	1.00☐	0.60☐
755	75c Satellite Rose	1.20☐	1.00☐
	First Day Cover (4) AP		3.00☐

757. ABC Logo

756. Announcer

50th Anniversary of A.B.C   198216 Jun

No.	Description	MUH	FU
756	27c Announcer	0.50☐	0.30☐
757	27c ABC Logo	0.50☐	0.30☐
758	Joined pair	1.00☐	1.00☐
758A	Gutter Pair	1.60☐	1.60☐
	First Day Cover (pair) AP		1.20☐
	First Day Cover (gutter pair) AP		3.50☐

759. Forbes N S W

760. Flemington Vic

761. Rockhampton Qld

762. Kingston SA

763. York WA

764. Launceston Tasmania

765. Alice Springs, NT

Historical Post Offices   1982 04 Aug

No.	Description	MUH	FU
759	27c Forbes N S W	0.50☐	0.30☐
760	27c Flemington Vic	0.50☐	0.30☐
761	27c Rockhampton Qld	0.50☐	0.30☐
762	27c Kingston SA	0.50☐	0.30☐
763	27c York WA	0.50☐	0.30☐
764	27c Launceston Tasmania	0.50☐	0.30☐
765	27c Alice Springs, NT	0.50☐	0.30☐
	First Day Cover (7) AP		3.00☐

766. Boxing

767. Archery

768. Weightlifting

769. Pole Vaulting

XIIth Commonwealth Games Brisbane — 1982 22 Sep

No.	Description	MUH	FU
766	27c Red Boxing	0.50	0.30
767	27c Green Archery	0.50	0.30
768	27c Brown Weightlifting	0.50	0.30
769	75c Blue Pole Vaulting	1.50	1.20
770	Miniature Sheet (3 x 27c)	1.60	1.60
	First Day Cover (4) AP		3.00
	First Day Cover (m/s) AP		3.00

771. 5/- Harbour Bridge repro.

National Stamp Week — 1982 27 Sep

No.	Description	MUH	FU
771	27c Harbour Bridge Stamp (5/- repro.)	0.50	0.30
	First Day Cover AP		1.00

772. Gurgurr, the Moon Man

Australian National Gallery — 1982 12 Oct

No.	Description	MUH	FU
772	27c Gurgurr the Moon Man	0.50	0.30
	First Day Cover AP		1.00

773. Bushman's Hotel

774. Spray of Wattle

775. Bush Christmas Scene

Christmas — 1982

(35c) 15 Sep - (21c, 75c) 38,292

No.	Description	MUH	FU
773	21c Bushman's Hotel	0.45	0.30
774	35c Spray of Wattle	0.70	0.30
775	75c Bush Christmas Scene	1.20	0.90
	First Day Cover (35c) AP		0.90
	First Day Cover (21c, 75c) AP		1.60

776. Mimi Spirits Dancing

777. Mimi Spirits Dancing

778. Mimi Spirits Dancing

779. Mimi Spirits Dancing

Aboriginal Music and Dance — 1982 17 Nov

No.	Description	MUH	FU
776	27c Buff Mimi Spirits Dance	0.50	0.30
777	40c Grey Mimi Spirits Dance	0.60	0.55
778	65c Grey Mimi Spirits Dance	1.00	0.70
779	75c Buff Mimi Spirits Dance	1.20	0.80
	First Day Cover (4) AP		4.00

780. Rosea 781. Caesia 782. Ficifolia 783. Globulus 784. Forrestiana

Eucalyptus 1982 17 Nov

NO.	DESCRIPTION	MUH	FU
780	1c Rosea	0.50	0.30
781	2c Caesia	0.50	0.30
782	3c Ficifolia	0.50	0.30
783	10c Globulus	0.50	0.40
784	27c Forrestiana	0.80	0.70
785	Joined strip of 5 values	2.60	2.60
785A	60c Booklet pane 6 (2 each: 1c, 2c,27c)	1.30	1.30
785B	$1 Booklet pane 9 plus label		
	(2 each: 1c, 2c - 1 each: 3c,10c -3 each: 27c)	3.00	3.60
	First Day Cover (strip of 5) AP		2.50

786. 1891 Shand Mason Steam 787. 1914 Hotchkiss

788. 1929 Arhrens Fox PS2 789. 1851 Merryweather

Historical Fire Engines 1983 12 Jan

NO.	DESCRIPTION	MUH	FU
786	27c 1891 Shand Mason Steam	0.50	0.30
787	40c 1914 Hotchkiss	0.60	0.60
788	65c 1929 Arhrens Fox PS2	1.10	0.70
789	75c 1851 Merryweather	1.20	0.80
	First Day Cover (4) AP		3.50

791. HMS Sirius 790. HM Brig Supply

Australia Day 1983 26 Jan

NO.	DESCRIPTION	MUH	FU
790	27c H M Brig Supply	0.50	0.30
791	27c H M S Sirius	0.50	0.30
792	Joined pair	1.00	1.00
792A	Gutter pair	1.50	1.50
	First Day Cover (pair) AP		2.00
	First Day Cover (gutter pair) AP		2.00

793. Kangaroo & Kiwi Graphic

Australia New Zealand
Closer Economic Relationship (ANZCER) 1983 02 Feb

NO.	DESCRIPTION	MUH	FU
793	27c Kangaroo & Kiwi Graphic	0.50	0.30
	First Day Cover AP		1.00

794. Lace Lizard 795. Crucifix Toad

796. Blue Tongued Lizard 797. Thorny Devil

Australian Animal Definitive Issues 1983 02 Feb

NO.	DESCRIPTION	MUH	FU
794	1c Lace Lizard	0.30	0.30
795	70c Crucifix Toad	1.20	0.40
796	85c Blue Tongued Lizard	1.40	0.80
797	95c Thorny Devil	1.50	0.70
	First Day Cover (4) AP		4.00

798. Equality & Dignity

799. Social Justice

800. Liberty & Freedom   801. Peace

Commonwealth Day — 1983 09 Mar

798	27c Equality & Dignity	0.50	0.30
799	27c Social Justice	0.50	0.30
800	27c Liberty & Freedom	0.50	0.30
801	75c Peace	1.20	0.80
	First Day Cover (4) AP		3.00

802. HMY Britannia.

803. Communication Graphic

804. Star of St John

805. Australian Jaycees

Queen Elizabeth II Birthday — 1983 20 Apr

| 802 | 27c HMY Britannia. | 0.50 | 0.30 |
| | First Day Cover AP | | 1.00 |

World Communication Year — 1983 18 May

| 803 | 27c Communication Graphic | 0.50 | 0.30 |
| | First Day Cover AP | | 1.00 |

Centenary St John Ambulance — 1983 08 Jun

| 804 | 27c Star of St John | 0.50 | 0.30 |
| | First Day Cover AP | | 1.00 |

50th Anniversary Australian Jaycees — 1983 08 Jun

| 805 | 27c Brown Buff Jaycees | 0.50 | 0.30 |
| | First Day Cover AP | | 1.00 |

806. Regent Skipper   807. Cairns Birdwing   808. Macleay's Swallowtail

809. Ulysses   810. Chlorinda Hairstreak   811. Blue Tiger

812. Big Greasy   813. Wood White

814. Amaryllis Azure   815. Sword Grass Brown

Australian Butterflies Definitive Issue — 1983 15 Jun

806	4c Regent Skipper	0.30	0.30
807	10c Cairns Birdwing	0.30	0.30
808	20c Macleay's Swallowtail	0.35	0.30
809	27c Ulysses	0.50	0.30
810	30c Chlorinda Hairstreak	0.60	0.30
811	35c Blue Tiger	0.55	0.30
812	45c Big Greasy	1.00	0.30
813	60c Wood White	1.20	0.55
814	80c Amaryllis Azure	1.40	0.70
815	$1 Sword Grass Brown	2.00	0.80
	First Day Cover (9) AP 2 covers		8.00

| 816. The Bloke | 817. Doreen - The Intro | 818. The Stror at Coot | 819. Hitched | 820. The Mooch of Life |

Australian Folklore Issue   1983 03 Aug

816	27c The Bloke	0.50☐	0.30☐
817	27c Doreen - The Intro	0.50☐	0.30☐
818	27c The Stror at Coot	0.50☐	0.30☐
819	27c Hitched	0.50☐	0.30☐
820	27c The Mooch of Life	0.50☐	0.30☐
821	Joined Strip of 5	2.50☐	2.30☐
	First Day Cover (Strip of 5) AP		2.50☐

| 822. Nativity Scene | 823. Kookaburra | 824. Santa/Beach Scene |

Christmas   1983

(35c) 14 Sep - (24c, 85c) 02 Nov

822	24c Nativity Scene	0.50☐	0.30☐
823	35c Kookaburra	0.50☐	0.30☐
824	85c Santa/Beach Scene	0.90☐	1.10☐
	First Day Cover (35c) AP		0.90☐
	First Day Cover (24c & 85c) AP		2.50☐

| 825. Robert O'Hara Burke & William John Wills | 826. Alexander Forrest | 827. Ludwig Leichhardt | 828. Paul Edmund de Strzelecki |

Australian Explorers   1983 26 Sep

825	30c Burke & Wills	0.50☐	0.30☐
826	30c Alexander Forrest	0.50☐	0.30☐
827	30c Ludwig Leichhardt	0.50☐	0.30☐
828	30c Paul Edmund de Strzelecki	0.50☐	0.30☐
	First Day Cover (4) AP		2.50☐

829. Cook's Cottage

Australia Day   1984 26 Jan

| 829 | 30c Cook's Cottage | 0.50☐ | 0.30☐ |
| | First Day Cover AP | | 1.00☐ |

830. Australia NZ Flight   831. Australia PNG Flight

50th Anniversary 1st Official Air Mail   **1984 22 Feb**

Australia and New Zealand, Australia and Papua New Guinea

830	45c Australia NZ Flight	0.90	0.60
831	45c Australia PNG Flight	0.90	0.60
832	Joined pair	2.50	2.00
	First Day Cover (joined pr) AP		2.50

833. 1898 Thomson

834. 1906 Tarrant

835. 1919 Australian Six

836. 1923 Summit

837. 1924 Chic

839. A Holiday at Mentone
(Charles Conder 1888)

Australian Painting Definitive   **1984 04 Apr**

A Holiday at Mentone (Charles Conder 1888)

| 839 | $5 A Holiday at Mentone (C Conder) | 8.00 | 2.00 |
| | First Day Cover AP | | 9.00 |

840. Queen Elizabeth

Queen Elizabeth II Birthday   **1984 18 Apr**

| 840 | 30c Queen Elizabeth | 0.50 | 0.30 |
| | First Day Cover AP | | 1.00 |

Australian Veteran & Vintage Cars   **1984 14 Mar**

833	30c 1898 Thomson	0.50	0.30
834	30c 1906 Tarrant	0.50	0.30
835	30c 1919 Australian Six	0.50	0.30
836	30c 1923 Summit	0.50	0.30
837	30c 1924 Chic	0.50	0.30
838	Joined strip of 5	2.50	2.50
	First Day Cover (strip of 5) AP		3.50

841. Cutty Sark

842. Orient

843. Sobraon

844. Thermopylae

Clipper Ships   **1984 23 May**

841	30c Cutty Sark	0.50☐	0.30☐
842	45c Orient	0.90☐	0.70☐
843	75c Sobraon	1.30☐	0.90☐
844	85c Thermopylae	1.50☐	0.90☐
	First Day Cover (4) AP		4.00☐

849. Coral Hopper

850. Orange Tipped Cowrie

851. Choat's Wrasse

852. Blue Lined Surgeon Fish

853. Bennett's Nudibranch

854. Regal Angel Fish

Marine Life Series, The Great Barrier Reef   **1984 18 Jun**

849	2c Coral Hopper	0.30☐	0.30☐
850	25c Orange Tipped Cowrie	0.50☐	0.30☐
851	30c Choat's Wrasse	0.50☐	0.30☐
852	50c Blue Lined Surgeon Fish	1.10☐	0.40☐
853	55c Bennett's Nudibranch	1.20☐	0.40☐
854	85c Regal Angel Fish	1.35☐	0.80☐
	First Day Cover (6) AP		4.50☐

845. Downhill Racer

846. Slalom

847. Nordic

848. Freestyle

Skiing in Australia   **1984 06 Jun**

845	30c Downhill Racer	0.50☐	0.30☐
846	30c Slalom	0.50☐	0.30☐
847	30c Nordic	0.50☐	0.30☐
848	30c Freestyle	0.50☐	0.30☐
	First Day Cover (4) AP		3.00☐

855. Pre Start

856. The Event

857. Post Event

Olympic Games (Los Angeles)   **1984 25 Jul**

855	30c Pre Start - Blue	0.60☐	0.40☐
856	30c The Event - Orange	0.60☐	0.40☐
857	30c Post Event - Green	0.60☐	0.40☐
	First Day Cover (3) AP		3.00☐

✪ RENNIKS

NO.	DESCRIPTION	MUH	FU	NO.	DESCRIPTION	MUH	FU

858. 1d Kangaroo reproduction on stamp

Ausipex 1984   **1984 22 Aug**
World Philatelic Exhibition: Melbourne 21-30 Sep 1984

| 858 | 30c 1d Kangaroo repro | 0.50 ☐ | 0.30 ☐ |
| | First Day Cover | | 1.00 ☐ |

Ausipex 1984 (miniature sheet)   **1984 21 Sep**
World Philatelic Exhibition: Melbourne 21-30 Sep 1984

| 859 | 30c Ausipex, Sheet 7 Stamps | 5.00 ☐ | 5.00 ☐ |
| | First Day Cover | | 5.00 ☐ |

Note individual stamps from this sheet (except No. 858, catalogued at 0.60 used) are worth approximately 65 cents in MUH to FU condition)

859. Sheet 7 reproductions on stamps

860. Angel & Child

861. Virgin & Child

862. Angel

869. Rock Python - Kimberleys

870. Wandjina Spirit &
Snake Babies - Kimberleys

863. Three Kings

864. Madonna & Child

871. Silver Barramundi -
Alligator River

872. Rock Possum-
Alligator River

Christmas   1984

Sacred Stained Glass Windows (40c) 17 Sep - (24c, 30c, 50c, 85c) 31 Oct

860	24c Angel & Child	0.50☐	0.30☐
861	30c Virgin & Child	0.55☐	0.30☐
862	40c Angel	0.60☐	0.30☐
863	50c Three Kings	0.95☐	0.50☐
864	85c Madonna & Child	1.60☐	0.80☐
	First Day Cover (40c) AP		1.00☐
	First Day Cover (others) AP		4.00☐

Australian Bicentennial Collection   1984 07 Nov

The First Australians - Rock Paintings

865	30c Bicentennial Symbol	0.60☐	0.30☐
866	30c Stick figures	0.60☐	0.30☐
867	30c Bunjil's Cave	0.60☐	0.30☐
868	30c Quinkan Gallery	0.60☐	0.30☐
869	30c Rock Python	0.60☐	0.30☐
870	30c Wandjina Spirit & Snake Babies	0.60☐	0.30☐
871	30c Silver Barramundi	0.60☐	0.30☐
872	85c Rock Possum	2.50☐	2.00☐
	First Day Cover (8) AP		6.00☐

865. Bicentennial Symbol

866. Stick figures - Cobar

873. Leadbeater's Possum   874. Helmeted Honeyeater

150th Anniversary of Victoria   1984 19 Nov

873	30c Leadbeater's Possum	0.50☐	0.40☐
874	30c Helmeted Honeyeater	0.50☐	0.40☐
875	Joined pair	1.00☐	1.00☐
875A	Gutter pair	1.50☐	1.50☐
	First Day Cover (gutter pair)		2.00☐

867. Bunjil's Cave - Grampians

868. Quinkan Gallery - Cape York

876. Musgrave Ranges
(Sydney Nolan)

877. Walls of China
(Russel Drysdale)

879. Youth Symbolised

International Youth Year   1985 13 Feb
Theme: Participation-Development-Peace

| 879 | 30c Youth Symbolised | 0.50□ | 0.30□ |
| | First Day Cover AP | | 1.00□ |

Australia Day: 1985 25 Jan
Lines from Dorothea MacKellers Poem 'My Country'

876	30c Musgrave Ranges painting	0.60□	0.30□
877	30c Walls of China painting	0.60□	0.30□
878	Joined pair	1.50□	1.50□
878A	Gutter pair	2.50□	2.50□
	First Day Cover (gutter pair) AP		3.00□

Colonial Military Uniforms   1985 25 Feb

880	33c Volunteer Artillery	0.60□	0.30□
881	33c WA Pinjarrah Cavalry	0.60□	0.30□
882	33c NSW Lancers	0.60□	0.30□
883	33c NSW Contingent in Sudan	0.60□	0.30□
884	33c Victorian Mounted Rifles	0.60□	0.30□
885	Joined strip of 5	3.00□	3.00□
	First Day Cover (strip) AP		3.00□

880. Volunteer Artillery   881. WA Pinjarrah Cavalry   882. NSW Lancers   883. NSW Contingent in Sudan   884. Victorian Mounted Rifles

886. Melbourne District Nurse

887. Cockatoo Pink

888. Cockatoo Aqua

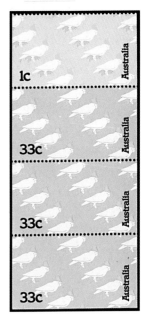

Centenary of District Nursing Services   1985 13 Mar

| 886 | 33c Melbourne District Nurse | 0.60□ | 0.30□ |
| | First Day Cover AP | | 1.00□ |

Vending Machines Folders   1985 13 Mar
Containing 1 x 1c & 3 x 33c Stamps in vertical Strip

887	1c Cockatoo - Pink	1.00□	1.00□
888	33c Cockatoo - Aqua	1.00□	0.50□
889	Joined strip of 4	4.50□	4.00□
	First Day Cover (4) AP		4.50□

891. Eendracht

892. William Dampier

890. Abel Tasman

893. World Globe

Australian Bicentennial Collection   1985 10 Apr
Terra Australis - Navigators

890	33c Abel Tasman	0.60☐	0.40☐
891	33c Eendracht	0.60☐	0.40☐
892	33c William Dampier	0.60☐	0.40☐
893	90c World Globe	2.00☐	1.20☐
894	Miniature Sheet 33c x 3 & 90c x 1	5.00☐	4.50☐
	First Day Cover (Miniature Sheet) AP		5.00☐
	First Day Cover (4) AP		5.00☐

894. Terra Australis - Navigators Miniature Sheet

The background of the miniature sheet is one of
the earliest known charts of Australia

901. Tasselled Anglerfish   902. Red Handfish

895. Leafy Sea Dragon   896. Order of Australia Medal

Marine Life Series II: Rare and Unusual   1985 20 Mar
895	33c Leafy Sea Dragon	0.60☐	0.30☐
	First Day Cover AP		1.00☐

Queen Elizabeth II Birthday   1985 22 Apr
896	33c Order of Australia Medal	0.60☐	0.30☐
	First Day Cover AP		1.00☐

903. Red Velvet Fish   904. Pineapple Fish

905. Crab-eyed Goby

897. Soil   898. Air

Marine Life Definitives   1985 12 Jun
901	5c Tasselled Anglerfish	0.30☐	0.30☐
902	20c Red Handfish	0.50☐	0.35☐
903	40c Red Velvet Fish	0.70☐	0.30☐
904	80c Pineapple Fish	1.30☐	0.60☐
905	90c Crab-eyed Goby	1.40☐	0.70☐
	First Day Cover (5) AP		4.50☐

899. Water   900. Energy

Conservation   1985 15 May
897	33c Soil	0.60☐	0.30☐
898	50c Air	1.10☐	0.80☐
899	80c Water	1.50☐	0.80☐
900	90c Energy	1.70☐	1.50☐
	First Day Cover (4) AP		4.50☐

Australiana   1985 17 Jul
Children's Books - Classical
906	33c Elves & Fairies	0.60☐	0.30☐
907	33c Magic Pudding	0.60☐	0.30☐
908	33c Ginger Meggs	0.60☐	0.30☐
909	33c Blinky Bill	0.60☐	0.30☐
910	33c Snugglepot & Cuddlepie	0.60☐	0.30☐
	Joined strip of 5	3.00☐	3.00☐
	First Day Cover (strip of 5) AP		4.00☐

906. Elves & Fairies   907. Magic Pudding   908. Ginger Meggs   909. Blinky Bill   910. Snugglepot & Cuddlepie

912. Angel Ship & Candle

913. Angel & Holly

914. Angel & Bells

915. Angel & Star

916. Angel & Bauble

Christmas

1,985

(45c) 18 Sep - (27c, 33c, 55c, 90c) 01 Nov

912	27c Angel & Holly	0.50☐	0.30☐
913	33c Angel & Bells	0.60☐	0.30☐
914	45c Angel Ship & Candle	0.70☐	0.40☐
915	55c Angel & Star	1.10☐	0.50☐
916	90c Angel & Bauble	1.50☐	1.30☐
	First Day Cover (45c only) AP		1.00☐
	First Day Cover (all values)		3.00☐

917. Electronic Mail Graphic

Electronic Mail

1985 18 Sep

917	33c Electronic Mail Graphic	0.60☐	0.30☐
	First Day Cover AP		1.00☐

918. Astrolabe

919. Jug

920. Scissors & Bobbins

921. Silver Buckle

Australian Bicentennial Series II:

1985 02 Oct

Terra Australis - Coastal Shipwrecks

918	33c Astrolabe	0.60☐	0.30☐
919	50c Jug	1.00☐	1.00☐
920	90c Scissors & Bobbins	1.60☐	1.00☐
921	$1 Silver Buckle	1.80☐	1.00☐
	First Day Cover (4) AP		6.00☐

922. An Aboriginal Perspective

Australia Day: An Aboriginal Perspective

1986 24 Jan

922	33c An Aboriginal Perspective	0.60☐	0.30☐
	First Day Cover AP		1.00☐

923. 3 Disc Satellite

924. Cylinder Satellite

AUSSAT

1986 24 Jan

923	33c 3 Disc Satellite	0.60☐	0.40☐
924	80c Cylinder Satellite	1.50☐	1.00☐
	First Day Cover (2) AP		2.50☐

925. Festive Design | 926. Buffalo

150th Anniversary of South Australia   **1986 12 Feb**

925	33c Festive Design	0.60☐	0.40☐
926	33c Buffalo	0.60☐	0.40☐
927	Se-tenant pair	1.20☐	1.10☐
927A	Gutter pair	1.60☐	1.60☐
	First Day Cover (gutter pair) AP		2.00☐

934. Radio Telescope

935. Queen Elizabeth II

Halley's Comet   **1986 09 Apr**

| 934 | 33c Radio Telescope | 0.60☐ | 0.40☐ |
| | First Day Cover AP | | 1.00☐ |

60th Birthday of Queen Elizabeth II   **1986 21 Apr**

| 935 | 33c Queen Elizabeth II | 0.60☐ | 0.40☐ |
| | First Day Cover AP | | 1.00☐ |

928. Banksia serrata | 929. Hibiscus merankensis

930. Dillenia alata | 931. Correa reflexa

932. Joseph Banks | 933. Sydney Parkinson

Australian Bicentennial Collection   **1986 12 Mar**
New Holland - Cook's Voyage

928	33c Banksia serrata	0.70☐	0.40☐
929	33c Hibiscus merankensis	0.70☐	0.40☐
930	50c Dillenia alata	1.00☐	0.60☐
931	80c Correa reflexa	1.40☐	0.80☐
932	90c Joseph Banks	2.00☐	1.00☐
933	90c Sydney Parkinson	2.00☐	1.00☐
	First Day Covers (2) AP		7.00☐

936. Brumbies

937. Mustering | 938. Show Jumping

939. Australian Pony

Horses   **1986 28 May**

936	33c Brumbies	0.60☐	0.40☐
937	80c Mustering	1.30☐	0.90☐
938	90c Show Jumping	1.40☐	0.90☐
939	$1 Australian Pony	1.60☐	1.20☐
	First Day Cover (4) AP		5.00☐

| 940. Jimble | 941. Stonefish | 942. Cone Shell | 943. Lionfish | 944. Stingaree |

Marine Life Definitives   **1986 11 Jun**

940	3c Jimble	0.30☐	0.30☐
941	10c Stonefish	0.30☐	0.30☐
942	45c Cone Shell	0.80☐	0.30☐
943	60c Lionfish	1.00☐	0.40☐
944	65c Stingaree	1.00☐	0.50☐
945	70c Octopus	1.20☐	0.50☐
946	$1 Crown of Thorns Starfish	1.00☐	0.60☐
	First Day Covers (7) AP 2 covers		7.50☐

945. Octopus   946. Crown of Thorns Starfish

| 947. The Old Shearer stands | 948. The Ringer looks around | 949. The Boss of the Board | 950. The Tarboy is there | 951. Shearing is all over |

'Click go the shears'   **1986 21 Jul**

947	33c The Old Shearer stands	0.60☐	0.40☐
948	33c The Ringer looks around	0.60☐	0.40☐
949	33c The Boss of the Board	0.60☐	0.40☐
950	33c The Tarboy is there	0.60☐	0.40☐
951	33c Shearing is all over	0.60☐	0.40☐
952	Joined strip of 5	3.00☐	3.00☐
	First Day Cover (strip of 5)AP		3.50☐

953. King George III   956. Capt John Hunter

954. Lord Sydney   955. Capt Arthur Phillip

Australian Bicentennial Series: The decision to settle

1986 06 Aug

953	33c King George III	0.60☐	0.40☐
954	33c Lord Sydney	0.60☐	0.40☐
955	33c Capt Arthur Phillip	0.60☐	0.40☐
956	$1 Capt John Hunter	2.50☐	1.80☐
	First Day Cover (4) AP		4.50☐

958. Tree Dwelling Orchid

959. Duck Orchid

957. Pink Enamel Orchid

960. Sun Orchid

Australian Native Orchids — 1986 18 Sep

957	36c Pink Enamel Orchid	0.70	0.40
958	55c Tree Dwelling Orchid	0.90	0.85
959	90c Duck Orchid	1.50	1.50
960	$1 Sun Orchid	1.50	1.20
	First Day Cover (4) AP		4.00

961. Red Kangaroo 962. Emu 963. Koala 964. Kookaburra 965. Platypus

Australian Wildlife - Definitives — 1986 13 Aug

961	36c Red Kangaroo	0.70	0.40
962	36c Emu	0.70	0.40
963	36c Koala	0.70	0.40
964	36c Kookaburra	0.70	0.40
965	36c Platypus	0.70	0.40
966	Joined strip of 5	4.00	3.30
	First Day Cover (strip) AP		3.50

968. Alpine Marsh Marigold 967. Royal Bluebell 970. Silver Snow Daisy

969. Mount Buffalo Daisy   967. Royal Bluebell   970. Silver Snow Daisy

Alpine Wildflowers. Vending machine booklets.   1986 25 Aug

Book 1: 80c (2 x 36c, 3c,5c) Book 2: $1 (25c, 3c, 2 x 36c)

No.	Description	MUH	FU
967	3c Royal Bluebell	0.60	0.40
968	5c Alpine Marsh Marigold	1.75	1.75
969	25c Mount Buffalo Daisy	1.75	1.25
970	36c Silver Snow Daisy	0.80	0.40
971	80c booklet - Strip x 4	4.00	4.00
972	$1 booklet -Strip x 4	4.50	4.50
	First Day Cover (strip) AP		4.50

974. Australia II Yacht

973. Fighting Kangaroo Symbol   975. Americas Cup

America's Cup Triumph 1983   1986 26 Sep

No.	Description	MUH	FU
973	36c Fighting Kangaroo Symbol	0.65	0.40
974	36c Australia II Yacht	0.65	0.40
975	36c America's Cup	0.65	0.40
	First Day Cover (3) AP		3.00

976. Peace Dove in Flight

International Year of Peace   1986 22 Oct

No.	Description	MUH	FU
976	36c Peace Dove in Flight	0.65	0.40
	First Day Cover AP		1.00

977. Mary & Joseph   978. Three Kings   979. Angels

Christmas   1986 03 Nov
Kindergarten Children Playing Christmas characters

977	30c Mary & Joseph	0.60	0.40
978	36c Three Kings	0.65	0.40
979	60c Angels	0.90	0.90
980	Miniature Sheet (5 x 30c)	3.00	3.00
	Individuals stamps from MS	0.60	0.60
	First Day Cover (3) AP		2.20
	First Day Cover (Miniature Sheet) AP		4.00

980. Miniature Sheet (5 x 30c)

981. Flag & Circuit Board   982. Australian Made Logo

Australia Day   1987 23 Jan

981	36c Flag & Circuit Board	0.70	0.40
982	36c Australian Made Logo	0.70	0.40
	First Day Cover (2) AP		2.25

983. View from Masthead

984. Yachts Tacking

991. Livestock

992. Farm Produce

985. Yachts Crossing

986. Yacht Sails

993. Sideshows

America's Cup   **1987 28 Jan**

983	36c View from Masthead	0.70☐	0.40☐
984	55c Yachts Tacking	1.00☐	0.90☐
985	90c Yachts Crossing	1.40☐	1.20☐
986	$1 Yacht Sails	1.70☐	1.40☐
	First Day Cover (4) AP		4.50☐

994. Competitions

Agricultural Show   **1987 10 Apr**

991	36c Livestock	0.60☐	0.40☐
992	65c Farm Produce	1.00☐	0.80☐
993	90c Sideshows	1.50☐	1.00☐
994	$1 Competitions	1.80☐	1.20☐
	First Day Cover (4) AP		5.00☐

987. Vine Fruit & Melons

988. Tropical & Subtropical Fruit

995. Queen Elizabeth II

Queens Birthday   **1987 21 Apr**

| 995 | 36c Queen Elizabeth II | 0.60☐ | 0.40☐ |
| | First Day Cover AP | | 1.00☐ |

989. Citrus Fruit Apples Pears

990. Stone & Berry Fruit

Fruit in Australia   **1987 11 Feb**

987	36c Vine Fruit & Melons	0.65☐	0.40☐
988	65c Tropical & Subtropical Fruit	1.10☐	1.00☐
989	90c Citrus Fruit Apples Pears	1.45☐	1.70☐
990	$1 Stone & Berry Fruit	1.60☐	1.90☐
	First Day Cover (4) AP		5.00☐

996. Convict   997. Officer & Wife   998. Sailors   999. Ferrying   1000. Fleet Setting Sail

First Fleet Bicentennial: Departure   1987 13 May

		MUH	FU
996	36c Convict	0.70	0.40
997	36c Officer & Wife	0.70	0.40
998	36c Sailors	0.70	0.40
999	36c Ferrying	0.70	0.40
1000	36c Fleet Setting Sail	0.70	0.40
1001	Joined strip 5	3.50	3.00
	First Day Cover (strip) AP		5.00

1002. Landfall   1003. Santa Cruz Ferrying   1004. Fishing

First Fleet Bicentennial: Anchoring at Teneriffe   1987 03 Jun

		MUH	FU
1002	$1 Landfall	1.50	1.00
1003	36c Santa Cruz Ferrying	0.70	0.40
1004	36c Fishing	0.70	0.40
1005	Joined pair (1003/1004)	1.80	1.00
	First Day Cover (3) AP		4.00

1006. At the Station   1007. Mountain Horse   1008. Terrible Descent   1009. At their heels   1010. Brought them back
                                    & Man

The Man from Snowy River   1987 24 Jun

		MUH	FU
1006	36c At the Station	0.70	0.50
1007	36c Mountain Horse & Man	0.70	0.50
1008	36c Terrible Descent	0.70	0.50
1009	36c At their heels	0.70	0.50
1010	36c Brought them back	0.70	0.50
1011	Joined strip of 5	3.50	3.50
	First Day Cover (strip) AP		4.00

1012. Possum   1013. Cockatoo   1014. Wombat   1015. Rosella   1016. Echidna

Australian Wildlife Series II: Definitives   1987 01 Jul

NO.	DESCRIPTION	MUH	FU
1012	37c Possum	0.70	0.40
1013	37c Cockatoo	0.70	0.40
1014	37c Wombat	0.70	0.40
1015	37c Rosella	0.70	0.40
1016	37c Echidna	0.70	0.40
1017	Joined strip of 5	3.50	3.00
	First Day Cover (strip) AP		4.00

1018. Stormy Seas   1019. Arrival   1020. Market Place   1021. Church Procession   1022. Departure

First Fleet Bicentennial: Rio de Janeiro   1987 06 Aug

NO.	DESCRIPTION	MUH	FU
1018	37c Stormy Seas	0.70	0.40
1019	37c Arrival	0.70	0.40
1020	37c Market Place	0.70	0.40
1021	37c Church Procession	0.70	0.40
1022	37c Departure	0.70	0.40
1023	Joined strip 5	3.50	3.00
	First Day Cover (strip) AP		4.00

1024. Bionic Ear

1025. Microchips

1026. Robotics   1027. Ceramics

1028. Boys with Yabbies   1029. Cats Cradle

1030. Barracking   1031. Playing with Roo

Australian Achievements in Technology   1987 19 Aug

NO.	DESCRIPTION	MUH	FU
1024	37c Bionic Ear	0.70	0.30
1025	53c Microchips	1.00	0.50
1026	63c Robotics	1.20	0.90
1027	68c Ceramics	1.30	1.00
	First Day Cover (4) AP		4.00

Aussie Kids   1987 16 Sep

NO.	DESCRIPTION	MUH	FU
1028	37c Boys with Yabbies	0.60	0.30
1029	55c Cats Cradle	1.00	0.90
1030	90c Barracking	1.40	1.20
1031	$1 Playing with Roo	1.80	0.90
	First Day Cover (4) AP		5.00

1032. Fishermen   1033. Livestock & Marine   1034. Loading

First Fleet Bicentennial: Cape of Good Hope   **1987 13 Oct**

No.	Description	MUH	FU
1032	37c Livestock & Marine	0.70☐	0.40☐
1033	37c Loading	0.70☐	0.40☐
1034	$1 Fishermen	1.80☐	0.80☐
1035	Joined pair (1033/1034)	1.50☐	1.50☐
	First Day Cover (3) AP		4.00☐

1036. Spear Thrower

1037. Basket

1038. Shield

1039. Bowl

1040. Belt

Aboriginal Art   **1987 13 Oct**

Booklet Panes
One booklet face value 80c contains 4 stamps (2x1036, 2x1037) as shown above. The other booklet face value $2.00 contains 6 stamps (1x1038, 3x1039, 2x1040) as shown at right.

No.	Description	MUH	FU
1036	3c Spear Thrower	2.00☐	1.80☐
1037	15c Shield	3.50☐	3.50☐
1038	37c Basket	1.20☐	1.20☐
1039	37c Bowl	1.20☐	1.20☐
1040	37c Belt	1.20☐	1.20☐
1041	Joined strip (80c: 2x3c, 2x37c)	7.00☐	6.00☐
1042	Joined strip ($2.00: 1x15c, 3x37c, 2x37c)	8.00☐	7.00☐
	First Day Cover (any strip) AP		9.50☐

| 1043. Grandmother | 1044. Father & Child | 1045. Children | 1046. Family | 1047. Teenagers |

1049. Senior Citizens

1050. Family

Christmas Issue: Carols by Candlelight — 1987 02 Nov

No.	Description	MUH	FU
1043	30c Grandmother	0.60	0.30
1044	30c Father & Children	0.60	0.30
1045	30c Children	0.60	0.30
1046	30c Family	0.60	0.30
1047	30c Teenagers	0.60	0.30
1048	Joined strip of 5	3.00	2.80
1049	37c Senior Citizens	0.70	0.40
1050	63c Family	1.40	1.10
	First Day Cover (7) AP		5.00

| 1051. Under Sail | 1052. Supply at Anchor | 1053. Sydney Cove | 1054. Marines Ferried Ashore | 1055 Raising the Flag |

First Fleet Bicentennial: Arrival — 1988 26 Jan

No.	Description	MUH	FU
1051	37c Under Sail	0.70	0.40
1052	37c Supply at Anchor	0.70	0.40
1053	37c Sydney Cove	0.70	0.40
1054	37c Marines Ferried Ashore	0.70	0.40
1055	37c Raising the Flag	0.70	0.40
1056	Joined strip of 5	4.00	3.00
	First Day Cover (strip) AP		4.50

1057. Koala & Eagle

Happy Bicentenary: Joint stamp issue with USA — 1988 26 Jan

No.	Description	MUH	FU
1057	37c Koala & Eagle	0.70	0.40
	First Day Cover AP		1.00

1058. Religion

1059. Industry

1060. Local Government

1061. Trade Unions

1062. Parliament

1063. Transport

1064. Sport

1065. Commerce

1066. Housing

1067. Welfare

1068. Postal Services

1069. Cycling

1070. Health

1071. Gold Mining

1072. Primary Industries

1073. Education

1074. Armed Services

1075. Police

1076. Telecommunications

1077. The Media

1078. Science

1079. Visual Arts

1080. Performing Arts

1081. Banking

1082. Law

1083. Rescue

Living Together Definitive
Part 1: 4c, 10c, 15c, 20c, 25c, 37c, 45c, 50c, 53c, 70c, 80c, 90c, $11988 17 Feb
Part 2: 1c, 2c, 3c, 5c, 30c, 40c, 55c, 60c, 63c, 65c, 68c, 75c, 95c1988 16 Mar

		MUH	FU
1058	1c Religion	0.40	0.30
1059	2cIndustry	0.40	0.30
1060	3cLocal Government	0.40	0.30
1061	4c Trade Unions	0.40	0.30
1062	5cParliament	0.55	0.30
1063	10c Transport	0.55	0.30
1064	15c Sport	0.30	0.30
1065	20c Commerce	0.55	0.30
1066	25c Housing	0.40	0.30
1067	30c Welfare	0.40	0.30
1068	37c Postal Services	1.10	0.40
1068a	Booklet Pane 10 x 37c	10.00	10.00
1069	40c Cycling	0.60	0.40
1070	45c Health	0.65	0.45
1071	50c Gold Mining	0.75	0.60
1072	53c Primary Industries	1.60	1.10
1073	55c Education	1.55	0.60
1074	60c Armed Services	1.10	0.80
1075	63c Police	2.00	1.00
1076	65c Telecommunications	2.00	0.70
1077	68c The Media	2.00	1.00
1078	70c Science	2.00	0.50
1079	75c Visual Arts	1.40	0.70
1080	80c Performing Arts	1.80	0.80
1081	90c Banking	2.00	0.80
1082	95c Law	2.00	0.90
1083	$1Rescue	2.30	0.90
	First Day Cover (Part 1 13 values) 3 Cover AP		10.00
	First Day Cover (Part 2 13 values) 2 Cover AP		10.00

1084. Government House 1790   1085. Government Farm 1791   1086. Parramatta Road 1796   1087. The Rocks 1800   1088. Sydney Hospital

The Early Years of Settlement: 1788 -1809   1988 13 Apr

1084	37c Government House 1790	0.80	0.50
1085	37c Government Farm 1791	0.80	0.50
1086	37c Parramatta Road 1796	0.80	0.50
1087	37c The Rocks 1800	0.80	0.50
1088	37c Sydney Hospital	0.80	0.50
1089	Joined strip of 5	4.00	3.00
	First Day Cover (strip) AP		4.00

1090. Queen Elizabeth II

1091. Expo 88 'Logo'

1092. Parliament House

Birthday of H M Queen Elizabeth II   1988 21 Apr

| 1090 | 37c Queen Elizabeth II | 0.80 | 0.40 |
| | First Day Cover AP | | 1.50 |

Expo '88   1988 29 Apr

| 1091 | 37c Expo 88 'Logo' | 0.80 | 0.40 |
| | First Day Cover AP | | 1.50 |

Opening of New Parliament House   1988 09 May

| 1092 | 37c Parliament House | 0.80 | 0.40 |
| | First Day Cover AP | | 1.50 |

1093. Emigration

1094. Parliament Democracy

1096. Sport - Cricketer

1097. Performing Arts

Joint Issue with United Kingdom   1988 21 Jun

1093	37c Emigration	0.80	0.40
1094	37c Parliament Democracy	0.80	0.40
1095	Joined pair	2.00	1.50
1096	$1 Sport - Cricketer	1.80	1.00
1097	$1 Performing Arts	1.80	1.00
1098	Joined pair	4.00	2.50
	First Day Cover (2 joined pairs)		5.00

1099. Koala & Kiwi

Happy Bicentenary Koala & Kiwi   **1988 21 Jun**
| 1099 | 37c Koala & Kiwi | 0.80☐ | 0.40☐ |
| | First Day Cover AP | | 1.50☐ |

1100. Bush Potato Country

1101. Courtship Rejection

1102. Medicine Story

1103. Ancestor Dreaming

Aboriginal Paintings: Art of the Desert   **1988 01 Aug**
1100	37c Bush Potato Country	0.80☐	0.40☐
1101	55c Courtship Rejection	1.30☐	1.20☐
1102	90c Medicine Story	2.50☐	2.00☐
1103	$1Ancestor Dreaming	2.20☐	1.30☐
	First Day Cover (4) AP		6.00☐

1104. Basketball   1105. Track & Field

1106. Gymnastics

Seoul 1988 Olympic Games   **1988 14 Sep**
1104	37c Basketball	0.80☐	0.40☐
1105	65c Track & Field	1.80☐	1.80☐
1106	$1Gymnastics	2.00☐	1.50☐
	First Day Cover (3) AP		4.50☐

1107. Mace & Rod

34th Commonwealth Parliamentary Conference   **1988 19 Sep**
| 1107 | 37c Mace & Rod | 0.80☐ | 0.40☐ |
| | First Day Cover AP | | 1.30☐ |

1108. Tourism & Coat of Arms

Living Together additional value   **1988 28 Sep**
1108	39c Tourism & Coat of Arms	0.80☐	0.40☐
1108a	Book pane 10 stamps	10.00☐	10.00☐
	First Day Cover (1) AP		1.60☐

1110. Vase

1111. Teapot

1109. Necklace

Australian Crafts   **1988 28 Sep**

Booklet Panes
One booklet face value 80c contains 3 stamps (1x1109, 2x1111) as shown
above. The other booklet face value $2.00 contains 6 stamps (1x1110, 5x1111)
as shown at right.

1109	2c Necklace	4.00☐	3.50☐
1110	5c Vase	4.00☐	3.50☐
1111	39c Teapot	1.80☐	0.60☐
1111a	Booklet Pane 80c	8.00☐	8.00☐
1111b	Booklet Pane $2.00	8.00☐	8.00☐
	First Day Cover (3) AP		8.00☐

1112. The Desert   1113. The Top End

1114. The Coast   1115. The Bush

Panorama of Australia   1988 17 Oct

No.	Description	MUH	FU
1112	39c The Desert	0.85	0.40
1113	55c The Top End	1.10	1.05
1114	65c The Coast	2.00	1.45
1115	70c The Bush	2.00	1.50
	First Day Cover (4) AP		6.00

1116. Mary & Jesus   1117. Cuddly Koala with Santa Hat

1118. Cockatoo as Santa

Christmas: Kids designed stamps   1988 31 Oct

No.	Description	MUH	FU
1116	32c Mary & Jesus	0.70	0.40
1117	39c Cuddly Koala with Santa Hat	0.85	0.50
1118	63c Cockatoo as Santa	1.80	1.60
	First Day Cover (3) AP		3.50

1119. Sir Henry Parkes

Australia Day   1989 25 Jan

No.	Description	MUH	FU
1119	39c Sir Henry Parkes	0.80	0.40
	First Day Cover AP		2.00

1120. Bowls   1121. Ten Pin Bowling

1122. Football   1123. Fishing

1124. Boy Kite Flying   1125. Cricket

1126. Golf

Sports Series I - Definitives   1989 13 Feb

No.	Description	MUH	FU
1120	1c Bowls	0.30	0.30
1121	2c Ten Pin Bowling	0.30	0.30
1122	3c Football	0.30	0.30
1123	39c Fishing	1.00	0.30
1123a	Booklet Pane 10 x 39c Stamps	12.00	12.00
1124	55c Boy Kite Flying	1.00	0.40
1125	70c Cricket	1.00	0.40
1126	$1.10 Golf	1.80	0.50
	First Day Cover (2) AP		6.50

1128. Poll Dorset

1129. Polwarth

1127. Merino

1130. Corriedale

Sheep in Australia   **1989 27 Feb**

1127	39c Merino	0.80	0.70
1128	39c Poll Dorset	0.80	0.70
1129	85c Polwarth	1.90	1.60
1130	$1 Corriedale	2.00	1.60
	First Day Cover (4) AP		6.50

1131. Botanical Gardens Adelaide

1132. Queen Elizabeth

Adelaide Botanical Gardens: Definitive Issue   **1989 21 Apr**

| 1131 | $10 Botanical Gardens Adelaide | 16.00 | 3.00 |
| | First Day Cover AP | | 18.00 |

Queen Elizabeth II Birthday   **1989 21 Apr**

| 1132 | 39c Queen Elizabeth | 1.00 | 0.40 |
| | First Day Cover AP | | 1.00 |

1133. Immigrants   1134. Pioneers   1135. Squatters   1136. Shepherds   1137. Explorers

Colonial Collection - The Pastoral Era   **1989 10 May**

1133	39c Immigrants	0.80	0.50
1134	39c Pioneers	0.80	0.50
1135	39c Squatters	0.80	0.50
1136	39c Shepherds	0.80	0.50
1137	39c Explorers	0.80	0.50
1138	Se-tenant strip of 5	5.00	3.00
	First Day Cover (strip) AP		5.00

1140. Screen The Talkies

1141. Stage The 90's

1139. Stage the 20's

1142. Screen The Silents

Stage and Screen   1989 12 Jul

No.	Description	MUH	FU
1139	39c Stage the 20's	0.80☐	0.50☐
1140	85c Screen The Talkies	1.70☐	1.60☐
1141	$1 Stage The 90's	2.00☐	1.50☐
1142	$1.10 Screen The Silents	2.40☐	1.50☐
	First Day Cover (4) AP		6.00☐

1143. Cycling

1144. Cycling (self adhesive)

Sport Definitive - Additional Value   1989 23 Aug

No.	Description	MUH	FU
1143	41c Cycling	1.00☐	0.30☐
1143a	$4.10 Booklet Pane (10 x 41c)	10.00☐	10.00☐
1144	41c Cycling Experimental issue		
	Self Adhesive issued in strip of 100 in box.		
	First Day Cover (1143) AP		1.30☐
	First Day Cover (1144) AP		1.30☐

1145. Tom Roberts

1146. Arthur Streeton

1147. Frederick McCubbin

1148. Charles Conder

Australian Impressionist Painters   1989 23 Aug

No.	Description	MUH	FU
1145	41c Tom Roberts	0.80☐	0.50☐
1146	41c Arthur Streeton	0.80☐	0.50☐
1147	41c Frederick McCubbin	0.80☐	0.50☐
1148	41c Charles Conder	0.80☐	0.50☐
	First Day Cover (4) AP		3.50☐

1149. Freeway Views

1150. City Buildings

1151. Commuter Train

1153. Nooroo NSW

1154. Mawarra Victoria

Gardens - Definitive Issue		1989 13 Sep	
1153	$2 Nooroo NSW	3.50☐	1.00☐
1154	$5 Mawarra Victoria	9.00☐	2.00☐
	First Day Cover ($2) AP		3.50☐
	First Day Cover ($5) AP		10.00☐

1155. Young people

50th Anniversary of Australian Youth Hostels		1989 13 Sep	
1155	41c Young people	0.80☐	0.50☐
	First Day Cover AP		1.00☐

The Urban Environment Booklet   **1989 01 Sep**

containing 7 x 41c stamps sold for $3 - 13c above face value.

1149	41c Freeway Views	1.10☐	0.50☐
1150	41c City Buildings	1.10☐	0.50☐
1151	41c Commuter Train	1.10☐	0.50☐
1152	Booklet Pane strip 7	7.00☐	7.00☐
	First Day Cover (3) AP		4.50☐

1156. Adelaide Tram   1157. Sydney Tram

1158. Melbourne Tram   1159. Hobart Tram

1160. Brisbane Tram

Australian Historic Trams   1989 11 Oct

		MUH	FU
1156	41c Adelaide Tram	0.85	0.50
1157	41c Sydney Tram	0.85	0.50
1158	41c Melbourne Tram	0.85	0.50
1159	41c Hobart Tram	0.85	0.50
1160	41c Brisbane Tram	0.85	0.50
	First Day Cover (5) AP		4.00

1161. Radio Australia 1939-1989

50th Anniversary of Radio Australia   1989 01 Nov

		MUH	FU
1161	41c Radio Australia 1939-1989	0.80	0.50
	First Day Cover AP		1.00

1162. Annunciation   1163. Annunciation to Shepherds

1164. Adoration of the Magi

Christmas - Illustrated Manuscripts   1989 01 Nov

		MUH	FU
1162	36c Annunciation	0.70	0.40
1162a	$3.60 Booklet pane 10 x 36c	8.00	8.00
1163	41c Annunciation to Shepherds	0.80	0.50
1164	80c Adoration of the Magi	1.65	1.20
	First Day Cover (3) AP		3.00

1165. Golden Wattle

Australia Day   1990 17 Jan

		MUH	FU
1165	41c Golden Wattle	1.00	0.50
	First Day Cover AP		2.00

1166. Kayaking & Canoeing   1167. Sailboarding

1168. Tennis   1169. Rockclimbing

1170. Fun Run

Sport Series II - Definitives   1990 17 Jan

		MUH	FU
1166	5c Kayaking & Canoeing	0.30	0.30
1167	10c Sailboarding	0.30	0.30
1168	20c Tennis	0.40	0.30
1169	65c Rockclimbing	1.50	0.90
1170	$1 Fun Run	2.00	0.80
	First Day Cover (5) AP		4.00

1171. Bouquet of Wildflowers

1177. Smoking

1178. Alcohol

1179. Nutrition

1180. Screening

Thinking of You   **1990 07 Feb**

1171	41c Bouquet of Wildflowers	0.80☐	0.50☐
1171a	Booklet pane 10 x 41c stamps	8.00☐	8.00☐
	First Day Cover AP		2.00☐

1172. Dr Constance Stone

Centenary of Women in Medical Practice   **1990 07 Feb**

1172	41c Dr Constance Stone	0.80☐	0.50☐
	First Day Cover AP		2.00☐

Community Health   **1990 14 Mar**

1177	41c Smoking	0.80☐	0.50☐
1178	41c Alcohol	0.80☐	0.50☐
1179	41c Nutrition	0.80☐	0.50☐
1180	41c Screening	0.80☐	0.50☐
	First Day Cover (4) AP		3.00☐

1173. Greater Glider

1174. Spotted Tailed Quoll

1175. Mountain Pygmy Possum

1176. Brush Tailed Rock Wallaby

1181. At the Front

1182. They Also Serve

1183. Lest We Forget

1184. Casualties

1185. News from Home

ANIMALS of HIGH COUNTRY   **1990 21 Feb**

1173	41c Greater Glider	0.80☐	0.50☐
1174	65c Spotted Tailed Quoll	1.60☐	1.10☐
1175	70c Mountain Pygmy Possum	1.50☐	1.10☐
1176	80c Brush Tailed Rock Wallaby	1.60☐	1.10☐
	First Day Cover (4) AP		5.00☐

The ANZAC Tradition   **1990 12 Apr**

1181	41c At the Front	0.90☐	0.50☐
1182	41c They Also Serve	0.90☐	0.50☐
1183	65c Lest We Forget	1.50☐	1.00☐
1184	$1 Casualties	1.90☐	1.20☐
1185	$1.10 News from Home	2.30☐	1.50☐
	First Day Cover (5) AP		6.50☐

1186. Queen Elizabeth

Queen Elizabeth   1990 19 Apr

1186	41c Queen Elizabeth	0.80☐	0.40☐
	First Day Cover AP		1.00☐

1193ms. Miniature Sheet
A special souvenir card was produced by Australia Post for the London 1990 Stamp
World Exhibition. The miniature sheet (shown below) was sold at the exhibition & in
Australia by mail order only. It is considered that this & other similar productions are
outside the scope of this catalogue

1187. NSW 5/- Coin

1188. SA 1/- Queen

1189. Van Diemens Land 4d
Queen

1190. Victoria 5/-
"Laureate"

1191. Qld 6d
Queen

1192. 1854 4d
"Inverted Frame"

150th Anniversary of First Adhesive Postage Stamp

		1990 1 May	
1187	41c Purple NSW 5/-	0.90☐	0.50☐
1188	41c Violet SA 1/-	0.90☐	0.50☐
1189	41c Orange Van Diemens Land 4d	0.90☐	0.50☐
1190	41c Blue Yellow 5/-	0.90☐	0.50☐

1191	41c Green Qld 6d	0.90☐	0.50☐
1192	41c Blue WA 4d	0.90☐	0.50☐
1193	Block of 6 Above	5.00☐	5.00☐
1193ms	Miniature Sheet	5.50☐	5.50☐
	First Day Cover (Block 6) AP		5.00☐
	First Day Cover (Miniature Sheet) AP		5.50☐

1194. Off to the Diggings   1195. The Diggings   1196. Panning for Gold   1197. Commissioners Tent   1198. The Gold Escort

Gold fever   1990 16 May

1194	41c Off to the Diggings	0.80☐	0.50☐
1195	41c The Diggings	0.80☐	0.50☐
1196	41c Panning for Gold	0.80☐	0.50☐
1197	41c Commissioners Tent	0.80☐	0.50☐
1198	41c The Gold Escort	0.80☐	0.50☐
1199	Se-tenant strip of 5	4.50☐	3.50☐
	First Day Cover (5) AP		5.00☐

1200. Analysis of Ice Cores

1201. Marine Biology

1201ms. Miniature Sheet

Scientific Co-operation in Antarctica Joint Issue — 1990 13 Jun

No.	Description	MUH	FU
1200	41c Analysis of Ice Cores	0.90☐	0.50☐
1201	$1.10 Marine Biology	1.70☐	1.20☐
1201ms	Miniature Sheet	2.80☐	2.80☐
	First Day Cover (2) AP		3.00☐
	First Day Cover (Miniature Sheet) AP		3.50☐

1202. Land Boom   1203. Building Boom   1204. Investment Boom   1205. Retail Boom   1206. Factory Boom

Boomtime — 1990 12 Jul

No.	Description	MUH	FU
1202	41c Land Boom	0.80☐	0.50☐
1203	41c Building Boom	0.80☐	0.50☐
1204	41c Investment Boom	0.80☐	0.50☐
1205	41c Retail Boom	0.80☐	0.50☐
1206	41c Factory Boom	0.80☐	0.50☐
1207	Se-tenant strip of 5	5.00☐	4.50☐
	First Day Cover (strip) AP		5.00☐

1208. A view of the artist's house & garden in Mills Plains,
VDL (John Glover)

Gardens - Definitive Issue $20 — 1990 15 Aug

No.	Description	MUH	FU
1208	$20 Garden Painting	28.00☐	10.00☐
	First Day Cover AP		30.00☐

1209. Skateboarding

1210. Skateboarding - self adhesive

1211. Gliding

Sport Series II - Additional Definitive Values   1990 27 Aug

No.	Description	MUH	FU
1209	43c Skateboarding	0.80 ☐	0.40 ☐
1209a	Booklet pane 10 x 43c	9.00 ☐	9.00 ☐
1210	43c Skateboarding self adhesive - strip of 100 in box		
	Also strip of 200 in box.	1.20 ☐	0.80 ☐
1211	$1.20 Gliding	1.80 ☐	1.00 ☐
	First Day Cover (2) AP		4.00 ☐

1212. Salmon Gums
(Robert Juniper)

1213. The Blue Dress
(Brian Dunlop)

Sterner Vending Machine Folder   1990 03 Sep

No.	Description	MUH	FU
1212	28c Salmon Gums	1.80 ☐	1.80 ☐
1213	43c The Blue Dress	0.80 ☐	0.60 ☐
1214	$2 folder (1 x 28c, 4 x 43c)	6.00 ☐	4.50 ☐
	First Day Cover (strip 5) AP		4.50 ☐

1215. Bouquet of Wildflowers

1217. Kookaburra

1219. Nativity

Thinking of You: Reissue of Stamp 1171 (41c value)

No.	Description	MUH	FU
		1990 03 Sep	
1215	43c Bouquet of Wildflowers	0.80 ☐	0.50 ☐
1216	$4.30 Booklet (10 x 43c)	9.50 ☐	
	First Day Cover AP		2.00 ☐

Christmas Issue: The Bush Nativity

No.	Description	MUH	FU
		1990 31 Oct	
1217	38c Kookaburra	0.70 ☐	0.50 ☐
1218	$3.80 Booklet (10 x 38c)	10.00 ☐	
1219	43c Nativity	0.80 ☐	0.50 ☐
1220	80c Possum	1.50 ☐	1.00 ☐
	First Day Cover (3) AP		3.50 ☐

1220. Possum

☆ RENNIKS

NO.	DESCRIPTION	MUH	FU	NO.	DESCRIPTION	MUH	FU

1221. Local Government

150 Years of Local Government 　　　　　　**1990 31 Oct**

1221	43c Local Government	0.90	0.50
	First Day Cover AP		1.00

1229. Chestnut Teal

Australian Waterbirds 　　　　　　**1991 14 Feb**

1226	43c Black Necked Stork	0.80	0.50
1227	43c Black Swan	0.80	0.50
1228	85c Cape Barren Goose	1.80	1.50
1229	$1 Chestnut Teal	2.00	1.60
	First Day Cover (4) AP		5.50

1222. Australian National Flag 　　　1223. White Ensign (RAN)

1224. Blue Ensign RAAF 　　　1225. Red Ensign (Merchant Navy)

Australia Day 　　　　　　**1991 10 Jan**

1222	43c Australian National Flag	0.80	0.50
1223	90c White Ensign (RAN)	1.70	1.40
1224	$1 Blue Ensign RAAF	2.00	1.60
1225	$1.20 Red Ensign (Merchant Navy)	2.50	1.60
	First Day Cover (4) AP		6.00

1230. Wartime Women's Services

1231. Siege of Tobruk

1232. Australian War Memorial

In Memory of Those Who Served: 50th Anniversaries

　　　　　　1991 14 Mar

1230	43c Wartime Women's Services	0.80	0.50
1231	43c Siege of Tobruk	0.80	0.50
1232	$1.20 Australian War Memorial	2.50	1.50
	First Day Cover (3) AP		4.00

1226. Black Necked Stork

1227. Black Swan

1228. Cape Barren Goose

1233. Queen Elizabeth

Queen's Birthday 　　　　　　**1991 11 Apr**

1233	43c Queen Elizabeth	0.80	0.50
	First Day Cover AP		1.00

1234. Cotton Harlequin Bug

1235. Hawk Moth

1243. Musical Group

1244. Serials

1236. Leichhardt's Grasshopper

1237. Jewel Beetle

Australian Insects   **1991 11 Apr**

		MUH	FU
1234	43c Cotton Harlequin Bug	0.80☐	0.50☐
1235	43c Hawk Moth	0.80☐	0.50☐
1236	80c Leichhardt's Grasshopper	1.80☐	1.40☐
1237	$1 Jewel Beetle	2.00☐	1.50☐
	First Day Cover (4) AP		6.00☐

1245. Quiz Shows

1246. Children's Shows

The Golden Days of Radio   **1991 13 Jun**

		MUH	FU
1243	43c Musical Group	0.80☐	0.50☐
1244	43c Serials	0.80☐	0.50☐
1245	85c Quiz Shows	1.80☐	1.60☐
1246	$1Children's Shows	2.00☐	1.75☐
	First Day Cover (4) AP		5.50☐

1238. Max Dupain

1239. Wolfgang Sievers

1247. Puppy

1248. Kitten

1241. Harold Carneaux

1242. Olive Cotton

Anniversary of Australian Photography   **1991 13 May**

		MUH	FU
1238	43c Max Dupain Bondi 1939	0.80☐	0.50☐
1239	43c Wolfgang Sievers Melbourne 1967	0.80☐	0.50☐
1240	Joined pair 1238/1239	1.80☐	1.60☐
1240A	Gutter pair 1238/1239	10.00☐	10.00☐
1241	70c Harold Cazneaux Youth 1929	1.50☐	1.20☐
1242	$1.20 Olive Cotton Teacups 1935	2.50☐	1.50☐
	First Day Cover (4) AP		5.50☐

1249. Pony

1250. Cockatoo

Australian Pets   **1991 25 Jul**

		MUH	FU
1247	43c Puppy	0.80☐	0.50☐
1248	43c Kitten	0.80☐	0.50☐
1249	70c Pony	1.50☐	1.00☐
1250	$1Cockatoo	2.00☐	1.50☐
	First Day Cover (4) AP		5.50☐

1252. Squash

1253. Diving

Sport Series III - Definitives   **1991 22 Aug**

1251	75c Netball	1.20	0.40
1252	80c Squash	1.30	0.50
1253	85c Diving	1.40	0.50
1254	90c Soccer	1.50	0.50
	First Day Cover (4) AP		6.30

1251. Netball

1254. Soccer

1255. Vancouver/Eyre

1255ms. Miniature Sheet

Exploration: Albany Western Australia   **1991 25 Sep**

1255	$1.05 Vancouver/Eyre	2.00	1.20
1255ms	$1.05 Miniature Sheet	2.50	2.00
	First Day Cover AP		2.30
	First Day Cover Miniature Sheet		2.50

1257. On Our Selection

1258. Clancy of the Overflow

1256. Seven Little Australians

1259. The Drover's Wife

Literary Legends   **1991 10 Oct**

1256	43c Seven Little Australians	0.80	0.50
1257	75c On Our Selection	1.75	0.90
1258	$1 Clancy of the Overflow	2.00	1.30
1259	$1.20 The Drover's Wife	2.40	1.60
	First Day Cover (4) AP		6.00

1262. Infant Jesus

1263. One of the Three Wise Men

1260. Shepherd

Christmas   1991 01 Nov

Ancient Bible Art imitating Renaissance Frescos

1260	38c Shepherd	0.75□	0.40□
1261	Booklet - 2 x panes (10 x 38c)	13.00□	11.00□
1262	43c Infant Jesus	0.80□	0.40□
1263	90c One of the Three Wise Men	1.80□	1.30□
	First Day Cover (3) AP		3.60□

1264. Bouquet of Wildflowers

Thinking of You   1992 02 Jan

1264	45c Bouquet of Wildflowers	0.90□	0.30□
1265	$4.50 Booklet pane (10 x 45c)	8.00□	
	First Day Cover (1) AP		2.00□

1266. Parma Wallaby   1268. Ghost Bat   1270. Dunnart

1272. Pygmy Possum   1274. Hopping Mouse   1276. Squirrel Glider

Threatened Species - Definitive Set   1992 02 Jan

1266	45c Parma Wallaby	0.80□	0.40□
1267	45c Parma Wallaby self adhesive	1.10□	0.30□
1268	45c Ghost Bat	0.80□	0.40□
1269	45c Ghost Bat self adhesive	1.10□	0.30□
1270	45c Dunnart	0.80□	0.40□
1271	45c Dunnart self adhesive	1.10□	0.30□
1272	45c Pygmy Possum	0.80□	0.40□
1273	45c Pygmy Possum self adhesive	1.10□	0.30□
1274	45c Hopping Mouse	0.80□	0.40□
1275	45c Hopping Mouse self adhesive	1.10□	0.30□
1276	45c Squirrel Glider	0.80□	0.40□
1277	45c Squirrel Glider self adhesive	1.10□	0.30□
1278	Block 6 (Se-tenant)	5.00□	5.00□
1279	$4.50 Booklet pane (10 self adhesive)	10.00□	
1280	$2.25 pane of 5 stamps self adhesive	6.00□	
	First Day Cover (2x6) AP		10.50□

Formats released:

1. Gummed stamps/sheets of 100/blocks 6 - 3x2 (shown above)
2. Self adhesive/rolls of 100, rolls of 200 (with tabs to alert user to number of remaining stamps).
3. Self adhesive/booklet of 10
4. Self adhesive/booklet of 5 - inc: 1269, 1271, 1273, 1275, 1277 (1267-wallaby was replaced on sheet with a tab showing value of sheet and contents). These designs originally prepared for the combined scale/calculator labels were originally scheduled for release in 1991.

1281. Noosa River
Queensland

1282. Lake Eildon
Victoria

1284. Young Endeavour

1285. Britannia

1286. Arkarana

1287. John Louis

Sterner Vending Machine Booklet: Wetlands and Waterways

1992 2 Jan

	Folder contains (1 x 20c & 4 x 45c)		
1281	20c Noosa River - Queensland	1.00☐	1.00☐
1282	45c Lake Eildon - Victoria	0.80☐	0.40☐
1283	$2.00 Booklet	5.00☐	
	First Day Cover (2) AP		2.20☐

Australia Day - Stamp plus miniature sheet

1992 15 Jan

1284	45c Young Endeavour	0.90☐	0.50☐
1285	45c Britannia	0.90☐	0.50☐
1286	$1.05 Arkarana	2.00☐	1.80☐
1287	$1.20 John Louis	2.40☐	1.50☐
1288	Miniature Sheet 4 stamps	7.00☐	7.00☐
	First Day Cover (4) AP		5.60☐
	First Day Cover (Miniature Sheet) AP		7.00☐

1289. Bombing of Darwin   1290. Battle of Milne Bay

1291. Battle of Kokoda Trail   1292. Battle of Coral Sea

1293. Battle of El Alamein

Australians Under Fire — 1992 19 Feb

NO.	Description	MUH	FU
1289	45c Bombing of Darwin	0.80☐	0.50☐
1290	75c Battle of Milne Bay	1.50☐	1.20☐
1291	75c Battle of Kokoda Trail	1.50☐	1.20☐
1292	$1.05 Battle of Coral Sea	2.00☐	1.60☐
1293	$1.20 Battle of El Alamein	2.40☐	1.70☐
	First Day Cover (5) AP		7.00☐

1294. Boxlink Symbol

Box Link New Stamp Label — 1992 02 Mar

A new stamped label - limited business use only. Initially introduced in Sydney, Brisbane, Melbourne for delivery to boxholders at a Box Link Post Office only. Issued in boxes of 100 ($38). Single stamps available in special packs.Self adhesive.

NO.	Description	MUH	FU
1294	38c Boxlink Symbol	1.50☐	2.00☐
	First Day Cover AP		11.00☐

1295. Helix Nebula   1296. The Pleiades

1297. Spiral Galaxy NGC 2997

International Space Year — 1992 19 Mar

NO.	Description	MUH	FU
1295	45c Helix Nebula	1.00☐	0.50☐
1296	$1.05 The Pleiades	2.00☐	1.90☐
1297	$1.20 Spiral Galaxy NGC 2997	2.40☐	2.20☐
1298	Miniature Sheet 3 Stamps	5.20☐	5.20☐
	First Day Stamps (3) AP		5.50☐
	First Day Cover (Miniature Sheet) AP		6.00☐

1299. Queen Elizabeth II

Queen Elizabeth II: Birthday — 1992 09 Apr

NO.	Description	MUH	FU
1299	45c Queen Elizabeth II	1.00☐	0.50☐
	First Day Cover AP		2.00☐

NO.	DESCRIPTION	MUH	FU	NO.	DESCRIPTION	MUH	FU

1300. Hunter Valley NSW

1301. North Eastern Victoria

1302. Barossa Valley SA

1303. Coonawarra SA

1311. Cycling

1312. High Jumping

1313. Weight Lifting

Olympic and Paralympic Games Barcelona 1992

1992 02 Jul

NO.	DESCRIPTION	MUH	FU
1311	45c Cycling	1.00☐	0.50☐
1312	$1.20 High Jumping	2.20☐	1.80☐
1313	$1.20 Weight Lifting	2.60☐	1.80☐
	First Day Cover (AP)		5.50☐

1314. Echidna

1315. Koala

1316. Brushtail Possum

1317. Common Wombat

1304. Margaret River WA

Vineyard Regions

1992 09 Apr

NO.	DESCRIPTION	MUH	FU
1300	45c Hunter Valley NSW	0.80☐	0.40☐
1301	45c North Eastern Victoria	0.80☐	0.40☐
1302	45c Barossa Valley SA	0.80☐	0.40☐
1303	45c Coonawarra SA	0.80☐	0.40☐
1304	45c Margaret River WA	0.80☐	0.40☐
	First Day Cover (5) AP		5.00☐

Australian Wildlife Definitive

1992 13 Aug

NO.	DESCRIPTION	MUH	FU
1314	35c Echidna	0.70☐	0.40☐
1315	50c Koala	0.95☐	0.40☐
1316	60c Brushtail Possum	0.90☐	0.40☐
1317	95c CommonWombat	1.40☐	0.40☐
	First Day Cover (4) AP		5.00☐

| 1305. Salt Action | 1306. Farm Planning | 1307. Erosion Control | 1308. Tree Planting | 1309. Dune Control |

Landcare

1992 11 Jun

NO.	DESCRIPTION	MUH	FU
1305	45c Salt Action	0.80☐	0.50☐
1306	45c Farm Planning	0.80☐	0.50☐
1307	45c Erosion Control	0.80☐	0.50☐
1308	45c Tree Planting	0.80☐	0.50☐
1309	45c Dune Control	0.80☐	0.50☐
1310	Strip of 5 Se-tenant	4.50☐	4.00☐
	First Day Cover (strip x 5) AP		5.00☐

1326. Cricket in the 1890's   1325. Cricket in the 1890's

Centenary of the Sheffield Shield Cricket

1318.   1319.
Opening of Harbour Tunnel

Official Opening of Sydney Harbour Tunnel - 29th Aug

			1992 28 Aug
1318	45c Opening of Harbour Tunnel	1.00☐	0.50☐
1319	45c Opening of Harbour Tunnel	1.00☐	0.50☐
1320	Pair se-tenant	3.00☐	2.00☐
	First Day Cover (pair)		2.50☐

Centenary of the Sheffield Shield Cricket

			1992 15 Oct
1325	45c Cricket in the 1890's	1.00☐	0.50☐
1326	$1.20 Cricket in the 1890's	2.40☐	2.20☐
	First Day Cover (2) AP		3.00☐

1321. Warden's Court House

1322. Post Office Kalgoorlie

1323. York Hotel Kalgoorlie

1324. Town Hall Kalgoorlie

1327. Christmas Playing

1329. Christmas Morning

1330. Christmas Carols

Discovery of Gold at Kalgoorlie and Coolgardie in the 1890's

			1992 17 Sep
1321	45c Warden's Court House	0.80☐	0.40☐
1322	45c Post Office Kalgoorlie	0.80☐	0.40☐
1323	$1.05 York Hotel Kalgoorlie	2.20☐	1.50☐
1324	$1.20 Town Hall Kalgoorlie	2.40☐	1.60☐
	First Day Cover (4) AP		5.00☐

Christmas

			1992 30 Oct
1327	40c Christmas Playing	0.90☐	0.40☐
1328	$8.00 Booklet 20 x 40c	15.00☐	
1329	45c Christmas Morning	0.90☐	0.40☐
1330	$1.00 Christmas Carols	1.70☐	1.40☐
	First Day Cover (3) AP		3.50☐

1331. Ghost Gum   1332. Mount Giles

Australia Day   **1993 14 Jan**

1331	45c Ghost Gum	1.00☐	0.50☐
1332	45c Mount Giles	1.00☐	0.50☐
1333	Joined pair	1.50☐	1.50☐
	First Day Cover (2) AP		2.50☐

1334. Wild Onion Dreaming

1335. Yam Plants

1336. Goose Egg Hunt

1337. Kalumpiwarra Ngulaintji

Dreaming   **1993 04 Feb**

1334	45c Wild Onion Dreaming	0.90☐	0.50☐
1335	75c Yam Plants	1.40☐	1.00☐
1336	85c Goose Egg Hunt	1.70☐	1.40☐
1337	$1 Kalumpiwarra Ngulaintji	2.00☐	1.80☐
	First Day Cover (4) AP		5.00☐

1338. Uluru Northern Territory

1339. Fraser Island

1340. Shark Bay

1341. Kakadu

World Heritage Sites   **1993 04 Mar**

1338, 1339, 1340 were short term issues. 1341 remained on sale as a definitive (replacing 1153).

1338	45c Uluru Northern Territory	0.90☐	0.50☐
1339	85c Fraser Island	1.70☐	1.10☐
1340	95c Shark Bay	1.80☐	1.30☐
1341	$2 Kakadu	3.80☐	1.90☐
	First Day Cover (4) AP		7.50☐

1342. Sydney II Cruiser

1344. Arunta Destroyer

1343. Bathurst Corvette

1345. Centaur Hospital Ship

Naval and Maritime War Vessels   **1993 07 Apr**

1342	45c Sydney II Cruiser	0.90☐	0.50☐
1343	85c Bathurst Corvette	1.60☐	1.10☐
1344	$1.05 Arunta Destroyer	1.90☐	1.60☐
1345	$1.20 Centaur Hospital Ship	2.10☐	1.50☐
	First Day Cover (4) AP		6.50☐

1346. Queen Elizabeth II

1347. Work in the Home

1348. Work in the Cities

1349. Work in the Country

1350. Trade Union Banners

Queen Elizabeth II: Birthday   1993 07 Apr

NO.	Description	MUH	FU
1346	45c Queen Elizabeth	0.80☐	0.50☐
	First Day Cover AP		2.00☐

Working Life in the 1890's   1993 07 May

NO.	Description	MUH	FU
1347	45c Work in the Home	0.90☐	0.50☐
1348	45c Work in the Cities	0.90☐	0.50☐
1349	$1 Work in the Country	1.80☐	1.20☐
1350	$1.20 Trade Union Banners	2.00☐	1.60☐
	First Day Cover (4) AP		6.00☐

1351. Centenary Train   1353. Spirit of Progress Train   1355. Western Endeavour Train

1357. Silver City Comet   1359. Kuranda Tourist Train   1361. The Ghan

Trains in Australia   1993 01 Jun

Formats released:
1. Gummed stamps/sheets of 100/panes of 50/blocks 6 (shown above)
2. Self adhesive/rolls of 100 consecutive stamps (with tabs)
3. Self adhesive/booklet of 10

NO.	Description	MUH	FU
1351	45c Centenary Train	0.85☐	0.60☐
1352	45c Centenary Train self adhesive	1.00☐	0.50☐
1353	45c Spirit of Progress Train	0.85☐	0.60☐
1354	45c Spirit of Progress self adhesive	1.00☐	0.50☐
1355	45c Western Endeavour Train	0.85☐	0.60☐
1356	45c Western Endeavour self adhesive	1.00☐	0.50☐
1357	45c Silver City Comet	0.85☐	0.60☐
1358	45c Silver City Comet self adhesive	1.00☐	0.50☐
1359	45c Kuranda Tourist Train	0.85☐	0.60☐
1360	45c Kuranda Tourist Train self adhesive	1.00☐	0.50☐
1361	45c The Ghan	0.85☐	0.60☐
1362	45c The Ghan self adhesive	1.00☐	0.50☐
1363	Joined block of 6	6.50☐	6.50☐
1364	$4.50 Booklet 10 stamps self adhesive	14.00☐	
	First Day Cover (block 6) AP		6.00☐
	First Day Cover (strip of 6) AP self adhesive		7.00☐

1366. Ngarrgooroom Country

1367. Ngak Ngak

1365. Black Cockatoo Feather

1368. Untitled

Aboriginal Australia   1993. 01 Jul

NO.	Description	MUH	FU
1365	45c Black Cockatoo Feather	0.90☐	0.50☐
1366	75c Ngarrgooroom Country	1.40☐	1.00☐
1367	$1 Ngak Ngak	1.80☐	1.00☐
1368	$1.05 Untitled	1.90☐	1.50☐
	First Day Cover (4) AP		5.50☐

1369. Platypus

1370. Kookaburra

1371. Eastern Grey Kangaroo

1372. Pink Cockatoo

Whilst the pane is of considerable philatelic interest,
it is considered to be outside the scope of this catalogue

Australian Wildlife Definitives   1993 12 Aug

Whilst the pane is of considerable philatelic interest,it is considered to be outside the scope of this catalogueAustralian Wildlife Definitives 1993 12 Aug
Four different designs Threatened Species counter printed stamps produced in Melbourne on equipment able to print denominations of almost any value, were released on 21 June, 1993 as a field test at a single outlet, the National Philatelic Centre located at Australia Post Headquarters.At the time of sale, individual stamps are overprinted with a code number (NPC1) and value.Whilst of interest, these self - adhesive stamps, not readily available, are considered to be outside the scope of this simplified catalogue.

No.	Description	MUH	FU
1369	40c Platypus	0.70☐	0.50☐
1370	70c Kookaburra	1.20☐	0.60☐
1371	90c Eastern Grey Kangaroo	1.60☐	0.80☐
1372	$1.20 Pink Cockatoo	2.00☐	1.00☐
	First Day Cover (4) AP	5.50☐	

1376. Ornithocheirus

1378. Leaellynasaura

1382. Allosaurus

1383. Timimus

1374. Women in Parliament   1373. 90th Inter-Parliament conference

Parliamentary Issue   1993 02 Sep

An unusual pane format was used for the above issue - a central block of 9 stamps 1374 surrounded by a border of 16 of stamp 1373. A special pane was released on the 20th of November, reverse of the above - central block of 9 stamp 1373 surrounded by a border of 16 of stamp 1374. This reverse pane was only available for a very short period from the GPO.s and by mail order from Australia Post.It is believed more the of the Reverse Pane were sold than the Standard Pane.

No.	Description	MUH	FU
1373	45c 90th Inter-Parliament Conference	1.00☐	0.50☐
1374	45c Women in Parliament	1.00☐	0.50☐
1375	Joined pair (any position)	2.00☐	2.00☐
	First Day Cover (joined pair) AP	2.20☐	

1384.
Muttaburrasaurus

1385. Minmi

1386. Miniature Sheet

Issued in usual format, stamps 1376/1378 were also released in self-adhesive form (S/A) peel & stick in rolls of both 100 & 200 stamps with two special advertising tabs, also in booklets of 10 stamps.
A large number of special Australian Dinosaur Era products were produced by Australia Post – details in Australian Stamp Bulletin No. 222

Australian Dinosaurs Era 1993 01 Oct

		MUH	FU
1376	45c Ornithocheirus	0.90	0.50
1377	45c Ornithocheirus self adhesive	2.00	0.50
1378	45c Leaellynasaura	0.90	0.50
1379	45c Leaellynasaura self adhesive	2.00	0.50
1380	Pair 1377/1379 self adhesive	6.00	2.00
1381	$4.50 Booklet 10 x 45c	10.00	
1382	45c Allosaurus	0.90	0.50
1383	45c Timimus	0.90	0.50
1384	75c Muttaburrasaurus	1.50	1.50
1385	$1.05 Minmi	2.00	2.00
1386	Miniature Sheet	7.00	6.25
	First Day Cover (6 gummed) AP		6.00
	First Day Issue (2 self adhesive) AP		3.00
	First Day Issue (m/s) AP		6.00

1387. Goodwill

1389. Joy

1390. Peace

Christmas 1993 01 Nov

		MUH	FU
	Age Old Sentiments		
1387	40c Goodwill	0.80	0.40
1388	$8.00 Booklet 20 x 40c	16.00	
1389	45c Joy	0.80	0.40
1390	$1 Peace	2.00	1.20
	First Day Cover (3) AP		3.50

1391. Shoalhaven River Bank
(Arthur Boyd)

1392. Wimmera
(Sydney Nolan)

1393. Lagoon Wimmera
(Sydney Nolan)

1394. White Cockatoo with Flame Trees
(Arthur Boyd)

Australia Day: Paintings by Sydney Nolan and Arthur Boyd

1994 13 Jan

NO.	DESCRIPTION	MUH	FU
1391	45c Shoalhaven River Bank	0.80☐	0.50☐
1392	85c Wimmera	1.70☐	1.00☐
1393	$1.05 Lagoon Wimmera	2.20☐	1.80☐
1394	$2 White Cockatoos in paddock	4.00☐	1.80☐
	First Day Cover (4) AP		7.00☐

1395. Vigilance

1397. Education

1399. Drill

1400. Fitness

Centenary of Life Saving in Australia

1994 20 Jan

In addition to usual gummed format stamps 1395/1397 were issued in self adhesive (peel & stick) rolls of 100's plus a booklet (s/a) containing 10 x 45c stamps.

NO.	DESCRIPTION	MUH	FU
1395	45c Vigilance	0.90☐	0.50☐
1396	45c Vigilance self adhesive	1.50☐	0.50☐
1397	45c Education	0.90☐	0.50☐
1398	45c Education self adhesive	1.50☐	0.50☐
1398a	$4.50 Booklet 10 x 45c	12.00☐	
1399	95c Drill	1.80☐	1.20☐
1400	$1.20 Fitness	2.00☐	1.40☐
	First Day Cover (4) AP		5.00☐
	First Day Cover (2 self adhesive) AP		2.00☐

1401. Rose

1403. Poppies   1402. Tulips

'Thinking of You' – Love stamp flower designs

1994 03 Feb

NO.	DESCRIPTION	MUH	FU
1401	45c Rose	0.90☐	0.50☐
1402	45c Tulips	0.90☐	0.50☐
1403	45c Poppies	0.90☐	0.50☐
1404	Joined pair (1402/1403)	1.80☐	1.50☐
1405	Booklet pane + B1957 10 (5 joined pairs)	9.00☐	
	First Day Cover (3) AP		2.60☐

1406. Crocodile

1407. Pelican

1411. Family with Dog

1412. Family on Beach

1408. Emu

1413. Aboriginal Family

Australian Native Animals
1994 10 Mar

No.	Description	MUH	FU
1406	30c Crocodile	0.50□	0.30□
1407	85c Pelican	1.40□	0.70□
1408	$1.35 Emu	2.00□	1.50□
	First Day Cover (3) AP	5.00□	

International Year of the Family
1994 14 Apr

Winning entries from a national competition amongst children.
A fourth design was used on the First Day Cover.

No.	Description	MUH	FU
1411	45c Family with Dog	1.80□	0.50□
1412	75c Family on Beach	1.20□	0.90□
1413	$1 Aboriginal Family	1.80□	1.50□
	First Day Cover (3) AP		4.00□
PNC001	$3.95 Stamp & Coin Cover - Year of the Family	95.00□	

1409. Friendship Bridge

1410. Queen Elizabeth II

Opening of Friendship Bridge linking Thailand and Laos
1994 08 Apr

No.	Description	MUH	FU
1409	95c Friendship Bridge	2.00□	1.75□
	First Day Cover (1) AP		2.20□

Queen Elizabeth II: Birthday
1994 08 Apr

No.	Description	MUH	FU
1410	45c Queen Elizabeth II	0.80□	0.40□
	First Day Cover (1) AP		1.20□

Australian Wildlife: Koalas and Kangaroos
1994 12 May

Formats released:
1. Gummed stamps/sheets of 100/blocks 6 (shown on this page)
2. Self adhesive/rolls of 100, rolls of 200
3. Self adhesive/booklet of 10

No.	Description	MUH	FU
1414	45c Red Kangaroo	0.80□	0.30□
1415	45c Red Kangaroo self adhesive	0.80□	0.30□
1416	45c Kangaroo with Joey	0.80□	0.30□
1417	45c Kangaroo with Joey self adhesive	0.80□	0.30□
1418	45c Grey Kangaroos	0.80□	0.30□
1419	45c Grey Kangaroos self adhesive	0.80□	0.30□
1420	45c Koala Family	0.80□	0.30□
1421	45c Koala Family self adhesive	0.80□	0.30□
1422	45c Koala on Ground	0.80□	0.30□
1423	45c Koala on Ground self adhesive	0.80□	0.30□
1424	45c Koala in Tree	0.80□	0.30□
1425	45c Koala in Tree self adhesive	0.80□	0.30□
1426	Joined block of 6 (3 x 2)	8.00□	8.00□
1427	Sheetlet of 5 + B2050 self adhesive	8.00□	
1428	$4.50 Booklet 45c x 10 self adhesive	11.00□	
	First Day Cover (6) AP		5.00□
	First Day Cover (6) self adhesive AP		6.00□

1414. Red Kangaroo   1416. Kangaroo with Joey   1418. Grey Kangaroos

1420. Koala Family   1422. Koala on Ground   1424. Koala in Tree

1429. Women Campaigning

Centenary of Votes for Women — 1994 09 Jun

NO.	DESCRIPTION	MUH	FU
1429	45c Women Campaigning	0.80	0.50
	First Day Cover (1) AP		1.20

1430. Aboriginal Bunyip

1431. Nature Spirit Bunyip

1433. Bunyip of Berkeley's Creek

1434. Natural history Bunyip

Bunyips (Australia's own mythological monster) — 1994 14 Jul

NO.	DESCRIPTION	MUH	FU
1430	45c Aboriginal Bunyip	0.90	0.50
1431	45c Nature Spirit Bunyip	0.90	0.50
1432	Joined pair (1430/1431)	2.00	1.80
1433	90c Bunyip of Berkeley's Creek	1.80	1.20
1434	$1.35 Natural History Bunyip	2.70	2.00
	First Day Cover (4) AP		6.00

Wartime Prime Ministers of Australia — 1994 11 Aug

NO.	DESCRIPTION	MUH	FU
1435	45c Sir Robert Menzies	0.80	0.40
1436	45c Arthur Fadden	0.80	0.40
1437	45c John Curtin	0.80	0.40
1438	45c Frank Forde	0.80	0.40
1439	45c Ben Chifley	0.80	0.40
	Joined strip of 5	6.00	6.00
	First Day Cover (5) AP		6.00

1441. Lawrence Hargraves

1442. Ross & Keith Smith

1443. Stan Globe/Ivor McIntyre

1444. Freda Thompson

Aviation Feats — 1994 20 Aug

NO.	DESCRIPTION	MUH	FU
	Engraved and printed in Sweden		
1441	45c Lawrence Hargraves	1.00	0.50
1442	45c Ross & Keith Smith	1.00	0.50
1443	$1.35 Stan Globe/Ivor McIntyre	3.00	2.50
1444	$1.80 Freda Thompson	3.50	3.50
	First Day Cover (4) AP		6.50

1435. Sir Robert Menzies

1436. Arthur Fadden

1437. John Curtin

1438. Frank Forde

1439. Ben Chifley

1445. Scarlet Macaw

1447. Cheetah

1449. Fijian crested Iguana

1450. Orang-utang

1451. Asian Elephant

Zoos - Endangered Species — 1994 28 Oct

Issued in usual gummed format, stamps 1445/1447 were also issued in self adhesive (s/a) peel and stick

No.	Description	MUH	FU
1445	45c Scarlet Macaw	1.00 ☐	0.50 ☐
1446	45c Scarlet Macaw self adhesive	2.00 ☐	0.50 ☐
1447	45c Cheetah	1.00 ☐	0.50 ☐
1448	45c Cheetah self adhesive	2.00 ☐	0.50 ☐
1449	45c Fijian Crested Iguana	1.00 ☐	0.50 ☐
1450	45c Orang-utang	1.00 ☐	0.50 ☐
1451	$1.00 Asian Elephant	2.00 ☐	1.50 ☐
1452	$2.80 Miniature Sheet	6.00 ☐	5.00 ☐
1453	$4.50 Stamp Booklet (1448/1446) in alternate pairs x 10 stamps self adhesive	18.00 ☐	
	First Day Cover (5) AP		5.00 ☐
	First Day Cover m/s AP		5.00 ☐

1452. Miniature Sheet

AUSTRALIA **40**c

1454. Adoration of the Magi
(detail) G Toscani

Giovanni Toscani The Adoration of the Magi (detail) **45**c

1456. Adoration of the Magi (detail)
G Toscani

Giovanni Toscani The Adoration of the Magi (detail) **$1**

1457. Adoration of the Magi (detail)
G Toscani

AUSTRALIA **$1**·80

1458. Adoration of the Magi
G Toscani

Christmas - Adoration of the Magi by G Toscani

1994 31 Oct

NO.	DESCRIPTION	MUH	FU
1454	40c Madonna & Child	0.75☐	0.40☐
1455	$8Booklet 20 x 40c stamps	18.00☐	
1456	45c Magi, Horse & groom	0.90☐	0.40☐
1457	$1Magi with Joseph	2.00☐	1.10☐
1458	$1.80 Complete Painting	3.50☐	2.20☐
	First Day Cover (4) AP		6.50☐

1461. Aproaching Tasmania   1459. Leaving Sydney

50th Anniversary Sydney to Hobart Yacht Race

1994 31 Oct

Issued as gummed and self adhesive, in se-tenant pairs and rolls of 100 stamps (consecutive pairs)

NO.	DESCRIPTION	MUH	FU
1459	45c Leaving Sydney	1.00☐	0.50☐
1460	45c Leaving Sydney self adhesive	2.00☐	0.50☐
1461	45c Aproaching Tasmania	1.00☐	0.50☐
1462	45c Aproaching Tasmania self adhesive	2.00☐	0.50☐
1463	Joined pair (1459/1461)	3.00☐	3.00☐
	First Day Cover (1460/1462) self adhesive AP		3.00☐
	First Day Cover (2) AP		3.00☐

Triangular ATM Stamps

The issue of Australia's first Triangular Stamps is an item of significant philatelic interest. These Self Adhesive stamps were only available from a limited number of Advance Bank automatic teller machines (ATM) and through Australian Posts National Philatelic Centre in Melbourne and by mail order from the Australian Philatelic Bureau. Due to this limited release, the stamps are considered to be outside the scope of this catalogue. As the sheetlet is interesting to collectors, we illustrate it on a reduced scale below.

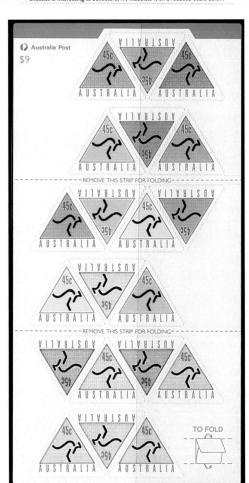

1464. Back Verandah (1942)
Russell Drysdale

1465. Skull Springs Country (1966)
Guy Grey Smith

1466. Outcamp (1977)
Robert Juniper

1467. Kite Flying (1958)
Ian Fairweather

Australia Day: **1995 12 Jan**
Paintings by Russell Drysdale, Guy Grey Smith, Robert Juniper & Ian Fairweather

1464	45c Back Verandah (1942)	0.80☐	0.50☐
1465	45c Skull Springs Country (1966)	0.80☐	0.50☐
1466	$1.05 Outcamp (1977)	2.20☐	2.20☐
1467	$1.20 Kite Flying(1958)	2.80☐	2.40☐
	First Day Cover (4) AP		5.50☐

1468. Heart   1469. Heart   1470. Heart

St Valentines Day   **1995 06 Feb**
1468	45c Red Heart & Gold	0.90☐	0.50☐
1469	45c Gold Heart & Red	0.90☐	0.50☐
1470	45c Gold Heart	0.90☐	0.50☐
1471	Se-tenant strip of 3	3.00☐	3.00☐
	First Day Cover strip (3) AP		3.00☐

1475. Endeavour Replica 20c

1473. Endeavour

1472. Endeavour Replica 45c   1473. Endeavour

Endeavour Replica: Photo   **1995 09 Feb**
Endeavour: Painting
Also issued as Sterner Stamp Booklet

1472	45c Endeavour (replica)	0.90☐	0.50☐
1473	45c Endeavour (original)	0.90☐	0.50☐
1474	Joined pair (1472/1473)	3.00☐	2.00☐
1475	20c Endeavour (replica) 1472 booklet	1.00☐	1.00☐
1475a	Joined pair from booklet (1472/1475)	3.00☐	3.00☐
1476	Booklet pair of 5 $2.00 folder - 1x		
	20c(1475), 4 x 45c(1473)	10.00☐	5.00☐
	First Day Cover (joined pair) AP		5.00☐

1477. Doll & Chair   1478. Plate & Clock

1480. Teapot & Statuette

1481. Bowl & Urn

Fifty years of the National Trust — 1995 16 Mar

NO.	DESCRIPTION	MUH	FU
1477	45c Doll & Chair	0.90	0.50
1478	45c Plate & Clock	0.90	0.50
1479	Joined pair (1477/1478)	2.00	2.00
1480	$1.00 Teapot & Statuette	2.50	1.90
1481	$2.00 Bowl & Urn	3.50	3.00
	First Day Cover (4) AP		6.50

1482. Light Opal

1483. Dark Opal

Opals, National Gemstones — 1995 05 Apr
(Australia Post first Holographic Stamps)

NO.	DESCRIPTION	MUH	FU
1482	$1.20 Light Opal	2.50	1.30
1483	$2.50 Dark Opal	4.00	3.00
	First Day Cover (2) AP		6.50

1484. Queen Elizabeth II

Queen Elizabeth II: Birthday — 1995 20 Apr

NO.	DESCRIPTION	MUH	FU
1484	45c Queen Elizabeth II	0.80	0.50
	First Day Cover AP		1.20

1485. Soldier Surgeon: 1487. War Widow's Guild:
Sir Edward 'Weary' Dunlop Mrs Jessie Vasey CBE

1489. Sergeant: 1491. Flight Sergeant:
Tom Derrick VC   Rawdon Hume Middleton

Australia Remembers — 1995 20 Apr
Issued in se-tenant block of four from gummed sheets of 100 (2 panes of 50). Also in rolls of 100 self- adhesive (S/A) peel and stick, with the 4 designs following one after the other. Issued in booklets of 10 - 2 of each design, except Sir Edward Dunlop which appears 4 times.

NO.	DESCRIPTION	MUH	FU
1485	45c Sir Edward 'Weary' Dunlop	0.90	0.50
1486	as above self adhesive	2.00	0.50
1487	45c Mrs Jessie Vasey CBE	1.90	0.50
1488	as above self adhesive	2.00	0.50
1489	45c Tom Derrick VC	0.90	0.50
1490	as above self adhesive	2.00	0.50
1491	45c Rawdon Middleton V.C	0.90	0.50
1492	as above self adhesive	2.00	0.30
1492a	Gutter pair (2 formats each)	3.00	2.00
1493	se-tenant block of 4	4.50	4.00
1494	Se-tenant strip of 4 self adhesive	6.00	6.00
1495	$4.50 booklet of 10 stamps	12.00	
	As above self adhesive block four B2236	9.00	
	First Day Cover (Block 4) AP		6.00
	As above self adhesive		7.00
	First Day Cover (3) AP		4.00
PNC002	$6.00 Stamp & Coin Cover - End of WWII Anniversary	30.00	

1497. UN 50th Anniversary Logo

1498. FAO

1499. UNESCO

1500. UNICEF

50th Anniversary of the United Nations — 1995 11 May

Se-tenant block 4 with tabs attached - as illustrated with differing tabs either to right of left of stamp.

1497	45c UN 50th Anniversary Logo	1.00☐	0.50☐
1498	45c FAO	1.00☐	0.50☐
1499	45c UNESCO	1.00☐	0.50☐
1500	45c UNICEF	1.00☐	0.50☐
1501	Se-tenant block of 4 (with tabs)	7.00☐	5.00☐
	First Day Cover (Block 4) AP		5.00☐

Used values quoted are for single stamps with tabs attached.
Stamps without tabs would be 30c each.

1502. The Story of the Kelly Gang

1504. On Our Selection

1506. Jedda

1508. Picnic at Hanging Rock

1510. Strictly ballroom

Centenary of the Cinema — 1995 08 Jun

1. Gummed/se-tenent strips of 5/sheets 100 (2 x panes 50)
2. Self adhesive/rolls of 100/5 consecutive
3. Self adhesive/Booklets 10/ 2 each of 5 stamps

1502	45c The Story of the Kelly Gang	1.00☐	0.60☐
1503	as above - self adhesive	2.00☐	0.50☐
1504	45c On Our Selection	1.00☐	0.60☐
1505	as above - self adhesive	2.00☐	0.50☐
1506	45c Jedda	1.00☐	0.60☐
1507	as above - self adhesive	2.00☐	0.50☐
1508	45c Picnic at Hanging Rock	1.00☐	0.60☐
1509	as above - self adhesive	2.00☐	0.50☐
1510	45c Strictly Ballroom	1.00☐	0.60☐
1511	as above - self adhesive	2.00☐	0.50☐
1512	Se-tenant strip of 5	6.00☐	5.00☐
1513	as above - self adhesive	20.00☐	15.00☐
1514	$4.50 booklet of 10 self adhesive	12.00☐	
	First Day Cover (strip) AP		5.00☐
	First Day Cover self adhesive AP		10.00☐

1516. Violin

1515. Kite

People with Disabilities — 1995 13 Jul

1515	45c Kite	1.00☐	0.50☐
1515A	Gutter pair	3.00☐	6.00☐
1516	45c Violin	1.00☐	0.50☐
1517	Se-tenant pair (1515/1516)	2.50☐	2.20☐
	First Day Cover (pair) AP		3.00☐

1518. Bomb Disposal:
Lt. Cr. Leon Goldworthy

1519.Fighter Pilot:
WO Ken Waters

1520. Army Nurse:
Sister Ellen Savage GM

1521. Ship's Stoker:
CPO Percy Collins DSM

Australia Remembers II   1995 10 Aug

1518	45c Lt. Commander Leon Goldworthy, GC, DSC, GM	0.90	0.50
1519	45c Warrant Officer Ken Waters	0.90	0.50
1520	45c Sister Ellen Savage GM	0.90	0.50
1521	45c CPO Percy Collins DSM	0.90	0.50
1522	Se-tenant block of 4	5.00	4.00
	First Day Cover (4) AP		5.00

1523. Star & Olive Wreath

1524. Peace, Motherhood &
Industry

1525. Australian Flag & Dove
of Peace

Peace and Victory   1995 10 Aug
50th Anniversary (reproduction of 1946 Issue)

1523	45c Star & Olive Wreath	1.20	0.60
1524	45c Peace, Motherhood, Industry	1.20	0.60
1525	$1.50 Australian Flag & Dove of Peace	3.00	2.50
	First Day Cover (3) AP		6.00

1526. Koala

1527. Panda

1529. Miniature Sheet: Koala

1530. Miniature Sheet: Panda

Australia and China Joint Issue   1995 01 Sep
1526, 1527 were printed in Australia. Same artwork as Miniature Sheets.
Miniature Sheets were printed in China.

1526	45c Koala	0.90	0.50
1527	45c Panda	0.90	0.50
1528	Se-tenant pair (1526, 1527)	3.00	2.50
1529	45c Koala Miniature Sheet	3.00	2.50
1530	45c Panda Miniature Sheet	3.00	2.50
	First Day Cover (pair) AP		2.50
	First Day Cover (1 Miniature Sheet) AP		2.50

1531. Radiology: J Slatery, T Lyle, W Filmer

1532. Viruses: J Macnamara, M Burnet

1534. Vision - F Hollows

1535. Antibiotics - H Florey

1536. Flatback Turtle

1538. Flame Angelfish

Celebrating Medical Science

1995 07 Sep

No.	Description	MUH	FU
1531	45c Radiology: J Slatery, T Lyle, W Filmer	1.00	0.50
1532	45c Viruses: J Macnamara, M Burnet	1.00	0.50
1533	Se-tenant pair 1531/1532	3.00	2.00
1534	45c Vision: F Hollows	1.00	0.50
1535	$2.50 Antibiotics: H Florey	5.00	5.00
	First Day Cover (4) AP		6.50

1541. Potato Cod

1543. Giant Trevally

The World Down Under

1995 03 Oct

Issued in gummed format sheets of 100, 3 different sheets of vertical se-tenant (joined) pairs. Also miniature sheets containing 3 x 2 vertical se-tenants. .This sheet contains stamps which are notably different from the standard issue (both gummed and self-adhesive). Refer to illustrations. The self adhesive were produced in rolls of 100 with the designs appearing one after the other. Also a booklet was issued in a self adhesive format.

No.	Description	MUH	FU
1536	45c Flatback Turtle	0.90	0.60
1537	45c Flatback Turtle self adhesive	1.50	0.50
1538	45c Flame Angelfish	0.90	0.60
1539	45c Flame Angelfish self adhesive	1.50	0.50
1540	Se-tenant pair (1536/1538)	3.00	2.40
1541	45c Potato Cod	0.90	0.60
1542	45c Potato Cod self adhesive	1.50	0.50
1543	45c Giant Trevally	0.90	0.60
1544	45c Giant Trevally self adhesive	1.50	0.50
1545	Se-tenant pair (1541/1543)	2.40	2.40
1546	45c Black Marlin	0.90	0.60
1547	45c Black Marlin self adhesive	1.50	0.50
1548	45c Tiger Shark	0.90	0.60
1549	45c Tiger Shark self adhesive	2.00	0.50
1550	Se-tenant pair (1546/1548)	2.40	2.40
1551	Miniature Sheet 1 x 6 values - gummed	6.00	6.00
1552	$4.50 booklet of 10 - self adhesive	13.00	
	First Day Cover 3 pairs AP		7.00
	First Day Cover 6 s/a AP		7.00
	First Day Cover Miniature Sheet		7.00

1546. Black Marlin

1548. Tiger Shark

1551. Miniature Sheet: The World Down Under

NO.	DESCRIPTION	MUH	FU

1553. Madonna & Child

1556. Three rejoicing Angels

1555. Angel with Banner

Christmas - Stained Glass Windows — 1995 01 Nov

NO.	DESCRIPTION	MUH	FU
1553	40c Madonna & Child	0.90	0.50
1554	$8.00 booklet 20 x 40c	14.00	
1555	45c Angel with Banner	0.90	0.50
1556	$1.00 Three rejoicing Angels	2.00	1.80
	First Day Cover (3) AP		4.00

1561. Hearts & Roses

Valentines Day: Hearts and Roses — 1996 30 Jan

NO.	DESCRIPTION	MUH	FU
	Heart in gold foil		
1561	45c Hearts & Roses	1.00	0.50
	First Day Cover AP		1.20

1562. Kittyhawk & Beaufighter   1563. Firefly & Sea Fury

1564. Bell Kiowa   1565. Hornet A21-101

Military Aviation — 1996 26 Feb

NO.	DESCRIPTION	MUH	FU
1562	45c Kittyhawk & Beaufighter	0.90	0.50
1563	45c Firefly & Sea Fury	0.90	0.50
1564	45c Bell Kiowa	0.90	0.50
1565	45c Hornet A21-101	0.90	0.50
1566	Se-tenant block of four	5.00	4.00
	First Day Cover AP		4.00

1557. Margaret Preston: Banksia, 1929

1558. Lisa Bryans:
The babe is wise, 1940

1559.
Grace Cossington Smith:
The Bridge in Curve, 1930

1560. Vids Lahey:
Beach Umbrellas, 1933

1567. Tasmanian Wilderness

1568. Willandra Lakes

Australia Day - Paintings by Australian Artists: — 1996 16 Jan

NO.	DESCRIPTION	MUH	FU
	Preston, Bryans, Cossington Smith, Lahey		
1557	45c Banksia 1929	1.00	0.60
1558	85c The babe is wise 1940	1.80	1.50
1559	$1.00 The Bridge in Curve 1930	2.00	1.80
1560	$1.20 Beach Umbrellas 1933	2.50	2.00
	First Day Cover (4) AP		6.50

1569. Naracoorte Cave

1570. Lord Howe Island

World Heritage Areas   **1996 14 Mar**

1567	45c Tasmanian Wilderness	1.00□	0.60□
1568	75c Willandra Lakes	1.50□	1.20□
1569	95c Naracoorte Cave	1.90□	1.40□
1570	$1 Lord Howe Island	2.00□	1.20□
	First Day Cover (4) AP		6.00□

1574. Miniature Sheet: Spotted Cuscus, Bear Cuscus

1571. Spotted Cuscus   1572. Bear Cuscus

Cuscuses joint issue Australia - Indonesia   **1996 22 Mar**

1571	45c Spotted Cuscus	0.90□	0.50□
1572	45c Bear Cuscus	0.90□	0.50□
1573	Se-tenant pair (1571/1572)	2.50□	2.00□
1574	Miniature Sheet	3.50□	3.00□
	First Day Cover (pair) AP		3.00□
	First Day Cover (m/s) AP		3.00□

1575. Queen Elizabeth II

Queen Elizabeth II: Birthday   **1996 11 Apr**

| 1575 | 45c Queen Elizabeth | 1.00□ | 0.50□ |
| | First Day Cover AP | | 2.00□ |

Above, from left to right:
1576. North Melbourne 'Roos'
1578. Brisbane 'Bears'
1580. Sydney 'Swans'
1582. Carlton 'Blues'
1584. Adelaide 'Crows'
1586. Fitzroy 'Lions'
1588. Richmond 'Tigers'
1590. St Kilda 'Saints'
1592. Melbourne 'Demons'
1594. Collingwood 'Magpies'
1596. Freemantle 'Dockers'
1598. Footscray 'Bulldogs'
1600. West Coast 'Eagles'
1602. Essendon 'Bombers'
1604. Geelong 'Cats'
1606. Hawthorn Hawks'

1608. Booklet: Australian Football League

1609. Leadbeaters Possum   1610. Powerful Owl

1611. Blackwood Wattle

1612. Mountain Ash Fern

Centenary of Australian Football League   1996 23 Apr

AFL - 16 Clubs - gummed and self adhesive

1576	45c North Melbourne 'Roos'	1.00☐	0.80☐
1577	45c North Melbourne 'Roos' self adhesive	1.00☐	0.50☐
1578	45c Brisbane 'Bears'	1.00☐	0.80☐
1579	45c Brisbane 'Bears' self adhesive	1.00☐	0.50☐
1580	45c Sydney 'Swans	1.00☐	0.80☐
1581	45c Sydney 'Swans self adhesive	1.00☐	0.50☐
1582	45c Carlton 'Blues'	1.00☐	0.80☐
1583	45c Carlton 'Blues' self adhesive	1.00☐	0.50☐
1584	45c Adelaide 'Crows'	1.00☐	0.80☐
1585	45c Adelaide 'Crows' self adhesive	1.00☐	0.50☐
1586	45c Fitzroy 'Lions'	1.00☐	0.80☐
1587	45c Fitzroy 'Lions' self adhesive	1.00☐	0.50☐
1588	45c Richmond 'Tigers'	1.00☐	0.80☐
1589	45c Richmond 'Tigers' self adhesive	1.00☐	0.50☐
1590	45c St Kilda 'Saints'	1.00☐	0.80☐
1591	45c St Kilda 'Saints' self adhesive	1.00☐	0.50☐
1592	45c Melbourne 'Demons'	1.00☐	0.80☐
1593	45c Melbourne 'Demons' self adhesive	1.00☐	0.50☐
1594	45c Collingwood 'Magpies'	1.00☐	0.80☐
1595	45c Collingwood 'Magpies' self adhesive	1.00☐	0.50☐
1596	45c Freemantle 'Dockers'	1.00☐	0.80☐
1597	45c Freemantle 'Dockers' self adhesive	1.00☐	0.50☐
1598	45c Footscray 'Bulldogs'	1.00☐	0.80☐
1599	45c Footscray 'Bulldogs' self adhesive	1.00☐	0.50☐
1600	45c West Coast 'Eagles'	1.00☐	0.80☐
1601	45c West Coast 'Eagles' self adhesive	1.00☐	0.50☐
1602	45c Essendon 'Bombers'	1.00☐	0.80☐
1603	45c Essendon 'Bombers' self adhesive	1.00☐	0.50☐
1604	45c Geelong 'Cats'	1.00☐	0.80☐
1605	45c Geelong 'Cats' self adhesive	1.00☐	0.50☐
1606	45c Hawthorn 'Hawks'	1.00☐	0.80☐
1607	45c Hawthorn 'Hawks' self adhesive	1.00☐	0.50☐
1608	4.50 Booklet: Centenary of the AFL		

Sixteen individual club stamp booklets were also issued, each containg ten
stamps (s/a) of that particular club, additionally showing the club logo & a
photographic reproduction of a nominated football hero. All booklets have equal
value & we have therefore grouped all these under a single catalogue number.

160.00☐

First Day Cover (4)
AP Gummed issue in Se-tenant block 16   16.00☐

Native of Australia - Definitive Issue   1996 09 May

1609	5cLeadbeaters Possum	0.30☐	0.30☐
1610	10c Powerful Owl	0.50☐	0.30☐
1611	$2Blackwood Wattle	3.50☐	1.00☐
1612	$5Mountain Ash Fern	9.00☐	5.00☐
	First Day Cover (4) AP		12.00☐

1614. Edwin Flack   1613. Fanny Durack

1616. Paralympics Athletics

Centenary of the Modern Olympics   1996 06 Jun

Edwin Flack & Fanny Durack were the first Australians
to win Olympic gold medals.

1613	45c Fanny Durack	0.90☐	0.50☐
1614	45c Edwin Flack	0.90☐	0.50☐
1615	Se-tenant pair (1613/1614)	2.00☐	2.00☐
1616	$1.05 Paralympics Athletics	2.00☐	1.90☐
	First Day Cover (3) AP		4.50☐

1617. Animalia   1619. Greetings from Sandy Beach

1621. Who sank the Boat?   1623. John Brown, Rose & Cat

Children's Book Council — 1996 04 Jul

NO.	Description	MUH	FU
1617	45c Animalia	0.90	0.70
1618	45c Animalia self adhesive	1.50	0.70
1619	45c Greetings from Sandy Beach	0.90	0.70
1620	45c Greetings from Sandy Beach self adhesive	1.50	0.70
1621	45c Who sank the Boat?	0.90	0.70
1622	45c Who sank the Boat? self adhesive	1.50	0.70
1623	45c John Brown, Rose & Cat	0.90	0.70
1624	45c John Brown, Rose & Cat self adhesive	1.50	0.70
1625	$4.50 selfadhesive booklet (10 x 45c)	12.00	
1626	Se-tenant block of 4 - gummed	6.00	4.00
	First Day Cover (4) AP self adhesive		5.00
	First Day Cover (4) AP gummed		10.00

1629. Margaret Windeyer

1630. Rose Scott

Centenary of National Council of Women — 1996 08 Aug

NO.	Description	MUH	FU
1629	45c Margaret Windeyer	1.00	0.50
1630	$1 Rose Scott	2.00	2.00
	First Day Cover (2) AP		2.50

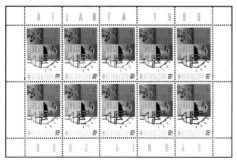

1627. Atlanta Handover

1631. Cultured Pearls

1632. Diamond

Handover of Olympic Flag at Atlanta — 1996 22 Jul

NO.	Description	MUH	FU
1627	Sheetlet of 10 x 45c stamps with special printed selvedge	10.00	10.00
1628	45c Atlanta Handover - single stamp	1.00	0.50
	First Day Cover (1 x 45c) AP		2.00
	Also available as self adhesive roll of 100		

Australia Pearls & Diamonds — 1996 05 Sep

Holographic stamps

NO.	Description	MUH	FU
1631	45c Cultured Pearls	1.00	0.80
1632	$1.20 Diamond	2.40	2.20
	First Day Cover (2) AP		3.00

1633. Arts Council

1634. Arts Council

1641. Ducks   1642. Cats & Dogs

1644. Cockatoo

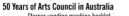

50 Years of Arts Council in Australia   1996 12 Sep

Sterner vending machine booklet
1 x 20c stamps - 4 x 45c stamps

		MUH	FU
1633	20c Performing Artists	0.60▢	0.50▢
1634	45c Performing Artists	1.00▢	0.50▢
1635	$2booklet (1 x 20c, 4 x 45c)	6.50▢	5.00▢
	First Day Cover (2) AP (1 x 20c - 1 x 45c)		2.00▢

1645. Horses

1646. Miniature Sheet: Pets

Pets Stamp Collecting Month   1996 01 Oct

Some stamps issued both gummed and self adhesive formats.
Booklet self adhesive only

		MUH	FU
1636	45c Blue Heelers	1.00▢	0.50▢
1637	45c Blue Heelers self adhesive	1.50▢	0.70▢
1638	45c Ginger Cats	1.00▢	0.50▢
1639	45c Ginger Cats self adhesive	1.50▢	0.70▢
1640	Se-tenant pair (1636/1638)	2.00▢	2.00▢
1641	45c Ducks	1.00▢	0.50▢
1642	45c Cats & Dogs	1.00▢	0.50▢
1643	Se-tenant pair (1641/1642)	2.00▢	2.00▢
1644	45c Cockatoo	1.00▢	0.50▢
1645	45c Horses	1.00▢	0.50▢
1646	$2.70 Miniature Sheet 1 x 6 values gummed	6.00▢	5.00▢
1647	$4.50 Stamp booklet 1637/1639 in pairs x 5	12.00▢	
	First Day Cover (6) AP		7.00▢
	First Day Cover (2) AP self adhesive		5.00▢
	First Day Cover Miniature Sheet AP		5.00▢

1636. Blue Heelers   1638. Ginger Cats

1649. Ferdinand von Mueller

Ferdinand von Mueller - Joint issue with Germany

1996 09 Oct

Von Mueller was a noted Australian 19th Century Scientist.
Stamps printed in Germany from an Australian design.

No.	Description	MUH	FU
1648	Sheetlet (10 x $1.20 stamps) with special printed selvedge	20.00☐	20.00☐
1649	$1.20 Von Mueller	2.50☐	2.00☐
	First Day Cover AP (1 x 20c)		3.00☐

1650. Wise man bearing Gifts

1651. Madonna & Child

1653. Shepherd Boy with Lamb

Christmas

1996 01 Nov

No.	Description	MUH	FU
1650	45c Wise Man bearing Gifts	0.80☐	0.40☐
1651	40c Madonna & Child	0.80☐	0.40☐
1652	$8 booklet (20x40c) self adhesive	20.00☐	
1653	$1 Shepherd Boy with Lamb	2.00☐	1.50☐
	First Day Cover (3) AP		4.00☐

1654. Willem de Vlamingh

Tercentenary of Dutchman Willem de Vlamingh's Voyage to East Coast of Australia

1996 01 Nov

Issued in Se-tenant pair design - 1654 printed AUSTRALIA, other stamp printed CHRISTMAS ISLAND AUSTRALIA. As at the present time, we do not catalogue Christmas Island issues, we show stamp above for interest.

No.	Description	MUH	FU
1654	45c Willem de Vlamingh	1.00☐	0.70☐
	First Day Cover AP		2.00☐

1655. Fred Williams: Landscape

1656. Brett Whiteley: The Balcony 2

1657. Lloyd Rees: Fire Haze

Australia Day - Paintings by Australian Artists:

1997 16 Jan

Fred Williams, Brett Whiteley, Lloyd Rees

No.	Description	MUH	FU
1655	85c Landscape	1.80☐	1.50☐
1656	90c The Balcony	2.00☐	1.60☐
1657	$1.20 Fire Haze	2.40☐	1.90☐
	First Day Cover (3) AP		6.00☐

NO.	DESCRIPTION	MUH	FU	NO.	DESCRIPTION	MUH	FU

1659. Sir Donald Bradman   1660. Sir Donald Bradman

Australian Legends: Sir Donald Bradman   1997 23 Jan
Issued in sheetlets of 10

NO.	DESCRIPTION	MUH	FU
1658	Sheetlet of 10 x 45c stamps		
	Special printing on selvedge	12.00	12.00
1659	45c Sir Donald Bradman	1.00	0.60
1660	45c Sir Donald Bradman	1.00	0.60
1661	Se-tenant pair 1659/1660	2.50	2.00
	First Day Cover AP (pair)		5.00
PNC003	$9.95 Stamp & Coin Cover - Sir Donald Bradman Tribute	45.00	

1662. Roses

Valentines Day: Roses   1997 29 Jan

NO.	DESCRIPTION	MUH	FU
1662	45c Roses	1.00	0.50
1663	$4.50 Booklet 10 x 45c self adhesive	12.00	
	First Day Cover AP		2.00

1664. Ford Utility   1666. Holden Sedan

1668. Austin Lancer   1670. Chrysler Valiant

Australia's Classic Cars   1997 27 Feb

NO.	DESCRIPTION	MUH	FU
1664	45c Ford Utility	1.00	0.60
1665	45c Ford Utility self adhesive	1.50	0.80
1666	45c Holden Sedan	1.00	0.60
1667	45c Holden Sedan self adhesive	1.50	0.80
1668	45c Austin Lancer	1.00	0.60
1669	45c Austin Lancer self adhesive	1.50	0.80
1670	45c Chrysler Valiant	1.00	0.60
1671	45c Chrysler Valiant self adhesive	1.50	0.80
1672	$4.50 booklet (10 x 45c)	12.00	
	First Day Cover gummed		5.00
	First Day Cover self adhesive		5.00

1673. Queen of the Arena   1674. Wizard of the Wire
May Wirth   Con Colleano

1675. Clowns   1676. Tumblers

Commemorating 150 years of Circus in Australia
               1997 13 Mar

NO.	DESCRIPTION	MUH	FU
1673	45c Queen of the Arena	1.00	0.60
1674	45c Wizard of the Wire	1.00	0.60
1675	45c Clowns	1.00	0.60
1676	45c Tumblers	1.00	0.60
1677	Se-tenant block of four	5.00	4.00
	First Day Cover (4) AP		5.00

1678. Saltwater Crocodile

1679. Dwarf Tree Frog

1680. Big Greasy Butterfly

1681. Kakadu Wetlands

1682. Miniature Sheet: Wetlands

1692. Jacana   1694. Little Kingfisher

1696. Brolga   1698. Jabiru

Native of Australia - Wetlands   1997 10 Apr

No.	Description	MUH	FU
1678	20c Saltwater Crocodile	0.60	0.30
1679	25c Dwarf Tree Frog	0.80	0.40
1680	$1 Big Greasy Butterfly	2.00	0.80
1681	$10 Kakadu Wetlands	16.00	7.00
1682	$10 Miniature Sheet	18.00	14.00
	First Day Cover (4) AP		16.00

Wetland Birds - definitive issue   1997 02 Jun

No.	Description	MUH	FU
1692	45c Jacana	0.80	0.40
1693	45c Jacana self adhesive	1.00	0.80
1694	45c Little Kingfisher	0.80	0.40
1695	45c Little Kingfisher self adhesive	1.00	0.80
1696	45c Brolga	0.80	0.40
1697	45c Brolga self adhesive	1.00	0.80
1698	45c Jabiru	0.80	0.40
1699	45c Jabiru self adhesive	1.00	0.80
1700	Se-tenant block (4)	4.00	4.00
1701	$4.50 booklet 10 x 45c self adhesive	10.00	
	First Day Cover (block 4) AP		5.00
	First Day Cover (block 4) self adhesive		5.00

1683. Queen Elizabeth

1684. Lions (1947 - 1997)

Queen Elizabeth II: Birthday   1997 17 Apr

No.	Description	MUH	FU
1683	45c Queen Elizabeth II	0.90	0.50
	First Day Cover AP		2.00

50th Anniversary of the Lions   1997 17 Apr

No.	Description	MUH	FU
1684	45c Lions (1947 - 1997)	0.90	0.50
	First Day Cover AP		2.00

1686. Billie Joe   1687. Woody   1688. McMahons Miniature   1689. Celeste   1690. Bentley

Dolls and Bears   1997 08 May

No.	Description	MUH	FU
1685	Sheetlet of 10 x 45c with special printed selvedge	9.00	9.00
1686	45c Billie Joe	0.90	0.60
1687	45c Woody	0.90	0.60
1688	45c McMahons Miniature	0.90	0.60
1689	45c Celeste	0.90	0.60
1690	45c Bentley	0.90	0.60
1691	Se-tenant strip of five	5.00	5.00
	First Day Cover (strip 5) AP		6.50

NO.	DESCRIPTION	MUH	FU	NO.	DESCRIPTION	MUH	FU

1702. Search & Rescue 1703. Police Rescue

1705. Fire Services 1706. Ambulance Services

1711. Dumbi the Owl

Emergency Services   1997 10 Jul

		MUH	FU
1702	45c Search & Rescue	0.90☐	0.60☐
1703	45c Police Rescue	0.90☐	0.60☐
1704	Se-tenant pair (1702/1703)	2.00☐	2.00☐
1705	$1.05 Fire Services	2.20☐	1.80☐
1706	$1.20 Ambulance Services	2.40☐	2.00☐
	First Day Cover (4) AP		5.00☐

1712. Two Williy Willies 1713. How Brolga becomes a Bird

1707. George Peppin Jnr 1708. 'Pepe' Chair

1714. Tuggan Tuggan

Bicentenary of arrival of merino sheep in Australia

     1997 07 Aug

		MUH	FU
1707	45c George Peppin Jnr	0.90☐	0.60☐
1708	45c 'Pepe' Chair	0.90☐	0.60☐
1709	Se-tenant pair (1707/1708)	2.50☐	2.00☐
1710	$4.50 sheetlet of 10 x 45c		
	with special printed selvedge	8.00☐	7.50☐
	First Day Cover (pair) AP		3.00☐

'The Dreaming'   1997 21 Aug
Designs are from stills of animated stories for children

		MUH	FU
1711	45c Dumbi the Owl	0.90☐	0.70☐
1712	$1 Two Willii- Willies	1.80☐	1.50☐
1713	$1.20 How Brolga becomes a Bird	2.40☐	1.90☐
1714	$1.80 Tuggan Tuggan	3.50☐	3.00☐
	First Day Cover (4) AP		8.00☐

1715. Rhoetosaurus brownei 1716. Mcnamaraspis kaprios 1717. Ninjemysoweni 1718. Paracylotosaurus davidi 1719. Woolung-asaurus glendowerensis

Prehistoric animals that roamed ancient Australia

     1997 04 Sep

		MUH	FU
1715	45c Rhoetosaurus brownei	0.90☐	0.60☐
1716	45c Mcnamaraspis kaprios	0.90☐	0.60☐
1717	45c Ninjemysoweni	0.90☐	0.60☐
1718	45c Paracylotosaurus davidi	0.90☐	0.60☐
1719	45c Woolung-asaurus glendowerensis	0.90☐	0.60☐
1720	Se-tenant strip of 5	6.00☐	5.00☐
1721	4.50 sheetlet + B2484 with printed selvedge	9.00☐	9.00☐
	First Day Cover (strip 5) AP		5.00☐

1732. Miniature Sheet

1722. Platypus 1723. Brown Antechinus 1724. Dingo

1731. Yellow Bellied Glider

1726. Barking Owl 1728. Spotted Tail Quoll

Creatures of the night   **1997 1 Oct**

No.	Description	MUH	FU
1722	45c Platypus	0.90	0.60
1723	45c Brown Antechinus	0.90	0.60
1724	45c Dingo	0.90	0.60
1725	Se-tenant strip of 3	3.00	3.00
1726	45c Barking Owl	0.90	0.60
1727	45c Self Adhesive	0.90	0.60
1727/29	in pairs x 5. Also issued in rolls of 100 self adhesive		
	First Day Cover AP 6 gummed stamps		6.00
	First Day Cover AP 2 self adhesive		3.00
	First Day Cover AP miniature sheet		6.00
1728	45c Spotted Tail Quoll	0.90	0.60
1729	45c Self Adhesive	1.50	1.00
1730	Se-tenant pair 1726/1728	2.00	2.00
1731	45c Yellow Bellied Glider	0.90	0.60
1732	$2.70 Miniature Sheet 6 x 45c Gummed	6.00	5.00
1733	$4.50 Stamp Booklet	10.00	

1734. Female Figure

Breast Cancer Awareness   **1997 27 Oct**

No.	Description	MUH	FU
1734	45c Female Figure	0.90	0.50
1735	Sheetlet 10 x 45c stamps	9.00	9.00
	First Day Cover AP		2.00

1736. Nativity Play

1738. Nativity Play

1739. Nativity Play

Christmas School Children in Play — 1997 3 Nov

1736	40c Nativity Play	0.80	0.40
1737	$8 Booklet - 20 x 40c	15.00	
1738	45c Nativity Play	0.90	0.40
1739	$1 Nativity Play	2.00	1.50
	First Day Cover (3) AP		4.00

1740. Flying Cloud

1741. Marco Polo

1742. Chusan

1743. Heather Belle

Australian Maritime Heritage — 1998 15 Jan

1740	45c Flying Cloud	0.90	0.60
1741	85c Marco Polo	1.60	1.50
1742	$1 Chusan	2.00	1.60
1743	$1.20 Heather Belle	2.40	1.90
	First Day Cover (4) AP		6.00

1744. Sheet of 12 stamps (cropped to fit this book)
- shown below as complete sheet.

1745. Betty Cuthbert

1748. Herb Elliott

1751. Dawn Fraser

1754. Marjorie Jackson

1757. Murray Rose

1760. Shirley Strickland

Australian Legends Olympics   **1998 21 Jan**

No.	Description	MUH	FU
1744	Sheetlet of 12 stamps x 45c		
	Special printed selvedge. All issues in adhesive rolls x 100		
	Catalogue values are identical to gummed stamps	14.00☐	14.00☐
1745	45c Betty Cuthbert photo portrait	1.25☐	0.70☐
	Self Adhesive	1.50☐	0.60☐
1746	45c Betty Cuthbert	1.25☐	0.70☐
	Self Adhesive	1.50☐	0.60☐
1747	Se-tenant pair (1745/1746)	2.50☐	2.50☐
	Self Adhesive	3.00☐	
1748	45c Herb Elliott photo portrait	1.25☐	0.70☐
	Self Adhesive	1.50☐	0.60☐
1749	45c Herb Elliott	1.25☐	0.70☐
	Self Adhesive	1.50☐	0.60☐
1750	Se-tenant pair (1748/1749)	2.50☐	2.50☐
	Self Adhesive	3.00☐	
1751	45c Dawn Fraser photo portrait	1.25☐	0.70☐
	Self Adhesive	1.50☐	0.60☐
1752	45c Dawn Fraser	1.25☐	0.70☐
	Self Adhesive	1.50☐	0.60☐
1753	Se-tenant pair (1751/1752)	2.50☐	2.50☐
	Self Adhesive	3.00☐	
1754	45c Marjorie Jackson photo portrait	1.25☐	0.70☐
	Self Adhesive	1.50☐	0.60☐
1755	45c Marjorie Jackson	1.25☐	0.70☐
	Self Adhesive	1.50☐	0.60☐
1756	Se-tenant pair (1754/1755)	2.50☐	2.50☐
	Self Adhesive	3.00☐	
1757	45c Murray Rose photo portrait	1.25☐	0.70☐
	Self Adhesive	1.50☐	0.60☐
1758	45c Murray Rose	1.25☐	0.70☐
	Self Adhesive	1.50☐	0.60☐
1759	Se-tenant pair (1757/1759	2.50☐	2.50☐
	Self Adhesive	3.00☐	
1760	45c Shirley Strickland photo portrait	1.25☐	0.70☐
	Self Adhesive	1.50☐	0.60☐
1761	45c Shirley Strickland	1.25☐	0.70☐
	Self Adhesive	1.50☐	0.60☐
1762	Se-tenant pair (1760/1761)	2.50☐	2.50☐
	Self Adhesive	3.00☐	
1763	$5.40 12 x 45c - Self adhesive stamps .	15.00☐	
	First Day Cover (2) AP with all gummed issues.		9.00☐
	Identical designs to gummed stamps.		
	In this instance & other following issues we have not		
	illustrated the self adhesive stamps.		

1764. Roses

1766. Queen Elizabeth

Greetings: Champagne Roses   **1998 12 Feb**

No.	Description	MUH	FU
1764	45cRoses	0.90☐	0.50☐
1765	$4.50 Booklet 10 x 45c Self adhesive	10.00☐	
	First Day Cover AP		2.00☐

Birthday of Queen Elizabeth   **1998 09 Apr**

No.	Description	MUH	FU
1766	45c Queen Elizabeth	0.90☐	0.50☐
	First Day Cover AP		2.00☐

1767. Sea Hawk Helicopter

50th Anniversary of Fleet Air Arm   **1998 09 Apr**

No.	Description	MUH	FU
1767	45c Sea Hawk Helicopter	0.90☐	0.50☐
	First Day Cover AP		2.00☐

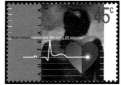

1775. Heart Health

Heart Health   **1998 4 May**

No.	Description	MUH	FU
1775	45c Heart Health	0.90☐	0.50☐
1776	$4.50 sheetlet 10 x 45c	9.00☐	
	First Day Cover (1) AP		2.00☐

1768. Wool	1769. Wheat	1770. Beef	1771. Sugar	1772. Dairy

Farming Australia   **1998 21 Apr**

No.	Description	MUH	FU
1768	45c Wool	0.90☐	0.70☐
1769	45c Wheat	0.90☐	0.70☐
1770	45c Beef	0.90☐	0.70☐
1771	45cSugar	0.90☐	0.70☐
1772	45c Dairy	0.90☐	0.70☐
1773	Se-tenant strip of 5	6.00☐	5.00☐
1774	$4.50 booklet 10 x 45c Self adhesive	15.00☐	
	First Day Cover (strip 5) AP		7.00☐

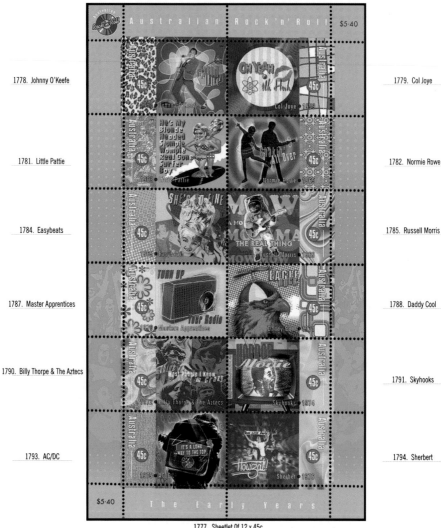

1778. Johnny O'Keefe
1779. Col Joye
1781. Little Pattie
1782. Normie Rowe
1784. Easybeats
1785. Russell Morris
1787. Master Apprentices
1788. Daddy Cool
1790. Billy Thorpe & The Aztecs
1791. Skyhooks
1793. AC/DC
1794. Sherbert

1777. Sheetlet Of 12 x 45c

Australian Rock' n' Roll — 1998 26 May

NO.	DESCRIPTION	MUH	FU
1777	Sheetlet of 12 x 45c Special Selvedge	12.00☐	12.00☐
1778	45c Johnny O'Keefe	1.00☐	0.80☐
1779	45c Col Joye	1.00☐	0.80☐
1780	Se-tenant pair (1778/1779)	2.50☐	2.00☐
1781	45c Little Pattie	1.00☐	0.80☐
1782	45c Normie Rowe	1.00☐	0.80☐
1783	Se-tenant pair (1781/1782)	2.50☐	2.00☐
1784	45c Easybeats	1.00☐	0.80☐
1785	45c Russell Morris	1.00☐	0.80☐
1786	Se-tenant pair (1784/1785)	2.50☐	2.00☐
1787	45c Master Apprentices	1.00☐	0.80☐
1788	45c Daddy Cool	1.00☐	0.80☐
1789	Se-tenant pair (1787/1788)	2.50☐	2.00☐
1790	45c Billy Thorpe & The Aztecs	1.00☐	0.80☐
1791	45c Skyhooks	1.00☐	0.80☐
1792	Se-tenant pair (1790/1791)	2.50☐	2.00☐
1793	45c AC/DC	1.00☐	0.80☐
1794	45c Sherbert	1.00☐	0.80☐
1795	Se-tenant pair (1793/1794)	2.50☐	2.00☐
	All issues in self adhesive rolls of 100		
	Cataloguevalues are identical with gummed stamps		
	First Day Cover AP Sheetlet		12.00☐
	First Day Cover AP SA strip 6 x 2		14.00☐

Australia 99 Maritime Heritage Sheetlet   **1998 17 Jun**

Re issue of stamp 1740 but in sheetlet of 10 stamps with
Australia 99 Logo printed in gold around shelvedge
No AP issue

| 1796 | Sheetlet of 10 x 45c | 8.00☐ | 8.00☐ |

1797. Helmeted Honeyeater   1798. Orange Bellied Parrot

1801. Red Tailed Black Cockatoo   1802. Gouldian Finch

1805. Dance   1806. Music

First Day CoverYouth Arts Australia   **1998 16 Jul**

1805	45c Dance	0.90☐	0.50☐
1806	45c Music	0.90☐	0.50☐
1807	Se-tenant pair (1805/1806)	2.20☐	2.00☐
	First Day Cover AP Se-tenant pair		3.00☐

Australian Endangered Birds   **1998 25 Jun**

1797	5cHelmeted Honeyeater	0.50☐	0.50☐
1798	5c Orange Bellied Parrot	0.50☐	0.50☐
1799	Se-tenant pair (1797/1798)	1.00☐	1.00☐
1800	Sheetlet 10 x 5c	5.00☐	5.00☐
1801	45c Red Tailed Black Cockatoo	1.00☐	0.70☐
1802	45c Gouldian Finch	1.00☐	0.70☐
1803	Se-tenant pair (1801/1802)	2.00☐	2.00☐
1804	Sheetlet 10 x 45c	8.00☐	8.00☐
	First Day Cover AP (2 x se-tenant pairs)		3.00☐

1812. Miniature Sheet

1808. Moth Orchid   1809. Bamboo Orchid   1810. Tiger Orchid   1811. Cooktown Orchid

Native Orchids - Joint issue with Singapore   **1998 6 Aug**

1808	45c Moth Orchid	0.90☐	0.70☐
1809	85c Bamboo Orchid	2.00☐	1.80☐
1810	$1Tiger Orchid	2.20☐	2.00☐
1811	$1.20 Cooktown Orchid	2.50☐	2.20☐
1812	$3.50 Miniature Sheet	7.00☐	7.00☐
	First Day Cover AP set		7.00☐
	First Day Cover AP Miniature Sheet		8.00☐

1813. Leunig Characters

1814. Leunig Characters

1815. Leunig Characters

1816. Leunig Symbol

Teapot of Truth   1998 13 Aug

1813	45c Leunig Characters	2.00	1.50
1814	45c Leunig Characters	2.00	1.50
1815	45c Leunig Characters	2.00	1.50
1816	$1 Leunig Symbol	3.00	2.00
1817	$1.20 Leunig Symbol	3.50	2.40
	First Day Cover (5) AP		12.00

1823. Se-tenant strip of 5

1817. Leunig Symbol

1818. Red Lacewing   1819. Dull Oakblue   1820. Meadow Argus   1821. Ulysses Butterfly   1822. Common Redeye

Australian Butterflies   1998 3 Sep

1818	45c Red Lacewing	1.00	0.70
	Self Adhesive	1.20	0.80
1819	45c Dull Oakblue	1.00	0.70
	Self Adhesive	1.20	0.80
1820	45c Meadow Argus	1.00	0.70
	Self Adhesive	1.20	0.80
1821	45c Ulysses Butterfly	1.00	0.70
	Self Adhesive	1.20	0.80
1822	45c Common Redeye	1.00	0.70
	Self Adhesive	1.20	0.80
1823	Se-tenant strip of 5	6.00	5.00
	Self Adhesive	6.00	
1824	Sheetlet of 10 stamps 5 x 2	8.00	8.00
	First Day Cover Strip (5) AP		4.00
	First Day Cover AP Self adhesive 5		5.00
	Also issued in rolls of 100 self adhesive		

1825. Sextant & Map

1827. Se-tenant pair

1826. Telescope & Map

Bass and Flinders   1998 10 Sep

1825	45c Sextant & Map	1.00	0.80
1826	45c Telescope & Map	1.00	0.80
1827	Se-tenant pair (1825/1826)	3.00	2.20
	First Day Cover AP (Se-tenant pair)		3.00
PNC004	$5.95 Stamp & Coin Cover		
	- Bass & Flinders Commemorative	45.00	

1835. Miniature Sheet

| 1830. Weedy Seadragon | 1828. Southern Right Whale | 1829. Manta Ray | 1834. White Pointer Shark | 1831. Bottlenose Dolphin | 1833. Fiery Squid |

Planet Ocean   1998 1 Oct

1828	45c Southern Right Whale	1.00	0.90
1829	45c Manta Ray	1.00	0.90
1830	45c Weedy Seadragon	1.00	0.90
1831	45c Bottlenose Dolphin	1.00	0.90
1832	Se-tenant pair (1830/1831)	2.00	2.00
1833	45c Fiery Squid	1.00	0.90
1834	45c White Pointer Shark	1.00	0.90
1835	$2.70 Miniature Sheet	6.00	6.00
1836	$4.50 Booklet 10 x 45c - 5 each (1830/1831)	10.00	
	Also issued in rolls of 100 self adhesive (1830/1831)		
	First Day Cover AP gummed stamps 6		7.00
	First Day Cover AP self adhesive 2		3.00
	First Day Cover Miniature Sheet		7.00

1832. Se-tenant pair

1837. Rose & Wire

50th Anniversary of UN Declaration of Human Rights

                                                   1998 22 Oct

| 1837 | 45c Rose & Wire | 0.90 | 0.70 |
| | First Day Cover AP | | 2.00 |

1838. Three Kings

1840. Nativity Scene

1841. Mary & Joseph

Christmas   1998 2 Nov

1838	40c Three Kings	0.90	0.50
1839	$8 Booklet 20 x 40c self adhesive	15.00	
1840	45c Nativity Scene	0.90	0.50
1841	$1 Mary & Joseph	1.90	1.80
	First Day Cover (3) AP		5.00

NO.	DESCRIPTION	MUH	FU	NO.	DESCRIPTION	MUH	FU

1842. Commonwealth Coat of Arms

50th Anniversary of Australian Citizenship — 1999 14 Jan

1842	45c Commonwealth Coat of Arms	1.00☐	0.70☐
	Also issued in rolls of 100 self adhesive		
	First Day Cover AP		2.00☐

1843. Arthur Boyd, Artist   1844. Nebuchadnezzar
1845. Se-tenant pair

Australian Legend - Arthur Boyd: Painter — 1999 22 Jan

1843	45c Arthur Boyd, Artist	1.00☐	0.70☐
1844	45c Nebuchadnezzar	1.00☐	0.70☐
1845	Se-tenant pair (1843/1844)	2.00☐	2.00☐
1846	Sheetlet of 10 x 45c	8.50☐	8.00☐
1847	$4.50 Booklet 10 x 45c	10.00☐	
	Self Adhesive identical designs to gummed stamps		
	First Day Cover (pair) AP		3.00☐

1848. Roses

Greetings: Romance Red Roses — 1999 4 Feb

1848	45c Roses	1.00☐	0.60☐
1849	$4.50 Booklet 10 x 45c Self Adhesive	8.00☐	
	First Day Cover AP		2.00☐

1850. Male   1851. Female
1852. Se-tenant pair

Celebrating Long Life — 1999 11 Feb

1850	45c Male	1.00☐	0.70☐
1851	45c Female	1.00☐	0.70☐
1852	Se-tenant pair (1850/1851)	2.50☐	2.00☐
1852a	Sheetlet of 10 x 45c (1850/1851)	10.00☐	8.00☐
	First Day Cover (pair) AP		3.00☐
PNC005	$3.95 Stamp & Coin Cover - Sir Donald Bradman Tribute	45.00☐	

1853. Polly Woodside   1854. Alma Doepel

1855. Enterprise   1856. Lady Nelsona

Sailing Ships of Australia — 1999 19 Mar

Issued on opening day of Australia '99 World Stamp Expo.
Melbourne 19 - 24 March.

1853	45c Polywooside	1.00☐	0.70☐
1854	85c Alma Doepel	1.50☐	1.50☐
1855	$1 Enterprise	2.00☐	1.90☐
1856	$1.05 Lady Nelson	2.20☐	1.80☐
	First Day Cover		7.00☐

1857. Tasman, Cook, Flinders

1858. Dampier, Bass, King

Navigators of Australia — 1999 19 Mar

1857	Navigators Miniature Sheet	6.00☐	6.00☐
1858	Navigators Miniature Sheet	6.00☐	6.00☐
	First Day Cover 1857		6.00☐
	First Day Cover 1858		6.00☐

1869. Here's Humphrey   1870. Bananas In   1871. Mr Squiggle   1872. Play School   1873. Play School
                      Pyjamas

1859. Olympic Torch

Olympic Torch   1999 22 Mar
Commemorating 1956 Olympic Games held in Melbourne

1859	$1.20 Olympic Torch	2.50☐	2.00☐
	First Day Cover AP		3.00☐

Children's Television   1999 06 May

1869	45c Here's Humphrey	0.90☐	0.70☐
1870	45c Bananas In Pyjamas	0.90☐	0.70☐
1871	45c Mr Squiggle	0.90☐	0.70☐
1872	45c Play School	0.90☐	0.70☐
1873	45c Play School	0.90☐	0.70☐
1874	Se-tenant strip of 5	5.00☐	5.00☐
1875	Sheetlet of 10 x 45c	8.00☐	8.00☐
1876	$4.50 Booklet of 10 x 45c - self adhesive	15.00☐	
	First Day Cover (strip 5) AP		5.00☐

1877. Replica of Gold Sovereign

Centenary of Perth Mint   1999 13 May
Gold embossed stamp

1877	$2.00 Replica of Gold Sovereign	4.00☐	3.00☐
	First Day Cover AP		4.50☐

1860. Native Fuschia (Correa reflexa)

1861. Guinea Flower (Hibbertia scandens)

1862. Beach Morning Glory (Ipomea pes-caprea)

1863. Australian Bluebells (Wahlenbergia stricta)

Nature of Australia: Coastal Flowers   1999 08 Apr

1860	45c Native Fuschia (Correa reflexa)	0.90☐	0.50☐
1861	45c Guinea Flower (Hibbertia scandens)	0.90☐	0.50☐
1862	45c Beach Morning Glory (Ipomea pes-caprea)	0.90☐	0.50☐
1863	45c Australian Bluebells (Wahlenbergia stricta)	0.90☐	0.50☐
1864	Se-tenant block of 4	4.00☐	4.00☐
1865	$4.50 Booklet of 10 x 45c - self adhesive	9.00☐	
1865A	$9.00 Booklet 20 x 45c - self adhesive	15.00☐	
1866	$2 25 sheetlet of 5 x 45c - self adhesive	5.00☐	
	Also issued in rolls of both 100 & 200 self adhesive stamps.		
	First Day Cover AP block of 4 gummed		4.00☐

1881. Try

1878. Line Out   1879. Kicking

1882. Passing

100 Years of Test Rugby   1999 08 Jun

1878	45c Line Out	0.90☐	0.70☐
1879	45c Kicking	0.90☐	0.70☐
1880	Se-tenant pair 1878/1879	2.20☐	1.70☐
1881	$1.00 Wallaby Try Against South Africa	2.20☐	1.80☐
1882	$1.20 Wallaby Passing Against Wales	2.60☐	2.00☐
	Also available in rolls of 100 x 45c self adhesive		
	First Day Cover Strip AP 2 x 45c		3.00☐
	First Day Cover Strip AP set of 4		6.00☐

1867. Queen Elizabeth II & The Queen Mother

Queens Birthday   1999 15 Apr

1867	45c Queen Elizabeth II & The Queen Mother	1.00☐	0.70☐
1868	Sheetlet of 10 x 45c	8.00☐	8.00☐
	First Day Cover AP 1		2.00☐

NO.	DESCRIPTION	MUH	FU	NO.	DESCRIPTION	MUH	FU

1883. Humpback Whales   1884. Brahminy Kite   1885. Fraser Island

1887. Loggerhead Turtle   1888. White Bellied Sea Eagle

Coastal Nature of Australia -Birds and Animals

1999 08 July

1883	70c Humpback Whales	1.30☐	0.70☐
1884	90c Brahminy Kite	1.50☐	1.00☐
1885	90c Fraser Island (Eagle)	1.50☐	1.00☐
1886	Se-tenant pair (1884 & 1885)	3.50☐	2.50☐
1887	$1.05 Loggerhead Turtle	2.00☐	1.20☐
1888	$1.20 White Bellied Sea Eagle	2.50☐	1.40☐
	First Day Cover (5) AP		9.00☐

1889. Carpenters (1951) & Island Bend Dam   1890. Tunnel (1960) & Eucumbene Dam (1959)

1891. English language class at Cooma (1951)   1892. Drilling & rock bolting (1959)

50th Anniversary Of Snowy Mountains Scheme

1999 12 Aug

1889	45c Carpenters (1951) & Island Bend Dam	0.90☐	0.60☐
1890	45c Tunnel (1960) & Eucumbene Dam (1959)	0.90☐	0.60☐
1891	45c English language class at Cooma (1951)	0.90☐	0.60☐
1892	45c Drilling & rock bolting (1959)	0.90☐	0.60☐
1893	Block of four	5.00☐	3.50☐
	Also issued in rolls 100 x 4 types		
	First Day Cover AP block of 4 gummed		3.50☐
	First Day Cover AP self adhesive x 4		3.50☐

1894. Teddy Bear with New Baby tab   1895. Birthday Cake with Happy Birthday tab

1896. Rings with Congratulations tab   1897. Pen with Thinking of You tab

1898. Bauble with Happy Christmas tab   1899. Koala with Greetings tab

Personal Greetings with Tabs

1999 01 Sept

1894	45c Teddy Bear with New Baby tab	1.00☐	1.00☐
1895	45c Birthday Cake with Happy Birthday tab	1.00☐	1.00☐
1896	45c Rings with 'Congratulations' tab	1.00☐	1.00☐
1897	45c Pen with 'Thinking of You' tab	1.00☐	1.00☐
1898	45c Bauble with 'Happy Christmas' tab	1.00☐	1.00☐
1899	$1 Koala with 'Greetings' tab	2.00☐	1.70☐
1900	45c 'Polly Woodside' (see 1853)		
	with 'Best Wishes'tab	1.00☐	1.00☐
	First Day Cover (5 with tabs) AP		8.50☐

1901. Emblem over Sydney Landmarks

Sydney '2000 Games' Emblem		1999 14 Sept
1901	45c Emblem over Sydney Landmarks	1.00	0.70
	$4.50 Sheetlet (10 x 45c)	12.00	9.00
	First Day Cover AP		2.00

1902. Australia Post Symbol

1903. Embryo Chair

1904. Possum Skin Textile

1905. RMIT Storey Hall

Design Australia		1999 16 Sept
1902	45c Australia Post Symbol	0.90	0.70
1903	90c Embryo Chair	1.70	1.50
1904	$1.35 Possum Skin Textile	2.50	1.80
1905	$1.50 RMIT Storey Hall	2.80	2.40
	First Day Cover (4) AP		8.00

1906. Roths Tree Frog   1907. Dragonfly

1912. Northern Dwarf   1913. Javelin Frog
Tree Frog (1909/1910)

1909. Sacred Kingfisher   1910. Magnificent Tree Frog

1915. Miniature Sheet

Small Pond   **1999 Oct 1**

1906	45c Roths Tree Frog	0.90	0.70
1907	45c Dragonfly	0.90	0.70
1908	Se-tenant pair (1906/1907)	2.00	1.80
1909	45c Sacred Kingfisher	0.90	0.70
1910	45c Magnificent Tree Frog	0.90	0.70
1911	Se-tenant pair from sheet	2.00	1.80
1912	50c Northern Dwarf Tree Frog (1909/1910)	1.00	0.70
1913	50c Javelin Frog	1.00	0.70
1914	Se-tenant pair from sheet (1912/1913)	2.50	1.80
1915	$2.80 Miniature Sheet	6.00	6.00
1916	$5 Booklet 10 x 50c self adhesive	9.00	
	Also issued in rolls 100 x 45c & strips 2 x 45c		
	First Day Cover AP Miniature Sheet		7.00

40c australia

1917. Madonna & Child

$1   australia

1918. Abstract painting Tree of Life

Christmas 1999   **1999 Nov1**

1917	40c Madonna & Child	0.65	0.30
1918	$1 Abstract painting 'Tree of Life'	1.40	0.80
1919	$8 Booklet 20 x 40c self adhesive	14.00	
	First Day Cover (2) AP		2.40

1920. Hologram with background colours
& fireworks

Celebrate 2000   **1999 Nov1**

1920	45c Hologram with background colours & fireworks	1.00	0.70
1921	$4.50 Sheetlet 10 x 45c	9.00	9.00
	Also issued in sheetlet 20 x 45c		
	First Day Cover AP		2.50

1922. Nicholle & Meghan Triandis
1923. David Willis
1924. Natasha Bramley
1925. Cyril Watson
1926. Mollie Dowdall
1927. Robin Dicks
1928. Mary Simons
1929. Peta & Samantha Nieuwerth
1930. John Matthews
-1931. Edith Dizon-Fitzsimmons
1932. Philipa Weir
1933. John (Jack) Thurgar
1934. Miguel Alzona
1935. Rachael Thomson
1936. Necip Akarsu
1937. Justin Allan
1938. Wadad Dennaoui
1939. Jack Laity
1940. Kelsey Stubbin
1941. Gianna Rossi
1942. Paris Hansch
1943. Donald George Whatham
1944. Stacey Coull
1945. Alex Payne
1946. John Lodge

Faces of Australia 2000 Jan 1

1922	45c Nicholle & Meghan Triandis	1.00☐	0.70☐
1923	45c David Willis	1.00☐	0.70☐
1924	45c Natasha Bramley	1.00☐	0.70☐
1925	45c Cyril Watson	1.00☐	0.70☐
1926	45c Mollie Dowdall	1.00☐	0.70☐
1927	45c Robin Dicks	1.00☐	0.70☐
1928	45c Mary Simons	1.00☐	0.70☐
1929	45c Peta & Samantha Nieuwerth	1.00☐	0.70☐
1930	45c John Matthews	1.00☐	0.70☐
1931	45cEdith Dizon-Fitzsimmons	1.00☐	0.70☐
1932	45c Philipa Weir	1.00☐	0.70☐
1933	45c John (Jack) Thurgar	1.00☐	0.70☐
1934	45c Miguel Alzona	1.00☐	0.70☐
1935	45c Rachael Thomson	1.00☐	0.70☐
1936	45c Necip Akarsu	1.00☐	0.70☐
1937	45c Justin Allan	1.00☐	0.70☐
1938	45c Wadad Dennaoui	1.00☐	0.70☐
1939	45c Jack Laity	1.00☐	0.70☐
1940	45c Kelsey Stubbin	1.00☐	0.70☐
1941	45c Gianna Rossi	1.00☐	0.70☐
1942	45c Paris Hansch	1.00☐	0.70☐
1943	45c Donald George Whatham	1.00☐	0.70☐
1944	45c Stacey Coull	1.00☐	0.70☐
1945	45c Alex Payne	1.00☐	0.70☐
1946	45c John Lodge	1.00☐	0.70☐
1947	$11.25 Sheetlet 25 x 45c	19.00☐	19.00☐
	First Day Covers 5 issued by AP		
	each cover featuring 5 x stamps. Each		6.00☐

1954. Perth Festival - Black Swan Theatre Company   1955. Adelaide Festival - Rosas Dance Company   1956. Sydney Festival - Tharp Dance Company   1957. Melbourne Festival - Sekawari-Balinese Dance Society   1958. Brisbane Festival - Vusa Dance Company

1967. Queens Birthday

Australian Arts Festivals — 2000 24 Feb

1954	45c Perth Festival - Black Swan Theatre Company	1.00☐	0.70☐
1955	45c Adelaide Festival - Rosas Dance Company	1.00☐	0.70☐
1956	45c Sydney Festival - Tharp Dance Company	1.00☐	0.70☐
1957	45c Melbourne Festival - Sekawari-Balinese Dance Society	1.00☐	0.70☐
1958	45c Brisbane Festival - Vusa Dance Company	1.00☐	0.70☐
1959	Se-tenant strip of 5	5.00☐	4.00☐
	First Day Cover AP		6.00☐

Queens Birthday — 2000 13 Apr

1967	45c Queen's Birthday	0.90☐	0.70☐
	First Day Cover AP		2.00☐

1960. Banksia-Sarsparilla-Bloodwood   1961. Bottlebrush with Eastern Spinebill   1962. Garden Cannas   1963. Roses with Swamphen   1964. Hibiscus

1968. Korean Landscape

Gardens of Australia — 2000 23 Mar

1960	45c Banksia-Sarsparilla-Bloodwood	0.90☐	0.70☐
1961	45c Bottlebrush with Eastern Spinebill	0.90☐	0.70☐
1962	45c Garden Cannas	0.90☐	0.70☐
1963	45c Roses with Swamphen	0.90☐	0.70☐
1964	45c Hibiscus	0.90☐	0.70☐
1965	Se-tenant strip of 5	6.00☐	4.00☐
1966	$4.50 Booklet, 10 x 45c self adhesive	10.00☐	
	Also issued in rolls 100 x 45 self adhesive		
	First Day Cover AP, both gummed & self adhesive		6.00☐

50th Anniversary of Korean War — 2000 18 Apr

1968	45c Korean Landscape	0.90☐	0.70☐
	Also issued in rolls 100 x 45 self adhesive		
	First Day Cover AP, both gummed & self adhesive		4.50☐
	First Day Cover AP		2.00☐

1969. Daisy - with tab   1970. Australia & Globe - with tab

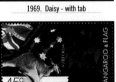

1948. Walter Parker   1949. Roy Longmore

1950. Alex Campbell   1951. World War 1914-1915 Star

1971. Kangaroo & Flag - with tab   1972. Sand & Sea Sky - with tab

1973. Rainforest - with tab

Australian Legends -The Last ANZACS — 2000 Jan 21

1948	45c Walter Parker	0.90☐	0.70☐
1949	45c Roy Longmore	0.90☐	0.70☐
1950	45c Alex Campbell	0.90☐	0.70☐
1951	45c World War 1914-1915 Star	0.90☐	0.70☐
1952	$1.80 Block of 4	4.00☐	4.00☐
1953	$4.50 Booklet, 10 x 45c self adhesive	12.00☐	
	First Day Cover, block x 4 AP, gummed		4.00☐
PNC006	$7.90 Stamp & Coin Cover - Last of the Anzacs	140.00☐	

Nature and Nation — 2000 11 May

1969	45c Daisy - with tab	1.00☐	1.00☐
1970	45c Australia & Globe - with tab	1.00☐	1.00☐
1971	45c Kangaroo & Flag - with tab	1.00☐	1.00☐
1972	45c Sand & Sea Sky - with tab	1.00☐	1.00☐
1973	45c Rainforest - with tab	1.00☐	1.00☐
	First Day Cover (5 with tabs) AP		5.00☐

TOWARDS FEDERATION

1890s - Conventions were held culminating in the colonies agreeing to federate.

5 July 1900 - The Commonwealth of Australia Constitution Act is passed in the British Parliament.

17 September 1900 - Queen Victoria proclaims the Commonwealth of Australia will come into existence on 1 January 1901.

AUSTRALIA 45c — TAKING THE VOTE

AUSTRALIA 45c — WAITING FOR THE RESULTS

AUSTRALIA $1.50 — THE FAIR NEW NATION

AUSTRALIA $1.50 — QUEEN VICTORIA

Towards Federation — 2000 22 May

No.	Description	MUH	FU
1974	45c Taking the Vote	0.90	0.70
1975	45c Waiting for the Results	0.90	0.70
1976	Se-tenant pair (1974/1975)	2.50	2.00
1977	$1.50 The Fair New Nation	2.80	1.50
1978	$1.50 Queen Victoria	2.80	1.50
1979	Se-tenant pair (1977/1978)	6.00	4.50
1980	$3.90 Miniature Sheet	8.00	7.00
	First Day Cover AP - Miniature Sheet		9.00
	First Day Cover AP - stamps (4) only		7.50

1974. Taking the Vote
1975. Waiting for the Results
1977. The Fair New Nation
1978. Queen Victoria

1981. Sydney Opera House

1982. Nandroya Falls

1983. Sydney Harbour Bridge

1984. Cradle Mountain

1985. The Pinnacles

1986. Flinders Ranges

1987. Twelve Apostles

1988. Devils Marbles

International Stamps — 2000 20 Jun

No.	Description	MUH	FU
1981	50c Sydney Opera House	1.00	1.00
1982	$1 Nandroya Falls	1.80	1.80
1983	$1.50 Sydney Harbour Bridge	2.80	2.80
1984	$2 Cradle Mountain	3.50	3.50
1985	$3 The Pinnacles	5.50	5.50
1986	$4.50 Flinders Ranges	8.50	8.50
1987	$5 Twelve Apostles	9.00	9.00
1988	$10 Devils Marbles	18.00	18.00
	First Day Cover AP (Set x 3)		50.00

RENNIKS

NO.	DESCRIPTION	MUH	FU	NO.	DESCRIPTION	MUH	FU

1989. Tennis   1990. Track Running

1992. Basketball   1993. Cycling   1994. Shot Put

Sydney 2000 Paralympic Games   2000 3 Jul

1989	45c Tennis	0.90	0.60
1990	45c Track Running	0.90	0.60
1991	Se-tenant pair (1989/1990)	2.50	2.00
1992	49c Basketball	0.90	0.70
1993	49c Cycling	0.90	0.70
1994	49c Shot Put	0.90	0.70
1995	Se-tenant strip (1992/1995)	3.50	3.00
1996	$4.90 Booklet, 10 x .49c, self adhesive type	18.00	
	Also issued in rolls 100 x .45c, self adhesive type		
	First Day Cover AP, gummed type (5)		6.00

1997. Sir Neville Howse - Boer War 1900   1998. Sir Roden Cutler - Lebanon, WW11, 1941   1999. Victoria Cross   2000. Edward Kenna-WWII-New Guinea 1945   2001. Keith Payne - South Vietnam, 1969

Centenary of Australia's First Victoria Cross   2000 24 Jul

1997	45c Sir Neville Howse - Boer War 1900	0.90	0.70
1998	45c Sir Roden Cutler - Lebanon, WW11, 1941	0.90	0.70
1999	45c Victoria Cross	0.90	0.70
2000	45c Edward Kenna-WWII-New Guinea 1945	0.90	0.70
2001	45c KeithPayne - South Vietnam, 1969	0.90	0.70
2002	Se-tenant strip (5)	6.00	4.50
	First Day Cover (strip 5) AP		5.00
PNC007	$9.85 Stamp & Coin Cover - Victoria Cross for Valour	270.00	

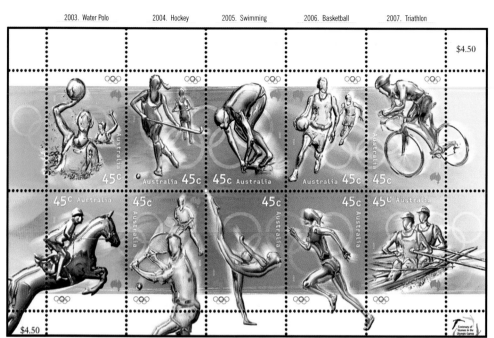

2003. Water Polo   2004. Hockey   2005. Swimming   2006. Basketball   2007. Triathlon

$4.50

2008. Equestrian   2009. Tennis   2010. Gymnastics   2011. Athletics   2012. Rowing

Olympic Sports — 2000 17 Aug

No.	Description	MUH	FU
2003	45c Water Polo	0.90☐	0.70☐
2004	45c Hockey	0.90☐	0.70☐
2005	45c Swimming	0.90☐	0.70☐
2006	45c Basketball	0.90☐	0.70☐
2007	45c Triathlon	0.90☐	0.70☐
2008	45c Equestrian	0.90☐	0.70☐
2009	45c Tennis	0.90☐	0.70☐
2010	45c Gymnastics	0.90☐	0.70☐
2011	45c Athletics	0.90☐	0.70☐
2012	45c Rowing	0.90☐	0.70☐
2013	$4.50 Sheetlet 10 x .45c	9.00☐	8.00☐
2014	$4.50 Booklet 10 x .45c, self adhesive type	15.00☐	
	First Day Cover, sheetlet, AP		10.00☐
PNC008	$10.85 Stamp & Coin Cover - Olympic Sports - Swimming	100.00☐	
PNC009	$7.85 Stamp & Coin Cover - Olympic Sports - Athletics	100.00☐	

2015. Flame, Flag, Athens - with tab

2016. Flame, Flag, Sydney - with tab

Sydney/Athens Joint Issue — 2000 15 Sep

No.	Description	MUH	FU
2015	45c Flame, Flag, Athens - with tab	1.30☐	1.00☐
2016	$1.50 Flame, Flag, Sydney - with tab	4.00☐	4.00☐
	First Day Cover (2) AP		6.50☐

2017. Ian Thorpe

2018. Mens 4 x 100m Freestyle Relay

2019. Michael Diamond

2020. Equestrian Team

2021. Susie ONeill

2022. Mens 4 x 200m Freestyle Relay

2023. Simon Fairweather

2024. Cycling: Mens Madison

2025. Grant Hackett

2026. Womens Water Polo

2027. Womens Beach Volley Ball

2028. Cathy Freeman

2029. Lauren Burns

2030. Womens Hockey

2031. Sailing - Womens 470 class

2032. Sailing - Mens 470 Class

Australian Gold Medalists 2000		Sept 17	Oct 1
2017	45c Ian Thorpe	1.00 ☐	0.85 ☐
2018	45c Men's 4 x 100m Freestyle Relay	1.00 ☐	0.85 ☐
2019	45c Michael Diamond	1.00 ☐	0.85 ☐
2020	45c Equestrian Team	1.00 ☐	0.85 ☐
2021	45c Susie O'Neill	1.00 ☐	0.85 ☐
2022	45c Men's 4 x 200m Freestyle Relay	1.00 ☐	0.85 ☐
2023	45c Simon Fairweather	1.00 ☐	0.85 ☐
2024	45c Cycling: Men's Madison	1.00 ☐	0.85 ☐
2025	45c Grant Hackett	1.00 ☐	0.85 ☐
2026	45c Women's Water Polo	1.00 ☐	0.85 ☐
2027	45c Women's Beach Volley Ball	1.00 ☐	0.85 ☐
2028	45c Cathy Freeman	1.00 ☐	0.85 ☐
2029	45c Lauren Burns	1.00 ☐	0.85 ☐
2030	45c Women's Hockey	1.00 ☐	0.85 ☐
2031	45c Sailing - Women's 470 class	1.00 ☐	0.85 ☐
2032	45c Sailing - Men's 470 Class	1.00 ☐	0.85 ☐

The above were printed in Off-Set & Digital format with both types having identical values. Various non AP First Day Covers exist in the Market place

2033. Flight Crew

2034. Robots

2042. Lighting the Olympic

Sydney Olympic Games Opening Ceremony   **2000 10 Oct**

| 2042 | 45c Lighting the Olympic Flame | 1.50☐ | 0.80☐ |
| | First Day Cover AP | | 2.50☐ |

2035. Astronaut   2036. Terrain

2039. Launch site

2038. Spacecraft

2043. Torch Logo

2040. Minature Sheetlet

2044. Torch with Runner

Paralympic Torch   **2000 18 Oct**

2043	45c Torch Logo–with tabs	1.00☐	0.90☐
2044	45c Torch with Runner -with tabs	1.00☐	0.90☐
	First Day Cover (2) AP		3.00☐

Space   **2000 3 Oct**

2033	45c Flight Crew	1.00☐	0.80☐
2034	45c Robots	1.00☐	0.80☐
2035	45c Astronaut	1.00☐	0.80☐
2036	45c Terrain	1.00☐	0.80☐
2037	Se-tenant pair (2035 & 2036)	3.00☐	3.00☐
2038	45c Spacecraft	1.00☐	0.80☐
2039	45c Launch site	1.00☐	0.80☐
2040	$2.70 Minature Sheetlet	6.00☐	6.00☐
2041	$4.50 Booklet, 10 x 45c self adhesive	10.00☐	
	Also issued in rolls 100 x .45c self adhesive format		
	First Day Cover, miniature sheetlet, AP		6.50☐

2045. Siobhan Paton

Paralympian of the Year   **2000 31 Oct**

| 2045 | 45c Siobhan Paton | 1.20☐ | 1.00☐ |
| | First Day Cover AP | | 2.00☐ |

2048. Silent Night Miniature Sheet

2050. Byron Bay - International stamp

Christmas 2000 — 2000 1 Nov

NO.	Description	MUH	FU
2046	40c Silent Night	0.90☐	0.40☐
2047	45c Silent Night	0.90☐	0.40☐
2048	85c Miniature Sheet	2.00☐	2.00☐
2049	$8. Booklet, 20 x 40c, self adhesive	15.00☐	
2050	80c Byron Bay - International stamp	1.80☐	1.80☐
	First Day Cover - Miniature Sheet AP		2.50☐
	First Day Cover AP (Stamps)		2.50☐
	First Day Cover - International Stamp		2.50☐

Centenary of Federation — 2001 1 Jan

NO.	Description	MUH	FU
2051	49cFederation Arch	1.00☐	0.90☐
2052	49c Edmund Barton	1.00☐	0.90☐
2053	Se-tenant pair (2051&2052)	2.50☐	2.00☐
2054	$2National Celebrations	4.00☐	3.00☐
2055	$2State Banquet	4.00☐	3.00☐
2056	$4.98 Miniature Sheetlet	10.00☐	9.00☐
2057	$4.90 Booklet, 10 x 49c, self adhesive	10.00☐	
	First Day Cover-Miniature sheetlet AP		9.00☐
	First Day Cover-stamps only (4) AP		8.50☐

2058. Slim Dusty circa 1957   2059. Slim Dusty circa 2001

Australian Legends Award - Slim Dusty — 2001 15 Feb

NO.	Description	MUH	FU
2058	45c Slim Dusty circa 1957	0.90☐	0.80☐
2059	45c Slim Dusty circa 2001	0.90☐	0.80☐
2060	Se-tenant pair (2058/2059)	2.50☐	2.00☐
2061	$4.50 Sheetlet x 10	9.00☐	9.00☐
2062	$4.50 Booklet x 10	15.00☐	
	First Day Cover (2) AP		2.50☐

2051. Federation Arch   2052. Edmund Barton   2055. State Banquet

2054. National Celebrations

2063. Historical Images   2064. Contemporary Images

Centenary of the Australian Army — 2001 15 Feb

NO.	Description	MUH	FU
2063	45c Historical Images	0.90☐	0.70☐
2064	45c Contemporary Images	0.90☐	0.70☐
2065	Se-tenant pair above	2.50☐	2.00☐
2066	$4.50 Sheetlet 10 x 45c	9.00☐	9.00☐
	First Day Cover (2) AP		2.50☐
PNC010	$17.85 Stamp & Coin Cover - Centenary of the Army	140.00☐	

NO.	DESCRIPTION	MUH	FU

2067. Site Plan	2068. Wallaby Sculpture Pangk

Opening National Museum of Australia   **2001 08 Mar**

2067	49c Site Plan	1.00☐	0.90☐
2068	49c Wallaby Sculpture 'Pangk'	1.00☐	0.90☐
2069	Se-tenant pair above (2067/2068)	2.50☐	2.00☐
	First Day Cover (2) AP		3.00☐

2070. Portrait	2071. Action at the Crease

Donald Bradman Memorial Issue   **2001 13 Mar**

2070	45c Portrait	1.00☐	0.90☐
2071	45c Action at the Crease	1.00☐	0.90☐
2072	Se-tenant pair above (2068/2069)	2.50☐	2.00☐
2073	$4.50 Sheetlet 10 x 45c	9.00☐	9.00☐
	First Day Cover (2) AP		3.00☐

2074. 1978 Cold Chisel	2075. 1981 Men at Work
2076. 1983 Midnight Oil	2077. 1984 INXS
2078. 1986 John Farnham	2079. 1986 Crowded House
2080. 1991 Yothu Yindi	2081. 1994 Silverchair
2082. 1994 Kylie Minogue	2083. 1997 Savage Garden

Rock Australia   **2001 20 Mar**

2074	45c 1978 Cold Chisel	1.00☐	0.70☐
2075	45c 1981 Men at Work	1.00☐	0.70☐
2076	45c 1983 Midnight Oil	1.00☐	0.70☐
2077	45c 1984 INXS	1.00☐	0.70☐
2078	45c 1986 John Farnham	1.00☐	0.70☐
2079	45c 1986 Crowded House	1.00☐	0.70☐
2080	45c 1991 Yothu Yindi	1.00☐	0.70☐
2081	45c 1994 Silverchair	1.00☐	0.70☐
2082	45c 1994 Kylie Minogue	1.00☐	0.70☐
2083	45c 1997 Savage Garden	1.00☐	0.70☐
2084	$4.50 Sheetlet 10 x 45c	9.00☐	9.00☐
2085	$4.50 Booklet 10 x 45c - self adhesive	14.00☐	
	Also issued in rolls 100 x 45c self adhesive		
	First Day Cover (2xcovers) AP		12.00☐

2086. QEII

Queens Birthday   **2001 12 Apr**

2086	45c QEII	0.90☐	0.70☐
	First Day Cover AP		2.00☐

2087. Celebrate 2001 with tab   2088. Lets Party with tab   2089. Smile with tab

2090. Leaps & Bounds - with tab   2091. Bayulu Banner - with tab

Colour My Day — 2001 24 Apr

		MUH	FU
2087	45c Celebrate 2001 with tab	1.00	1.00
2088	45c Let's Party with tab	1.00	1.00
2089	45c Smile with tab	1.00	1.00
2090	$1 Leaps & Bounds - with tab	2.50	2.00
2091	$1.50 Bayulu Banner - with tab	3.00	3.00
	Also all types issued in sheetlets x 20		
	First Day Cover (5) AP		8.00

2092. Charles Nuttals Painting

2094. Tom Roberts Painting

Federal Parliament Centenary — 2001 03 May

		MUH	FU
2092	45c Charles Nuttal's Painting	1.00	0.70
2093	45c Miniature Sheet of above	1.50	1.50
2094	$2.45 Tom Robert's Painting	5.00	4.50
2095	$2.45 Miniature Sheet of above	5.00	5.00
	First Day Cover AP stamps only		7.00
	First Day Cover AP miniature sheets only		6.00

2096. Telecommunications   2097. Transport   2098. School of the Air   2099. Postal Services   2100. Royal Flying Doctor Service

OutbackServices — 2001 05 Jun

		MUH	FU
2096	45c Telecommunications	0.90	0.70
2097	45c Transport	0.90	0.70
2098	45c School of the Air	0.90	0.70
2099	45c Postal Services	0.90	0.70
2100	45c Royal Flying Doctor Service	0.90	0.70
2101	Se-tenant strip x 5	6.00	4.00
	Also issued in rolls 100 x 45c self adhesive		

		MUH	FU
2102	$4.50 Booklet 10 x 45c - self adhesive	9.00	
	First Day Cover gummed or self adhesive (5) AP		5.00

2103. Dragon Boat with Hong Kong background

2104. International Post - Dragon Boat with Sydney background

Dragon Boat Racing   2001 25 Jun

No.	Description	MUH	FU
2103	45c Dragon Boat with Hong Kong background	1.00☐	0.70☐
2104	$1.00 International Post - Dragon Boat with Sydney background	2.00☐	1.80☐
2105	$1.45 Miniature Sheet with both issues	4.00☐	3.00☐
	First Day Cover AP - stamps only		4.00☐
	First Day Cover AP - Miniature Sheet only		4.50☐

2106. Three Sisters - Blue Mountains NSW

2107. Murrumbidgee River ACT

2108. Four Mile Beach, Port Douglas Qld

2109. Uluru NT

International Post Stamps - Panoramas of Australia

2001 12 Jul

No.	Description	MUH	FU
2106	50c Three Sisters - Blue Mountains NSW	1.00☐	0.90☐
2107	$1.00 Murrumbidgee River ACT	2.00☐	2.00☐
2108	$1.50 Four Mile Beach, Port Douglas Qld	3.50☐	3.00☐
2109	$20.00 Uluru NT	35.00☐	35.00☐
2110	$5.00 Booklet 10 x 50c - self adhesive	10.00☐	
	First Day Cover (4) AP		35.00☐

2111. Variegated Fairy-wren   2112. Painted Firetail

2113. Crimson Chat   2114. Budgerigar

Desert Birds of Australia

2001 09 Aug

No.	Description	MUH	FU
2111	45c Variegated Fairy-wren	0.90☐	0.70☐
2112	45c Painted Firetail	0.90☐	0.70☐
2113	45c Crimson Chat	0.90☐	0.70☐
2114	45c Budgerigar	0.90☐	0.70☐
2115	$1.80 Block of 4 stamps	4.50☐	4.00☐
2116	$4.50 Booklet of 10 - self adhesive	8.00☐	
2117	$9.00 Booklet of 20 - self adhesive	14.50☐	
	Also issued in rolls x 100 all types		
	First Day Cover (4) AP		4.50☐

2118. Daniel Solander & Barringtonia calyptrata

2119. Endeavour Aground with Cochlospermum Gillivraei

Joint Issue with Sweden

2001 16 Aug

No.	Description	MUH	FU
2118	45c Daniel Solander & Barringtonia calyptrata	1.00☐	0.70☐
2119	$1.50 Endeavour Aground with Cochlospermum Gillivraei	4.00☐	3.00☐
	First Day Cover (2) AP		4.50☐

RENNIKS

NO.	DESCRIPTION	MUH	FU	NO.	DESCRIPTION	MUH	FU

2120. 47th Common-   2121. CHOGM
wealth Parliament
Conference

Commonwealth Parliamentary Meetings   2001 04 Sept

2120	45c 47th Commonwealth Parliament Conference	0.90☐	0.70☐
2121	45c CHOGM	0.90☐	0.70☐
2122	Se-tenant pair, above	2.50☐	2.00☐
	First Day Cover (4) AP		4.00☐

2125. Wedge-tailed Eagle   2126. Nankeen Kestrel

2128. Red Goshawk   2129. Spotted Harrier

Australian Birds of Prey   2001 11 Sept

2125	49c Wedge-tailed Eagle	1.00☐	0.80☐
2126	49c Nankeen Kestrel	1.00☐	0.80☐
2127	Se-tenant pair (2125/2126)	2.50☐	2.00☐
2128	98c Red Goshawk	2.00☐	1.60☐
2129	98c Spotted Harrier	2.00☐	1.60☐
2130	Se-tenant pair (2128/2129)	4.00☐	4.00☐
	First Day Cover (4) AP		6.00☐

2123. Seasons Greetings   2124. International Post-Peace &
Good Will

Season'sGreetings   2001 04 Sept

2123	40c Seasons Greetings with tab	1.00☐	0.70☐
2124	80c International Post-Peace & Good Will-with tab	2.00☐	1.30☐
	First Day Cover (2) AP		2.50☐

2131. Cockatoo & Bush   2132. Kevin Koala &   2133. Possum Party
Musicians   his Cake

2136. Bilbies & Gifts   2137. Wombat & Friends   2138. Echidna & Wallaby

Wild Babies		2001 02 Oct	
2131	45c Cockatoo & Bush Musicians	1.00☐	0.70☐
2132	45c Kevin Koala & his Cake	1.00☐	0.70☐
2133	45c Possum Party	1.00☐	0.70☐
2134	Se-tenant strip (213½133)	3.00☐	3.00☐
2135	$1.35 Miniature Sheet (213½133)	3.50☐	2.80☐
2136	45c Bilbies & Gifts	1.00☐	0.70☐
2137	45c Wombat & Friends	1.00☐	0.70☐
2138	45c Echidna & Wallaby	1.00☐	0.70☐
2139	Se-tenant strip (2136/2138)	3.00☐	3.00☐
2140	$1.35 Miniature Sheet (2136/2138)	3.50☐	2.80☐
2141	$4.50 Booklet, 10 x 45c self adhesive	9.00☐	
	Also rolls 100 x 45c self adhesive		
	First Day Cover (6) AP		7.00☐

2142. Adoration of the Magi

2143. The Flight into Egypt

Christmas 2001		2001 01 Nov	
2142	40c Adoration of the Magi	0.80☐	0.60☐
2143	45c The Flight into Egypt	0.90☐	0.70☐
2144	$8.00 Booklet 20 x 40c - gummed	15.00☐	
	First Day Cover (2) AP		2.50☐

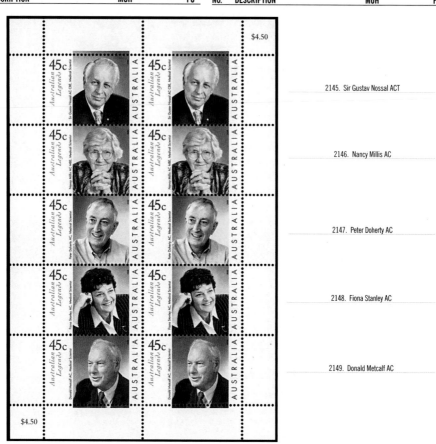

$4.50

$4.50

2145. Sir Gustav Nossal ACT

2146. Nancy Millis AC

2147. Peter Doherty AC

2148. Fiona Stanley AC

2149. Donald Metcalf AC

Australian Legends Award - Medical Science   **2002 23 Jan**

No.	Description	MUH	FU
2145	45c Sir Gustav Nossal ACT	1.00☐	0.70☐
2146	45c Nancy Millis AC	1.00☐	0.70☐
2147	45c Peter Doherty AC	1.00☐	0.70☐
2148	45c Fiona Stanley AC	1.00☐	0.70☐
2149	45c Donald Metcalf AC	1.00☐	0.70☐
2150	Se-tenant strip (2145/2149)	4.00☐	4.00☐
2151	$4.50 Sheetlet, 10 x 45c	9.00☐	9.00☐
2151a	$4.50 Booklet 10 x 45c self adhesive	16.00☐	
	First Day Cover (5) AP		6.00☐

2152. Queen   2153. Queen
Elizabeth II   Elizabeth II

Queens Golden Jubilee Year   **2002 06 Feb**

No.	Description	MUH	FU
2152	45c Queen Elizabeth II	0.90☐	0.70☐
2153	$2.45 Queen Elizabeth II	4.50☐	4.00☐
2154	$2.90 Miniature Sheet, above	5.50☐	5.50☐
	First Day Cover (2) AP - stamps alone		6.00☐
	First Day Cover AP - Miniature Sheet		6.00☐
PNC011	$9.95 Stamp & Coin Cover		
	- Queen Elizabeth II Accession	240.00☐	

2170. Nicholas Baudin   2171. Matthew Flinders

2155. Steven Bradbury -
Short Track Speed Skating

2156. Alisa Camplin - Womens Aerial
Freestyle

Flinders-Baudin Bicentenary
Joint Issue with France la Poste   **2002 24 Apr**

2172	45c Nicholas Baudin	1.00☐	0.70☐
2173	$1.50 Matthew Flinders	2.75☐	2.50☐
	First Day Cover (2) AP		5.00☐

2002 Winter Olympic Games
Australian Gold Medal Winners   **2002 20 & 22nd Feb**

2155	45c Steven Bradbury - Short Track Speed Skating	1.00☐	1.00☐
2156	45c Alisa Camplin - Womens Aerial Freestyle	1.00☐	1.00☐
	Issued in sheetlets x 10		
	NoFirst Day Covers issued by AP		

2157. 1928 Austin 7 &
Bugatti Type 40   2158. 1963 Jaguar MkII   2159. 1966 Repco Brabham

2160. 1972 Holden Torana XU1   2161. 1980 Ford FW07   2162. Benetton-Renault

Motor Racing Australia   **2002 27 Feb**

2157	45c 1928 Austin 7 & Bugatti Type 40	0.90☐	0.70☐
2158	45c 1963 Jaguar MkII	0.90☐	0.70☐
2159	45c 1966 Repco Brabham	0.90☐	0.70☐
2160	45c 1972 Holden Torana XU1	0.90☐	0.70☐
2161	45c 1980 Ford FW07	0.90☐	0.70☐
2162	45c Benetton-Renault	0.90☐	0.70☐
2163	Se-tenant block of six	5.00☐	5.00☐
2164	$4.50 Booklet, 10 x 45c	10.00☐	
	Also issued in roll 100 x 45c self adhesive type		
	First Day Cover (6) AP		7.50☐

2165. Macquarie Light,
South Head, Sydney, NSW   2167. Troubridge Island,
SA   2166. Cape Naturaliste,
WA   2169. Cape Bruny,
Tas

Lighthouses of Australia   **2002 12 Mar**

2165	45c Macquarie Light, South Head, Sydney, NSW	0.90☐	0.70☐
2166	49c Cape Naturaliste, WA	1.00☐	0.90☐
2167	49c Troubridge Island, SA	1.00☐	0.90☐
2168	Se-tennant pair (2166/2167)	2.50☐	2.00☐
2169	$1.50 Cape Bruny, Tas	2.75☐	2.25☐
2170	$4.90 Booklet, 10 x 49c	10.00☐	
2171	$9.95 Prestige Booklet also issued	15.00☐	
	First Day Cover (4) AP		7.00☐

2174. Walker Flat, Murray River SA   2175. Mt Roland Tas   2176. Cape Leveque WA

International Post - Panoramas of Australia   2002 23 Aug

No.	Description	MUH	FU
2174	50c Walker Flat, Murray River SA	1.00☐	0.90☐
2175	$1 Mt Roland Tas	1.80☐	1.80☐
2176	$1.50 Cape Leveque WA	2.80☐	2.50☐
2176B	$7 Booklet (6 x .50, 4 x $1) self adhesive	15.00☐	
	First Day Cover (3) AP		7.00☐

2177. Desert Star Flower   2178. Bilby   2179. Thorny Devil

2180. Great Sandy Desert

Nature of Australia Desert   2002 04 Jun

No.	Description	MUH	FU
2177	50c Desert Star Flower	1.00☐	0.30☐
2178	$1 Bilby	1.80☐	0.70☐
2179	$1.50 Thorny Devil	2.80☐	1.50☐
2180	$2Great Sandy Desert	3.50☐	3.00☐
2180B	$5 Booklet (10 x .50) self adhesive	9.00☐	
2180C	$10 Booklet (20 x .50) self adhesive	18.00☐	
	First Day Cover (4) AP		10.00☐

2181. Ghost Gum Mt Sonder   2182. Mt Hermannsburg

2187. Miniature Sheet

2183. Glen Helen Country   2184. Simpsons Gap

Birth Centenary Of Albert Namatjira   2002 02 Jul

No.	Description	MUH	FU
2181	45c Ghost Gum Mt Sonder	0.90☐	0.70☐
2182	45c Mt Hermannsburg	0.90☐	0.70☐
2183	45c Glen Helen Country	0.90☐	0.70☐
2184	45c Simpsons Gap	0.90☐	0.70☐
2185	Block of (4)	4.50☐	3.50☐
2186	$4.50 Booklet (10 x 45c) self adhesive	9.00☐	
2187	$1.80 Miniature Sheet	3.50☐	3.50☐
	First Day Cover (4) AP		5.00☐

2188. Nymphaea immutabilis orchid 2189. Nelumbo nucifer orchid

2190. Minature Sheet (2)

Diplomatic Relations With Thailand 2002 06 Aug

2188	45c Nymphaea immutabilis orchid	1.00☐	0.60☐
2189	$1.00 Nelumbo nucifer orchid	1.80☐	0.80☐
2190	$1.45 Minature Sheet (2)	2.80☐	2.80☐
	First Day Cover (2) AP		4.00☐

2192. Gariwerd Grampians-VIC

2191. Coonawarra-SA

2193. National Library-ACT

2194. Cape York-QLD

International Stamps - Panoramas Of Australia

2002 23 Aug

2191	$1.10 Coonawarra-SA	2.00☐	2.00☐
2192	$1.65 Gariwerd Grampians-VIC	3.00☐	3.00☐
2193	$2.20 National Library-ACT	4.00☐	4.00☐
2194	$3.30 Cape York-QLD	6.00☐	6.00☐
	First Day Cover (4) AP		15.00☐

2195. Tinsel Star with tab

2196. Koala with tab

2197. Aboriginal art with tab

International Greetings 2002 23 Aug

2195	90c Tinsel Star with tab	1.80☐	1.80☐
2196	$1.10 Koala with tab	2.20☐	2.20☐
2197	$1.65 Aboriginal art with tab	3.50☐	3.50☐
	First Day Cover (3) AP		8.00☐

NO.	DESCRIPTION	MUH	FU	NO.	DESCRIPTION	MUH	FU

AUSTRALIA 49c *Murnong* | AUSTRALIA 49c *Acacia seeds* | AUSTRALIA 49c *Quandong* | AUSTRALIA 49c *Honey grevillea* | AUSTRALIA 49c *Lilly-pilly*

2198. Lilly-pilly

2199. Honey grevillea

2200. Quandong

2201. Acacia

2202. Murnong

Bush Tucker — 2002 03 Sept

2198	49c Lilly-pilly	1.00☐	0.90☐
2199	49c Honey grevillea	1.00☐	0.90☐
2200	49c Quandong	1.00☐	0.90☐
2201	49c Acacia	1.00☐	0.90☐
2202	49c Murnong	1.00☐	0.90☐
2203	Se-tenant strip (5) 2196/2200	5.00☐	5.00☐
2204	$4.90 booklet (10 x 49c) self adhesive	10.00☐	
2205	Tete-Beche Block (10)	11.00☐	11.00☐
	First Day Cover (5) AP		6.50☐

2206. Bunyip	2207. Fairy	2208. Gnome

2222. Nativity

2223. Wise Men

Christmas — 2002 01 Nov

2222	40c Nativity	0.90☐	0.60☐
2223	45c Wise Men	0.90☐	0.65☐
2224	$8.00 booklet (20 x 40c) self adhesive	15.00☐	
	First Day Cover (2) AP		2.50☐

2210. Goblin	2211. Wizard	2212. Sprite

The Magic Rainforest — 2002 25 Sept

2206	45c Bunyip	1.00☐	0.70☐
2207	45c Fairy	1.00☐	0.70☐
2208	45c Gnome	1.00☐	0.70☐
2209	Se-tenant strip of 3 (2206-2209)	3.50☐	3.00☐
2210	45c Goblin	1.00☐	0.70☐
2211	45c Wizard	1.00☐	0.70☐
2212	45c Sprite	1.00☐	0.70☐
2213	Se-tenant strip of 3 (2210-2213)	3.50☐	3.00☐
2214	$4.50 booklet (10 x 45c) self adhesive	9.00☐	
2215	$2.70 Minature Sheet	7.00☐	5.00☐
	First Day Cover (6) AP		7.50☐

2216. Wakeful	2217. Rising Fast	2218. Manikato	2219. Might and Power	2220. Sunline

Champions Of Turf — 2002 15 Oct

2216	45c Wakeful	1.00☐	0.70☐
2217	45c Rising Fast	1.00☐	0.70☐
2218	45c Manikato	1.00☐	0.20☐
2219	45c Might and Power	1.00☐	0.70☐
2220	45c Sunline	1.00☐	0.70☐
2221	Se-tenant strip (5)	5.50☐	4.00☐
	First Day Cover (5) AP		6.50☐

2225. Daisy   2226. Wedding ring   2227. Hearts and roses

2229. Birthday cake   2230. Teddy Bear   2231. Party balloons

2233. Kangaroo & Flag   2234. Australia & Globe   2235. Sports car

Celebration And Nation — 2003 07 Jan

		MUH	FU
2225	50c Daisy with tab	1.00☐	0.90☐
2226	50c Wedding ring wih tab	1.00☐	0.90☐
2227	50c Hearts and roses with tab	1.00☐	0.90☐
2228	Se-tenant strip with tabs (3) (2225-2228)	3.00☐	3.00☐
2229	50c Birthday cake with tab	1.00☐	0.90☐
2230	50c Teddy Bear with tab	1.00☐	0.90☐
2231	50c Party balloons with tab	1.00☐	0.90☐
2232	Se-tenant strip with tabs (3) (2229/2231)	3.00☐	3.00☐
2233	50c Kangaroo & Flag with tab	1.00☐	0.90☐
2234	50c Australia & Globe with tab	1.00☐	0.90☐
2235	50c Sports car with tab	1.00☐	0.90☐
2236	Se-tenant strip (3) (2233/2236)	3.00☐	3.00☐
2237	$1.00 Silver rings with tab	2.00☐	2.00☐
	First Day Cover (10 x stamps/2 x cover) AP		12.00☐

2237. Silver rings

2244. Blue Orchid

2238. Margaret Court & trophy   2239. Margaret Court in action

2240. Rod Laver & trophy   2241. Rod Laver in action

Australian Legends Awards - Tennis — 2003 24 Jan

		MUH	FU
2238	50c Margaret Court & trophy	1.00☐	0.80☐
2239	50c Margaret Court in action	1.00☐	0.80☐
2240	50c Rod Laver & trophy	1.00☐	0.80☐
2241	50c Rod Laver in action	1.00☐	0.80☐
2242	Block (4) (2238/2241)	4.50☐	4.00☐
2243	$5.00 booklet (10 x 50c) self adhesive	12.00☐	
	First Day Cover (4) AP		5.00☐

Nature Of Australia - Rainforest — 2003 11 Feb

		MUH	FU
2244	$1.45 Blue Orchid	2.80☐	2.80☐
	First Day Cover AP		4.00☐

⦿RENNIKS

NO.	DESCRIPTION	MUH	FU	NO.	DESCRIPTION	MUH	FU

2245. Snapper   2246. Murray cod   2247. Brown trout   2248. Yellowfind tuna   2249. Barramundi

Fishing In Australia — 2003 11 Feb

No.	Description	MUH	FU
2245	50c Snapper	1.00	0.85
2246	50c Murray cod	1.00	0.85
2247	50c Brown trout	1.00	0.85
2248	50c Yellowfind tuna	1.00	0.85
2249	50c Barramundi	1.00	0.85
2250	Se-tenant strip 5 (2245/2249)	5.00	5.00
	First Day Cover (5) AP	10.00	

2251. Hari Withers' camellia   2252. Victoria Gold rose   2253. Superb grevillea   2254. Bush Tango kangaroo paw   2255. Midnight rhododendron

Blooms Australian Cultivars — 2003 25 Mar

No.	Description	MUH	FU
2251	50c Hari Withers' camellia	1.00	0.85
2252	50c Victoria Gold rose	1.00	0.85
2253	50c Superb grevillea	1.00	0.85
2254	50c Bush Tango kangaroo paw	1.00	0.85
2255	50c Midnight rhododendron	1.00	0.85
2256	Se-tenant strip 5 (2251/2255)	5.00	5.00
2257	$5.00 booklet (10 x 50c) self adhesive	10.00	
2258	Sheet-let (10 x 50c)	10.00	10.00
	Self adhesive issued in roll x 100		
	First Day Cover (5) AP	6.00	

2259. Sidney Nolan Ned Kelly   2260. Howard Arkley Family Home

2262. Robert Jacks Cord Long Drawn Expectant

2263. Joy Hester Girl

Australian Paintings — 2003 06 May

No.	Description	MUH	FU
2259	$1.00 Sidney Nolan Ned Kelly	1.80	1.80
2260	$1.00 Howard Arkley Family Home	1.80	1.80
2261	Se-tenant pair (2259-2260)	4.00	4.00
2262	$1.45 Robert Jacks Cord Long Drawn Expectant	2.80	2.80
2263	$2.45 Joy Hester Girl	4.80	4.80
	First Day Cover (4) AP	12.00	

2265. St Edward's Crown

2264. Cecil Beaton portrait

Golden Jubilee Of Queen Elizabeth II Coronation

2003 02 Jun

2264	50c Cecil Beaton portrait	1.00□	0.80□
2265	$2.45 St Edward's Crown	4.00□	4.00 1
2266	$2.95 Minature Sheet	5.00□	5.00□
2267	$5.00 booklet (10 x 50c) self adhesive	9.00□	
	First Day Cover (2) AP		6.00□
PNC012	$11.95 Stamp & Coin Cover		
	- Queen Elizabeth II Golden Jubilee	35.00□	

2266. Minature Sheet

2268. Ningura Napurrula

2269. Naata Nungurrayi

2270. Graham Tjupurrula

2271. Dini Campbell Tjampitjinpa

International Post - Art Of Papunya Tula

2003 17 Jun

2268	$1.10 Ningura Napurrula	2.00□	2.00□
2269	$1.65 Naata Nungurrayi	3.00□	3.00□
2270	$2.20 Graham Tjupurrula	4.00□	4.00□
2271	$3.30 Dini Campbell Tjampitjinpa	6.50□	6.00□
	First Day Cover (4) AP		16.00□

2272. DNA double helix   2273. Kangaroo chromosomes

Genetic And The Discovery Of DNA

2003 08 Jul

2272	50c DNA double helix	1.00□	0.80 1
2273	50c Kangaroo chromosomes	1.00□	0.80□
2274	Se-tenant pair (2270-2271)	2.00□	2.00□
	First Day Cover (2) AP		2.50□

2275. Orange-thighed tree frog

2276. Green-spotted triangle butterfly

2277. Striped possum   2278. Yellow-bellied sunbird

Nature Of Australia - Rainforests

2003 08 Jul

2275	50c Orange-thighed tree frog	1.00□	0.60□
2276	50c Green-spotted triangle butterfly	1.00□	0.60□
2277	50c Striped possum	1.00□	0.60□
2278	50c Yellow-bellied sunbird	1.00□	0.60□
2279	Se-tenant block x 4 (2275/2278)	4.00□	4.00□
2280	$5.00 booklet (10) self adhesive	9.00□	
2281	$10.00 booklet (20) self adhesive	18.00□	
	First Day Cover (4) AP		4.50□

⑦RENNIKS

NO.	DESCRIPTION	MUH	FU	NO.	DESCRIPTION	MUH	FU

2282. PS Oscar W built 1908

2283. PS Marion built 1897

2284. PS Ruby built 1907

2285. PV Pyap built 1896

2286. PS Adelaide built 1866

2291. Sir Samuel Griffith

2292. Text of High Court case

150th Anniversary Murray River Shipping — 2003 05 Aug

No.	Description	MUH	FU
2282	50c PS Oscar W built 1908	1.00▢	0.80▢
2283	50c PS Marion built 1897	1.00▢	0.80▢
2284	50c PS Ruby built 1907	1.00▢	0.80▢
2285	50c PV Pyap built 1896	1.00▢	0.80▢
2286	50c PS Adelaide built 1866	1.00▢	0.80▢
2287	Se-tenant strip x 5 (2282-2286)	5.00▢	5.00▢
2288	$5.00 booklet (10) self adhesive	9.00▢	
	First Day Cover (5) AP		7.00▢

2293. Minature sheet

Centenary High Court (1903-2003) — 2003 02 Sept

No.	Description	MUH	FU
2291	50c Sir Samuel Griffith	1.00▢	0.80▢
2292	$1.45 Text of High Court case	2.50▢	2.50▢
2293	$1.95 Minature sheet	4.00▢	4.00▢
	First Day Cover (2) AP		5.00▢

2289. Christmas tree

2290. International Christmas star

Peace And Goodwill — 2003 05 Aug

No.	Description	MUH	FU
2289	50c Christmas tree	1.00▢	0.70▢
2290	90c International Christmas star	1.60▢	1.60▢
	First Day Cover (2) AP		3.00▢

2294. Ulysses butterfly   2295. Leichhardt's grasshopper   2296. Vedalia ladybird

2297. Green mantid   2298. Emperor gum moth caterpillar   2299. Fiddler beetle

Bugs And Butterflies   2003 24 Sept

No.	Description	MUH	FU
2294	50c Ulysses butterfly	1.00	0.80
2295	50c Leichhardt's grasshopper	1.00	0.80
2296	50c Vedalia ladybird	1.00	0.80
2296a	Se-tenant strip x 3 (2294/2296)	3.50	2.40
2297	50c Green mantid	1.00	0.80
2298	50c Emperor gum moth caterpillar	1.00	0.80
2299	50c Fiddler beetle	1.00	0.80
2299a	Se-tenant strip x 3 (2297/2299)	3.50	2.40
2300	$3.00 Minature Sheet (6)	6.00	6.00
2301	$5.00 booklet (10) self adhesive	9.00	
	Self adhesive type issued in roll x 100		
	First Day Cover (6) AP		7.00

2302. Passing the ball   2303. William Webb Ellis Cup   2304. Try scoring & kicking

Rugby World Cup (10 Oct 2003/22 Nov 2003)   2003 08 Oct

No.	Description	MUH	FU
2302	50c Passing the ball	1.00	0.80
2303	$1.10 International Post William Webb Ellis Cup	2.00	2.00
2304	$1.65 International Post Try scoring & kicking	3.00	3.00
2305	$3.25 Minature sheet (3)	6.00	6.00
	First Day Cover (3) AP		7.00

2305. Minature sheet

Active With Asthma   2003 14 Oct

No.	Description	MUH	FU
2306	50c Active lifestyles	1.00	0.70
2307	$5.00 Sheetlet (10)	9.00	9.50
	First Day Cover (1) AP		2.00

2306. Active lifestyles

⦿RENNIKS

NO.	DESCRIPTION	MUH	FU	NO.	DESCRIPTION	MUH	FU

2308. Mary and baby Jesus

2309. Three Wise Men

2323. Minature sheet

2310. Angel & shepherds

2317. Cheshunt house   2318. Shell necklace

Christmas — 2003 31 Oct

2308	45c Mary and baby Jesus	0.80	0.40
2309	50c Three Wise Men	0.90	0.50
2310	90c Angel & shepherds	1.60	1.50
2311	$9.00 booklet (20 x 45c) self adhesive	16.00	
	First Day Cover (3) AP		3.50

2320. Mountain-Sth-West Tasmania   2321. Mt Wellington & Hobart Town

Tasmania 1804-2004 — 2004 03 Feb

2317	50c Cheshunt house	1.00	0.80
2318	50c Shell necklace	1.00	0.80
2319	Se-tenant pair (2317/2318)	3.50	3.50
2320	$1.00 Mountain-Sth-West Tasmania	2.00	1.60
2321	$1.00 Mt Wellington & Hobart Town	2.00	1.60
2322	Se-tenant pair (2320/2321)	5.00	3.50
2323	$3.00 Minature sheet (4)	6.00	5.00
	First Day Cover (4) AP		6.00

2312. Dame Joan Sutherland as Lucia   2313. Dame Joan Sutherland portrait

Australian Legends Award - Dame Joan sutherland — 2004 23 Jan

2312	50c Dame Joan Sutherland as Lucia	1.00	0.70
2313	50c Dame Joan Sutherland portrait	1.00	0.70
2314	Se-tenant pair (2312/2313)	2.50	2.00
2315	$5.00 Minature sheet (10 x 50c)	8.00	8.00
2316	$5.00 booklet (10 x 50c) self adhesive	8.00	
	First Day Cover (2) AP		3.00

Landmark Bridges — 2004 2 Mar

	2324	50c Ross Bridge, TAS	1.00	0.70
✓	2325	50c Lockyer Creek Bridge, QLD	1.00	0.70
✓	2326	50c Sydney Harbour Bridge, NSW	1.00	0.70
✓	2327	50c Birkenhead Bridge, SA	1.00	0.70
✓	2328	50c Bolte Bridge, VIC	1.00	0.70
	2329	$2.50 Se-tenant strip (5) (2324/2329)	5.50	5.00
	2330	$5.00 booklet (10 x 50c) self adhesive	9.00	
	2331	$10.95 Prestige booklet	19.00	
		Self adhesive type issued in roll x 100		
		First Day Cover (5) AP		4.50

2324. Ross Bridge, TAS

2325. Lockyer Creek Bridge, QLD

2326. Sydney Harbour Bridge, NSW

2327. Birkenhead Bridge, SA

2328. Bolte Bridge, VIC

2332. Southern Cross symbol

2342. Red lacewing

2343. Blue-banded eggfly

Celebrate 2004   **2004 16 Mar**

2332	50c Southern Cross symbol	1.00□	0.70□
	First Day Cover AP		2.00□

2344. Cruiser

2333. Solar energy   2334. Wind power

2336. Hydro electricity   2337. Biomass power

2345. Daintree rainforest

Nature Of Australia - Rainforest Butterflies   **2004 04 May**

2342	5c Red lacewing	0.20□	0.10□
2343	10c Blue-banded eggfly	0.30□	0.20□
2344	75c Cruiser	1.25□	1.25□
2345	$2.00 Daintree rainforest	3.50□	2.50□
	First Day Cover (4) AP		6.00□

Renewable Energy   **2004 30 Mar**

2333	50c Solar energy	1.00□	0.70□
2334	50c Wind power	1.00□	0.70□
2335	Se-tenant pair (2333/2334)	2.00□	2.00□
2336	50c Hydro electricity	1.00□	0.70□
2337	50c Biomass power	1.00□	0.70□
2338	$1.00 Se-tenant pair (2336/2337)	2.00□	2.00□
	Self adhesive issued in roll x 100		
	First Day Cover (4) AP		6.00□

2339. Queen Elizabeth II

1954 Royal Tour Jubilee   **2004 13 Apr**

2339	50c Queen Elizabeth II	1.00□	0.70□
2340	$5.00 Sheet-let (10 x 50c)	8.00□	8.00□
2341	$10.95 Prestige booklet (20 x 50c) self adhesive	15.00□	
	First Day Cover (1) AP		2.50□

2340. QEII Sheet-let

①RENNIKS

NO.	DESCRIPTION	MUH	FU	NO.	DESCRIPTION	MUH	FU

2346. Black Box Flight Recorder 1961	2347. Ultrasound Imaging 1976	2348. Racecam TV Sport Coverage 1979	2349. Baby Safety Capsule 1984	2350. Polymen Banknotes 1988

Australian Innovations — 2004 18 May

No.	Description	MUH	FU
2346	50c Black Box Flight Recorder 1961	1.00	0.70
2347	50c Ultrasound Imaging 1976	1.00	0.70
2348	50c Racecam TV Sport Coverage 1979	1.00	0.70
2349	50c Baby Safety Capsule 1984	1.00	0.70
2350	50c Polymen Banknotes 1988	1.00	0.70
2351	$2.50 Se-tenant strip (5) (2346/2350)	5.50	5.00
2352	$5.00 booklet (10 x 50c) self adhesive	9.00	
	First Day Cover (5) AP		4.50

2353. Dominion Monarch	2354. Awatea	2355. Ormonde	2356. Moreton Bay

Bon Voyage — 2004 1 Jun

No.	Description	MUH	FU
2353	50c Dominion Monarch	1.00	0.70
2354	$1.00 Awatea	1.75	1.75
2355	$1.45 Ormonde	2.50	2.00
2356	$2.00 Moreton Bay	3.50	3.50
2357	$5.00 booklet (10 x50c) self adhesive	9.00	
	First Day Cover (4) AP		8.00

2358. Eureka flag

2359. Peter Lalor

Eureka 1854 - 2004 — 2004 29 Jun

No.	Description	MUH	FU
2358	50c Eureka flag	1.00	0.70
2359	$2.45 Peter Lalor	4.50	4.00
2360	$2.95 Minature sheet	5.50	5.50
2361	$10.95 Prestige booklet (20 x 50c) self adhesive	20.00	
	First Day Cover (Min. sheet) AP		8.00
PNC013	$14.85 Stamp & Coin Cover - Eureka Stockade	30.00	

NO.	DESCRIPTION	MUH	FU

2362 Koala

2363 Little Penguin

2365 Clown anemone fish

2366 Main Beach, Gold Coast Queensland

Australian Impressions 2004 13 July

No.	Description	MUH	FU
2362	$1.00 Koala	1.50□	1.30□
2363	$1.00 Little Penguin	1.50□	1.30□
2364	Se-tenant pair (2362/2363)	3.50□	3.50□
2365	$1.45 Clown anemone fish	3.00□	2.20□
2366	$2.45 Main Beach, Gold Coast Queensland	4.50□	3.50□
	First Day Cover (4) AP		12.50□

2367 Swimming 2368 Athletics

2369 Cycling

Olympic Games Athens 2004 3 August

No.	Description	MUH	FU
2367	0.50c Swimming	0.80□	0.70□
2368	$1.65 International Post-Athletics	3.50□	3.50□
2369	$1.65 International Post-Cycling	3.50□	3.50□
	First Day Cover (3) AP		8.00□

NO.	DESCRIPTION	MUH	FU

2370 Ian Thorpe | 2371 Womens 4x100m Freestyle | 2372 Ian Thorpe 200m Freestyle

2373 Petria Thomas – 100m Butterfly | 2374 Jodie Henry – 100m Freestyle | 2375 Grant Hackett – 1500m F'style

2376 Womens 4x100m medley | 2377 Chantelle Newbery 10m diving | 2378 Sara Carvigan Cycling roadrace

2379 Anna Meares – 500m Cycling time trial | 2380 Mens 400m – Cycling Pursuit team | 2381 Ryan Bayley – Individual Sprint Cycling

2382 Graeme Brown & Stuart O'Grady – Cycling | 383 Ryan Bayley – Cycling Men's Keirin | 2384 James Tomkin & Drew Ginn – Rowing

2385 Suzanne Balogh – Trap shooting | 2386 Mens Hockey Team

OLYMPIC GAMES, ATHENS 2004 - Australian Gold Medalists 2004 16-30 August

No.	Description	MUH	FU
2370	.50c Ian Thorpe – 400m Freestyle swimming	1.00□	1.00□
2371	.50c Womens 4x100m Freestyle swimming relay	1.00□	1.00□
2372	.50c Ian Thorpe – 200m Freestyle swimming	1.00□	1.00□
2373	.50c Petria Thomas – 100m Butterfly swimming	1.00□	1.00□
2374	.50c Jodie Henry – 100m Freestyle swimming	1.00□	1.00□
2375	.50c Grant Hackett – 1500m Freestyle swimming	1.00□	1.00□
2376	.50c Womens 4x100m Swimming medley relay team	1.00□	1.00□
2377	.50c Chantelle Newbery – 10m Platform diving	1.00□	1.00□
2378	.50c Sara Carvigan – Cycling roadrace	1.00□	1.00□
2379	.50c Anna Meares – 500m Cycling time trial	1.00□	1.00□
2380	.50c Mens 400m – Cycling Pursuit Team	1.00□	1.00□
2381	.50c Ryan Bayley – Individual Sprint Cycling	1.00□	1.00□
2382	.50c Graeme Brown & Stuart O'Grady – Cycling Mens Madison	1.00□	1.00□
2383	.50c Ryan Bayley – Cycling Men's Keirin	1.00□	1.00□
2384	.50c James Tomkin & Drew Ginn – Rowing coxless pairs	1.00□	1.00□
2385	.50c Suzanne Balogh – Trap shooting	1.00□	1.00□
2386	.50c Mens Hockey Team	1.00□	1.00□
	First Day Cover – All Gold Medalists (17xcovers) AP		70.00□

NO.	DESCRIPTION	MUH	FU	NO.	DESCRIPTION	MUH	FU

2387 Entrance Beach-Broome W.A.

2388 Mt William National Park – Tas

2389 Potato Point-Bodalla NSW

2390 Point Gibbon – Eyre Peninsula - SA

2398 $5.00 Kangaroo & Map Australia

2399 $5.00 Kangaroo & Map Australia-self adhesive format

International Post – Australian Coast Lines 2004 6 September

2387	$1.20 Entrance Beach-Broome W.A.	2.20☐	2.00☐
2388	$1.80 Mt William National Park – Tas	3.00☐	3.00☐
2389	$2.40 Potato Point-Bodalla NSW	4.00☐	4.00☐
2390	$3.60 Point Gibbon – Eyre Peninsula - SA	6.00☐	6.00☐
	First Day Cover (4) AP		20.00☐

Treasures from Australia Post Archives 2004 7 September

2398	$5.00 Kangaroo & Map Australia	12.00☐	10.00☐
2399	$5.00 Kangaroo & Map Australia-self adhesive format	12.00☐	12.00☐
	First Day Cover (both types) AP		15.00☐

2391 Melbourne-Sandridge 1854   2392 Sydney-Parramatta 1855

2393 Helidon-Queensland 1867   2394 Kalgoorlie-W.A. 1917   2395 Alice Springs N.T. 2004

150th Anniversary of Railways in Australia 2004 7 September

2391	.50c Melbourne-Sandridge 1854	1.00☐	0.70☐
2392	.50c Sydney-Parramatta 1855	1.00☐	0.70☐
2393	.50c Helidon-Queensland 1867	1.00☐	0.70☐
2394	.50c Kalgoorlie-W.A. 1917	1.00☐	0.70☐
2395	.50c Alice Springs N.T. 2004	1.00☐	.70☐
2396	Se-tenant strip x 5 (2391/2395)	6.00☐	4.50☐
2397	$5.00 Booklet (10 x 0.50) self adhesive	9.00☐	
	First Day Cover (5) AP		6.00☐

2400 "Ezzie"

2408 Miniature Sheet

2401 "Tinkerbell"

2403 "Max"   2404 "Bridie" & "Lily"

2407 "Edward"

Cats & Dogs Stamp Collecting Month   2004 21 September

2400	.50c "Ezzie" black/white cat	1.00	0.70
2401	.50c "Tinkerbell" ginger/white kitten	1.00	0.70
2402	Se-tenant pairs (2400/2401)	2.50	1.80
2403	.50c "Max" a Labrador/Retriever pup	1.00	0.70
2404	.50c "Bridie" & "Lily" West Highland Terriers	1.00	0.70
2405	Se-tenant pair (2403/2404)	2.50	1.80
2406	$5.00 Booklet – 10x0.50c self adhesive	10.00	
2407	$1.00 "Edward" Jack Russell Terrier	2.00	1.50
2408	$3.00 Miniature Sheet	6.50	6.00
	First Day Cover (5) AP		6.50
	First Day Cover Mini/Sheet AP		6.50

2419 Three Wise Men

Christmas 2004   2004 1 November

2416	.45c Madonna & Child	0.80	0.60
2417	$9.00 Booklet – 20x.45c self adhesive	15.00	
2418	.50c Angel & Shepherd	1.00	0.70
2419	$1.00 International Post – Three Wise Men	2.00	2.00
	First Day Cover (3) AP		4.00

2416 Madonna & Child

2418 Angel & Shepherd

2411 Troy Bayliss   2412 Daryl Beattie   2413 Garry McCoy

2409 Mick Doohan   2410 Wayne Gardner

Australian Heroes of Grand Prix Motor Cycle Racing   2004 12 October

2409	.50c Mick Doohan (b.1965)	1.00	0.70
2410	.50c Wayne Gardner (b.1959)	1.00	0.70
2411	.50c Troy Bayliss (b.1969)	1.00	0.70
2412	.50c Daryl Beattie (b.1970)	1.00	0.70
2413	.50c Garry McCoy (b.1972)	1.00	0.70
2414	Se-tenant strip x 5 (2409/2413)	5.50	5.50
2415	$5.00 Booklet – 10x0.50c self adhesive	10.00	
	First Day Cover (5) AP		6.50

NO.	DESCRIPTION	MUH	FU	NO.	DESCRIPTION	MUH	FU

2423 Prue Acton

2424 Jenny Bannister

2420 Tennis Match early 1900's — 2421 picturing a modern match

Australian Open Tennis Championship – 100 Years   2005 11 January

2420	.50c Tennis Match early 1900's	1.00☐	0.80☐
2421	International Post picturing a modern match	3.00☐	3.00☐
2422	$10.95 Prestige booklet	18.00☐	
	First Day Cover (2) AP		6.00☐
PNC014	$12.95 Stamp & Coin Cover - Australian Tennis Open	30.00☐	

2427 Collette Dinnigan

2428 Akira Isogawa

2441 Sir Donald Bradman – Cap   2442 Lionel Rose – boxing gloves

2431 Joe Saba

2432 Carla Zampatti

2444 Marjorie Jackson – running spikes   2445 Phar Lap's – racing silks

Sports Treasures   2005 8 March

2441	.50c Sir Donald Bradman – Cap	1.00☐	0.70☐
2442	.50c Lionel Rose – boxing gloves	1.00☐	.70☐
2443	Se-tenant pair (2441/2442)	2.50☐	1.80☐
2444	$1.00 Marjorie Jackson – running spikes	2.00☐	1.40☐
2445	$1.00 Phar Lap's – racing silks	2.00☐	1.40☐
2446	Se-tenant pair (2444/2445)	4.50☐	3.50☐
	First Day Cover (4) AP		6.50☐

Australian Legends – Fashion Designers   2005 21 January

2423	.50c Prue Acton	1.00☐	0.70☐
2424	.50c Jenny Bannister	1.00☐	0.70☐
2425	Se-tenant pair (2423/2424)	2.20☐	1.70☐
2426	$5.00 Booklet of 10x0.50 (2423/2424) self adhesive	9.00☐	
2427	.50c Collette Dinnigan	1.00☐	0.70☐
2428	.50c Akira Isogawa	1.00☐	0.70☐
2429	Se-tenant pair (2427/2428)	2.20☐	1.70☐
2430	$5.00 Booklet of 10x0.50c (2427/2428) self adhesive	9.00☐	
2431	.50c Joe Saba	1.00☐	0.70☐
2432	.50c Carla Zampatti	1.00☐	0.70☐
2433	Se-tenant pair (2431/2432)	2.20☐	1.70☐
2434	$5.00 Booklet of 10x0.50c (2431/2433) self adhesive	9.00☐	
	First Day Cover (6) AP		6.50☐

Australian Parrots   2005 8 February

2435	.50c Princess Parrot	1.00☐	0.70☐
2436	.50c Rainbow Lorikeet	1.00☐	0.70☐
2437	.50c Green Rosella	1.00☐	0.70☐
2438	.50c Red-capped Parrot	1.00☐	0.70☐
2439	.50c Purple-crowned Lorikeet	1.00☐	0.70☐
2440	Se-tenant strip (5) (2435/2439)	5.50☐	4.50☐
	Also issued in roll of 100 self adhesive		
	First Day Cover (5) AP		6.50☐

2447 Bumble Bee   2449 Roses   2451 Party presents   2453 Kangaroos   2454 Wedding

2448 Bumble Bee self adhesive   2450 Roses self adhesive   2452 Party presents self adhesive   2455 Wedding self adhesive

2459 Koala   2461 Beach scene   2462 Sydney Opera House   2460 Koala self adhesive

2463 Booklet (Nos:2461/2462) self adhesive   2457 Wedding   2458 Wedding self adhesive

Marking the Occasion   2005   22 March

No.	Description	MUH	FU
2447	.50c Bumble Bee	1.00☐	0.70☐
2448	$10.95 Special Occasion Booklet (20x.50c) with personalised tabs-self adhesive	18.00☐	
2449	.50c Roses	1.00☐	0.70☐
2450	$10.95 Special Occasion Booklet (20x.50c) with personalised tabs-self adhesive	18.00☐	
2451	.50c Party presents	1.00☐	0.70☐
2452	$10.95 Special Occasion Booklet (20x.50c) with personalised tabs-self adhesive type–issued	18.00☐	
2453	.50c Kangaroos (also issued in self-adhesive format)	1.00☐	0.70☐
2454	.50c Wedding	1.00☐	0.70☐
2455	$10.95 Special Occasion Booklet (20x.50c) with personalised tabs-self adhesive	16.00☐	
2456	Se-tenant strip (5) (2447, 2449, 2451, 2453, 2454)	6.00☐	4.50☐
2457	$1.00 Wedding (non standard)	1.50☐	1.40☐
2458	$10.95 Special Occasion Booklet (20x$1) with personalised tabs self adhesive	30.00☐	
2459	$1.10 International Post-Koala	2.00☐	1.70☐
2460	$11.00 Special Occasion Booklet with (10x$1.10) personalized tabs self adhesive	20.00☐	
2461	$1.20 International Post – Beach scene	2.30☐	2.30☐
2462	$1.80 International Post – Sydney Opera House	3.50☐	3.50☐
2463	$15.00 International Post – Special Occasion booklet (Nos:2461/2462) self adhesive type	25.00☐	
	First Day Cover (9) 2 x AP Covers		20.00☐

2464 Greater Blue Mountains Area NSW   2465 Blenheim Place England

2467 Wet Tropics Queensland   2468 Stonehenge England

2470 Purnululu National Park WA   2471 Heart of Neolithic Orkney

2473 Uluru-Kata Tjuta National Park NT   2474 Hadrian's Wall England

World Heritage – Australia/United Kingdom Joint Issue   2005 21 April

2464	.50c Greater Blue Mountains Area NSW	1.00☐	0.70☐
2465	.50c Blenheim Place England	1.00☐	0.70☐
2466	Se-tenant pair (2464/2465)	2.50☐	1.80☐
2467	.50c Wet Tropics Queensland	1.00☐	0.70☐
2468	.50c Stonehenge England	1.00☐	0.70☐
2469	Se-tenant pair (2467/2468)	2.50☐	1.80☐
2470	$1.00 Purnululu National Park WA	2.00☐	1.40☐
2471	$1.00 Heart of Neolithic Orkney	2.00☐	1.40☐
2472	Se-tenant pair (2470/2471)	4.50☐	3.20☐
2473	$1.80 Uluru-kata Tjuta National Park NT	3.00☐	3.00☐
2474	$1.80 Hadrian's Wall England	3.00☐	3.00☐
2475	Se-tenant pair (2473/2474)	7.50☐	7.50☐
	First Day Covers (UK and Aust Stamp x 8) x 2 Covers AP	16.00☐	
PNC015	$39.60 Stamp & Coin Cover - World Heritage Sites	110.00	☐

2476 Tribrachidium   2477 Dickinsonia

2478 Spriggina   2479 Kimberella   2480 Inaria

Creatures of the Slime   2005 21 April

2476	.50c Tribrachidium	1.00☐	0.70☐
2477	.50c Dickinsonia	1.00☐	0.70☐
2478	.50c Spriggina	1.00☐	0.70☐
2479	.50c Kimberella	1.00☐	0.70☐
2480	.50c Inaria	1.00☐	0.70☐
2481	Se-tenant strip (5) (2476/2480)	6.00☐	4.50☐
2482	$1.00 Charnodiscus	2.00☐	1.40☐
2483	Miniature sheet (170mm x 210mm)- Overlarge	6.00☐	6.00☐
	First Day Cover (6) AP		8.00☐
	First Day Cover Miniature Sheet (170mmx86.8m)		8.00☐

2484 Rotary symbol

Centenary of Rotary International   2005 21 April

2484	.50c Rotary symbol	1.00☐	0.70☐
	$5.00 Booklet of (10x.50c) – self adhesive	10.00☐	
	First Day Cover AP		2.50☐

2486 Obverse image of first coin

2487 Reverse of coin

2488 Miniature Sheet

150TH Anniversary of the First Australian Coin   2005 21 April

2486	.50c Obverse image of first coin	1.00	0.70
2487	$2.45 Reverse of coin	5.00	4.40
2488	$2.95 Miniature Sheet	6.00	5.50
	First Day Cover Miniature Sheet	6.50	

2489 Photographic image of Queen

Queen's Birthday   2005 10 May

2489	.50c Photographic image of Queen	1.00	0.70
2490	$10.95 Prestiage booklet	19.00	
	First Day Cover AP		2.50
PNC016	$14.95 Stamp & Coin Cover - Melbourne Baton Relay 28/10/05		45.00

2502 Vineyard   2503 Grapes ready for picking

2505 Harvesting grapes   2506 Wine Casks

2508 Ready for Drinking

Australian Wine   2005 19 July

2502	.50c Vineyard	1.00	0.70
2503	.50c Grapes ready for picking	1.00	0.70
2504	Se-tenant pair (2502/2503)	2.50	1.80
2505	$1.00 Harvesting grapes	2.00	1.30
2506	$1.00 Wine Casks	2.00	1.30
2507	Se-tenant pair (2505/2506)	4.50	3.00
2508	$1.45 Ready for drinking	2.80	2.50
2509	$5.00 Booklet of (10x.50c) self adhesive	9.00	
	First Day Cover (5) AP		8.00

2491 Superb Lyrebird   2492 Laughing Kookaburra   2493 Koala   2494 Red Kangaroo

International Post – Australia's Bush Wildlife   2005 7 June

2491	$1.00 Superb Lyrebird	2.00	2.00
2492	$1.10 Laughing Kookaburra	2.20	2.20
2493	$1.20 Koala	2.40	2.40
2494	$1.80 Red Kangaroo	3.50	3.50
	Nos 2492/2494 also issued in self adhesive format		
	First Day Cover (4) AP		12.00

| 2495 Sturt's Desert Pea | 2496 Coarse-leaved Mallee | 2497 Common Fringe Lily | 2498 Swamp Daisy |

Australian Wildflowers — 2005 5 July

No.	Description	MUH	FU
2495	.50c Sturt's Desert Pea	1.00☐	0.70☐
2496	.50c Coarse-leaved Mallee	1.00☐	0.70☐
2497	.50c Common Fringe Lily	1.00☐	0.70☐
2498	.50c Swamp Daisy	1.00☐	0.70☐
2499	Se-tenant strip (2495/2498)	4.50☐	4.00☐
2500	$5.00 Booklet (10x.50c) self adhesive	9.00☐	
2501	$10.00 Booklet (10x.50c) self adhesive	17.50☐	
	First Day Dover (4) AP		4.00☐

| 2510 Snow Gum | 2511 Wollemi Pine | 2512 Boab Tree |

| 2513 Karri Tree | 2514 Moreton Bay Fig |

Australian Native Trees — 2005 8 August

No.	Description	MUH	FU
2510	.50c Snow Gum	1.00☐	0.70☐
2511	.50c Wollemi Pine	1.00☐	0.70☐
2512	.50c Boab Tree	1.00☐	0.70☐
2513	.50c Karri Tree	1.00☐	0.70☐
2514	.50c Moreton Bay Fig	1.00☐	0.70☐
2515	Se-tenant strip (2510/2514)	5.50☐	4.50☐
	Also issued self-adhesive format in roll x 100		
	First Day Cover (5) AP		6.00☐

Treasures from Australia Post Archives — 2005 6 September

No.	Description	MUH	FU
2516	$5.00 Copy of NSW 20/-stamp	10.00☐	9.00☐
	Stamp size 105mx70m		
	First Day Cover AP		12.00☐

2516 Copy of NSW 20/-stamp

NO.	DESCRIPTION	MUH	FU	NO.	DESCRIPTION	MUH	FU

2517 Christmas tree (card rate)   2518 Australiana

Marking the Occasion   **2005 6 September**

2517	.45c Christmas tree (card rate)	0.90☐	0.40☐
2518	.50c Australiana	1.00☐	0.50☐
	First Day Cover (2) AP		2.50☐

519 Chloe the Chicken   2520 Lucy the Lamb

2521 Gilbert the Goat   2522 Ralph the Pig   2523 Abigail the Cow

2525 Harry the Horse

Down on the Farm   **2005 4 October**

2519	.50c Chloe the Chicken	1.00☐	.70☐
2520	.50c Lucy the Lamb	1.00☐	.70☐
2521	.50c Gilbert the Goat	1.00☐	.70☐
2522	.50c Ralph the Pig	1.00☐	.70☐
2523	.50c Abigail the Cow	1.00☐	.70☐
2524	Se-tenant strip (2519/2523)	5.50☐	4.00☐
2525	$1.00 Harry the Horse	2.00☐	1.50☐
2526	$5.00 Booklet (10x.50c) self adhesive	10.00☐	
2527	$10.00 Booklet (20x.50c) self adhesive	17.00☐	
2528	$3.50 Miniature Sheet (6)	7.00☐	6.00☐
	First Day Cover – Miniature Sheet (6) AP		7.50☐

2528 Miniature Sheet

2530 Adoring Angel

2529 Madonna & Child

2541 .50c Romance – red rose

Christmas 2005   2005 4 October

2529	.45c Madonna & Child	0.90☐	0.40☐
2530	$1.00 International Post – Adoring Angel	2.00☐	2.00☐
2531	$9.00 Booklet (20x.45c) self adhesive	16.00☐	
	First Day Cover (2) AP		3.50☐

2532
Commonwealth Games Logo

2542 Booklet (10x50c) self adhesive

Roses   2006 27 January

2541	.50c Romance – red rose	1.00☐	0.70☐
2542	$5.00 Booklet (10x50c) self adhesive	9.00☐	
	First Day Cover AP		2.50☐

Melbourne 2006 Commonwealth Games Part 1   2006 12 January

2532	.50c Commonwealth Games Logo	1.00☐	0.70☐
	Also issued in self adhesive format		
	First Day Cover AP		2.50☐

2532A	Imperforate block x 10 included in Sports of the		
	Games Coin & Stamp Prestige Booklet issued		
	15-26 March 2006		
PNC017	$14.95 Stamp & Coin Cover - 2006.		
	- Commonwealth Nations	25.00☐	

2533 Mrs Norm Everage 1969   2534 Mrs Edna Everage 1973   2535 Dame Edna Everage 1982   2536 Dame Edna Everage 2004   2537 Barry Humphries

2540 Booklet (10x.50c) Set 2 self adhesive

Australian Legends – Dame Edna Everage   2006 20 January

2533	50c Mrs Norm Everage 1969	1.00☐	0.70☐
2534	.50c Mrs Edna Everage 1973	1.00☐	0.70☐
2535	.50c Dame Edna Everage 1982	1.00☐	0.70☐
2536	.50c Dame Edna Everage 2004	1.00☐	0.70☐
2537	.50c Barry Humphries	1.00☐	0.70☐
2538	Se-tenant strip (2533/2538)	5.50☐	4.50☐
2539	$5.00 Booklet (10x.50c) Set 1 self adhesive	9.00☐	
2540	$5.00 Booklet (10x.50c) Set 2 self adhesive	9.00☐	
	First Day Cover (5) AP		6.50☐
PNC019	$14.95 Stamp & Coin Cover - Dame Edna Everage	25.00☐	

2543 Pincushion Hakea 　　　　2544 Donkey Orchid

2545 Mangles Kangaroo Paw

2546 Waratah

2547 Miniature Sheet

Australian Wildflowers – Definitive Issue　　2006 7 February

2543	$1.00 Pincushion Hakea	2.00□	1.20□
2544	$2.00 Donkey Orchid	4.00□	1.60□
2545	$5.00 Mangles Kangaroo Paw	9.00□	4.00□
2546	$10.00 Waratah	18.00□	12.00□
2547	$10.00 Miniature Sheet	22.00□	15.00□
	First Day Cover (4xstamps) AP		30.00□
	First Day Cover – Miniature Sheet AP		25.00□

2548 Dale Begg-Smith – Mens Moguls

XX WINTER OLYMPICS, TORINO, ITALY　　2006 21 February
Australian Gold Medal Winner

2548	.50c Dale Begg-Smith – Mens Moguls	1.50□	1.30□
	Issued in sheetlets x 10		
	No First Day Covers issued by AP		

ROYAL VISIT TO AUSTRALIA　　2006   28 February
By Queen Elizabeth II

| | $15.95 Prestige Booklet including 2339, 2 x se-tenant pairs of 391/392 and 588/589 and .50c coin | 25.00□ | |

2550 Runner 　　　　2551 Cyclist

2552 Basketball

2553 Miniature Sheet

2554 Booklet (10x50c) self adhesive

Melbourne 2006 Commonwealth Games Part II　2006 1 March

2550	.50c Runner	1.00□	0.70□
2551	$1.20 International Post – cyclist	2.40□	2.40□
2552	$1.80 International Post – basketball	3.50□	3.50□
2553	$3.50 Miniature Sheet	5.30□	5.30□
2554	$5.00 Booklet (10x50c) self adhesive	9.00□	
	First Day Cover (4) AP		7.50□
	First Day Cover Miniature Sheet AP		7.50□

2561 Melbourne Tram

2562 Ceremonial Fish

2563 Stage

2564 Queen Elizabeth

2565 Ceremony

2567 Anna Meares –
Womens 500m Time
Trial

2568 Equality –
Humanity - Destiny

2569 Stephanie Rice –
Womens 200m
Individual Medley

2570 Destiny -
Equality - Humanity

2571 Ben Kersten –
Mens 100m time trial

XVII COMMONWEALTH GAMES MELBOURNE   2006 15 March

OPENING CEREMONY – WEDNESDAY 15 MARCH 2006
Printed in Sheetlet Format Sheetlet No. 1 (180mx200m) only

		MUH	FU
2561	.50c Melbourne Tram	1.00☐	1.00☐
2562	.50c Ceremonial Fish	1.00☐	1.00☐
2563	.50c Stage	1.00☐	1.00☐
2564	.50c Queen Elizabeth	1.00☐	1.00☐
2565	.50c Ceremony	1.00☐	1.00☐
2566	$2.50 Sheetlet No. 1 only	6.00☐	6.00☐

First Day Covers AP each stamp (5)   2.50☐

AUSTRALIAN CHAMPIONS – THURSDAY 16 MARCH
Printed in Sheetlet Format No. 2 (180mx200m) only

		MUH	FU
2567	.50c Anna Meares – Womens 500m Time Trial	1.00☐	1.00☐
2568	.50c Equality – Humanity - Destiny	1.00☐	1.00☐
2569	.50c Stephanie Rice – Womens 200m Individual Medley	1.00☐	1.00☐
2570	.50c Destiny - Equality - Humanity	1.00☐	1.00☐
2571	.50c Ben Kersten – Mens 100m time trial	1.00☐	1.00☐
2572	$2.50 Sheetlet No. 2 only	6.00☐	6.00☐

First Day Covers AP – stamps only (3) each   2.50☐

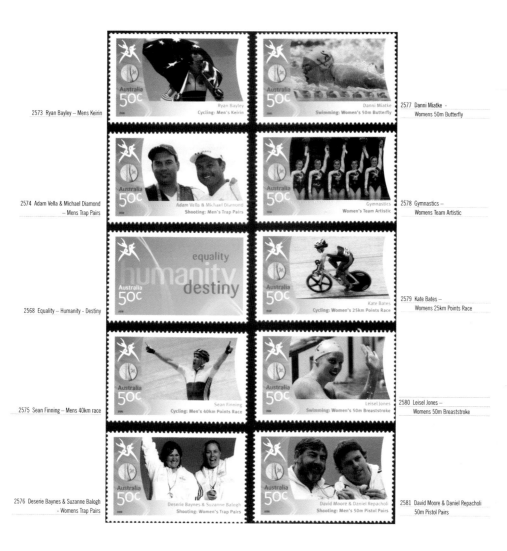

2573 Ryan Bayley – Mens Keirin

2577 Danni Miatke -
Womens 50m Butterfly

2574 Adam Vella & Michael Diamond
– Mens Trap Pairs

2578 Gymnastics –
Womens Team Artistic

2568 Equality – Humanity - Destiny

2579 Kate Bates –
Womens 25km Points Race

2575 Sean Finning – Mens 40km race

2580 Leisel Jones –
Womens 50m Breaststroke

2576 Deserie Baynes & Suzanne Balogh
– Womens Trap Pairs

2581 David Moore & Daniel Repacholi
50m Pistol Pairs

AUSTRALIAN CHAMPIONS – FRIDAY 17 MARCH
Printed in Sheetlet Format No. 3 (180mx200m) Only

No.	Description	MUH	FU
2573	.50c Ryan Bayley – Mens Keirin	1.00☐	1.00☐
2574	.50c Adam Vella & Michael Diamond – Mens Trap Pairs	1.00☐	1.00☐
2568	.50c Equality – Humanity - Destiny	1.00☐	1.00☐
2575	.50c Sean Finning – Mens 40km race	1.00☐	1.00☐
2576	.50c Deserie Baynes & Suzanne Balogh - Womens Trap Pairs	1.00☐	1.00☐
2577	.50c Danni Miatke - Womens 50m Butterfly	1.00☐	1.00☐
2578	.50c Gymnastics – Womens Team Artistic	1.00☐	1.00☐
2579	.50c Kate Bates – Womens 25km Points Race	1.00☐	1.00☐
2580	.50c Leisel Jones – Womens 50m Breaststroke	1.00☐	1.00☐
2581	.50c David Moore & Daniel Repacholi 50m Pistol Pairs	1.00☐	1.00☐
2582	$5.00 Sheetlet No. 3 only	12.00☐	10.00☐

First Day Covers AP – stamps only (9) each   2.50☐

2583 Brad Kahlefeldt
     – Mens Triathlon

2584 Libby Lenton
     – 100m Freestyle

2585 Josh Jefferis
     – Gymnastics Mens Artistic

2586 Equality – Humanity
     - Destiny

2587 Emma Snowsill
     – Womens Triathlon

2597 Katie Mactier
     - 3000m Individual Pursuit

2598 Russell Mark &
     Craig Trembath
     - Double Trap Pairs

2599 Jessicah Schipper
     - 100m Butterfly

2600 Kerryn McCann
     - Womens Marathon

2601 Lalita Yauhleuskaya &
     Dina Aspandiyarova
     - Air Pistol Pairs

AUSTRALIAN CHAMPIONS – SATURDAY 18 MARCH
Printed in Sheetlet Format No. 4 (180mx200m) Only

			MUH	FU
2583	.50c	Brad Kahlefeldt – Mens Triathlon	1.00☐	1.00☐
2584	.50c	Libby Lenton – 100m Freestyle	1.00☐	1.00☐
2585	.50c	Josh Jefferis – Gymnastics Mens Artistic	1.00☐	1.00☐
2586	50c	Equality – Humanity - Destiny	1.00☐	1.00☐
2587	.50c	Emma Snowsill – Womens Triathlon	1.00☐	1.00☐
2581	$2.50	Sheetlet No. 4 only	6.00☐	
		First Day Covers – AP stamps only (4) each		2.50☐

AUSTRALIAN CHAMPIONS - SUNDAY 19 MARCH
Printed in Sheetlet Format No. 6 (180mx200m) Only

			MUH	FU
2597	.50c	Katie Mactier - 3000m Individual Pursuit	1.00☐	1.00☐
2598	.50c	Russell Mark & Craig Trembath - Double Trap Pairs	1.00☐	1.00☐
2599	.50c	Jessicah Schipper - 100m Butterfly	1.00☐	1.00☐
2600	.50c	Kerryn McCann - Womens Marathon	1.00☐	1.00☐
2601	.50c	Lalita Yauhleuskaya & Dina Aspandiyarova - Air Pistol Pairs	1.00☐	1.00☐
2602	$2.50	Sheetlet No. 6 only	6.00☐	
		First Day Covers AP (5) each		2.50☐

2588 Leisel Jones
      – Womens 200m Breaststroke

2589 Ryan Bayley - Mens Sprint

2568 Equality – Humanity – Destiny

2590 Matthew Cowdrey – 50m Freestyle

2591 Chloe Sims
      – Gymnastics – Womens Artistic

2570 Destiny – Equality – Humanity

2592 Humanity – Destiny – Equality

2593 Sophie Edington – 100m backstroke

2594 Womens 200m Freestyle Relay

2595 Ben Turner – Weightlifting 69kg

AUSTRALIAN CHAMPIONS - SATURDAY 18 MARCH
Printed in Sheetlet Format No. 5 (180mx200m) Only

2588	.50c Leisel Jones – Womens 200m Breaststroke	1.00☐	1.00☐
2589	.50c Ryan Bayley - Mens Sprint	1.00☐	1.00☐
2568	.50c Equality – Humanity – Destiny	1.00☐	1.00☐
2590	.50c Matthew Cowdrey – 50m Freestyle	1.00☐	1.00☐
2591	.50c Chloe Sims – Gymnastics – Womens Artistic	1.00☐	1.00☐
2570	.50c Destiny – Equality – Humanity	1.00☐	1.00☐
2592	.50c Humanity – Destiny – Equality	1.00☐	1.00☐
2593	.50c Sophie Edington – 100m backstroke	1.00☐	1.00☐
2594	.50c Womens 200m Freestyle Relay	1.00☐	1.00☐
2595	.50c Ben Turner – Weightlifting 69kg	1.00☐	1.00☐
2596	$5.00 Sheetlet No. 5 only	15.00☐	

First Day Covers AP – stamps only (7) each	2.50☐
First Day Cover AP - stamp slogans on (3) each	2.50☐

⚙ RENNIKS

NO.	DESCRIPTION	MUH	FU	NO.	DESCRIPTION	MUH	FU

2603 Lauryn Mark &
   Natalia Rahman
   - Skeet Pairs

2619 Alex Karapetyan
   - Weightlifting 94kgs

2604 Jane Sevill – 20km Walk

2620 Jessicah Schipper
   - 200m Butterfly

2605 Libby Lenton
   - 50m Freestyle

2621 Nathan O'Neill
   - Individual Time Trial

2606 Nathan Deakes
   – 20km Walk

2568 Equality
   – Humanity – Destiny

2607 Lisa McIntosh
   - Womens 100m EAD

2622 Lalita Yauhleuskaya
   - 25m Pistol

AUSTRALIAN CHAMPIONS - MONDAY 20 MARCH
Printed in Sheetlet Format No. 7 (180mx200m) Only

2603	.50c Lauryn Mark & Natalia Rahman - Skeet Pairs	1.00☐	1.00☐
2604	.50c Jane Sevill – 20km Walk	1.00☐	1.00☐
2605	.50c Libby Lenton - 50m Freestyle	1.00☐	1.00☐
2606	.50c Nathan Deakes – 20km Walk	1.00☐	1.00☐
2607	.50c Lisa McIntosh - Womens 100m EAD	1.00☐	1.00☐
2608	$2.50 Sheetlet No. 7 only	6.00☐	
	First Day Covers AP (5) each		2.50☐

AUSTRALIAN CHAMPIONS - TUESDAY 21 MARCH
Printed in Sheetlet Format No. 9 (180mx200m) Only

2619	.50c Alex Karapetyan - Weightlifting 94kgs	1.00☐	1.00☐
2620	.50c Jessicah Schipper - 200m Butterfly	1.00☐	1.00☐
2621	.50c Nathan O'Neill - Individual Time Trial	1.00☐	1.00☐
2568	.50c Equality – Humanity – Destiny	1.00☐	1.00☐
2622	.50c Lalita Yauhleuskaya - 25m Pistol	1.00☐	1.00☐
2623	$2.50 Sheetlet No. 9 only	6.00☐	
	First Day Covers AP stamp only (4) each		2.50☐

2609 Leisel Jones - 100m Breaststroke

2610 Lawn Bowls Triples Team

2568 Equality – Humanity – Destiny

2611 Sophie Edington – 50m Breaststroke

2612 Matthew Cowdrey
 - 100m Freestyle

2613 Brooke Krueger-Billett
 - Hammer Throw

2614 Josh Jefferis - Mens Rings

2615 Natalie Grinham - Singles Squash

2616 Womens 4x100m Freestyle

2617 Joanna Fargus
 - 200m Backstroke

AUSTRALIAN CHAMPIONS - MONDAY 20 MARCH
Printed in Sheetlet Format No. 8 (180mx200m) Only

No.	Description	MUH	FU
2609	.50c Leisel Jones - 100m Breaststroke	1.00☐	1.00☐
2610	.50c Lawn Bowls Triples Team	1.00☐	1.00☐
2568	.50c Equality – Humanity – Destiny	1.00☐	1.00☐
2611	.50c Sophie Edington – 50m Breaststroke	1.00☐	1.00☐
2612	.50c Matthew Cowdrey - 100m Freestyle	1.00☐	1.00☐
2613	.50c Brooke Krueger-Billett - Hammer Throw	1.00☐	1.00☐
2614	.50c Josh Jefferis - Mens Rings	1.00☐	1.00☐
2615	.50c Natalie Grinham - Singles Squash	1.00☐	1.00☐
2616	.50c Womens 4x100m Freestyle	1.00☐	1.00☐
2617	.50c Joanna Fargus - 200m Backstroke	1.00☐	1.00☐
2618	$5.00 Sheetlet No. 8 only	15.00☐	
	First Day Covers AP stamp only (9) each		2.50☐

RENNIKS

NO.	DESCRIPTION	MUH	FU	NO.	DESCRIPTION	MUH	FU

2624 Hollie Dykes - Womens Gymnastics

2570 Destiny – Equality – Humanity

2625 Mens 4x100m Medley

2592 Humanity – Destiny – Equality

2568 Equality – Humanity – Destiny

2628 Stephanie Rice - 400m Medley

2626 Oenone Wood - Individual Time Trial

2629 Damian Istria - Horizontal Bar

2627 Womens 4x100m Medley

2630 Deborah Lovel - Weightlifting 75kg

AUSTRALIAN CHAMPIONS - TUESDAY 21 MARCH
Printed in Sheetlet Format No. 10 (180mx200m) Only

No.	Description	MUH	FU
2624	.50c Hollie Dykes - Womens Gymnastics	1.00☐	1.00☐
2625	.50c Mens 4x100m Medley	1.00☐	1.00☐
2568	.50c Equality – Humanity – Destiny	1.00☐	1.00☐
2626	.50c Oenone Wood - Individual Time Trial	1.00☐	1.00☐
2627	.50c Womens 4x100m Medley	1.00☐	1.00☐
2570	.50c Destiny – Equality – Humanity	1.00☐	1.00☐
2592	.50c Humanity – Destiny – Equality	1.00☐	1.00☐
2628	.50c Stephanie Rice - 400m Medley	1.00☐	1.00☐
2629	.50c Damian Istria - Horizontal Bar	1.00☐	1.00☐
2630	.50c Deborah Lovel - Weightlifting 75kg	1.00☐	1.00☐
2631	$5.00 Sheetlet No. 10 only	15.00☐	

First Day Covers AP stamp only (7) each		2.50☐

AUSTRALIAN CHAMPIONS - WEDNESDAY 22 MARCH
Printed in Sheetlet Format No. 11 (180mx200m) Only

2632	.50c Chantelle Newbery & Loudy Tourky		
	- Synchronised Diving	1.00☐	1.00☐
2633	.50c John Steffensen - 400 metres	1.00☐	1.00☐
2634	.50c Bree Cole & Sharleen Stratton		
	- Synchronised Diving	1.00☐	1.00☐
2568	.50c Equality – Humanity – Destiny	1.00☐	1.00☐
2635	.50c Lynsey Armitage & Karen Murphy		
	- Lawn Bowls Pairs	1.00☐	1.00☐
2636	$2.50 Sheetlet No. 11 only	6.00☐	
	First Day Covers AP stamps only (4) each		2.50☐

AUSTRALIAN CHAMPIONS - THURSDAY 23 MARCH
Printed in Sheetlet Format No. 12 (180mx200m) Only

2637	.50c Heath Francis - 200 metres	1.00☐	1.00☐
2638	.50c Jana Pittman - 400m Hurdles	1.00☐	1.00☐
2639	.50c Lalita Yauhleuskaya - 10m Air Pistol	1.00☐	1.00☐
2568	.50c Equality – Humanity – Destiny	1.00☐	1.00☐
2640	.50c Scott Martin - Mens Discus	1.00☐	1.00☐
2641	.50c Loudy Tourky - 10m Platform Diving	1.00☐	1.00☐
2570	.50c Destiny – Equality – Humanity	1.00☐	1.00☐
2642	.50c Womens Basketball	1.00☐	
2643	.50c Chris Rae - Weightlifting 105kg	1.00☐	1.00☐
2644	.50c Bruce Scott - Open Full Bore	1.00☐	1.00☐
2645	$5.00 Sheetlet No. 12 only	15.00☐	
	First Day Covers AP stamps only (8) each		2.50☐

2646 Nathan Deakes - 50km Walk

2570 Destiny – Equality – Humanity

2647 Bronwyn Thompson - Long Jump

2592 Humanity – Destiny – Equality

2568 Equality – Humanity - Destiny

2650 Stuart Rendell – Hammer Throw

2648 Robert Newbery & Mathew Helm
- Synchronised 10m Platform

2651 Kelvin Kerkow
- Singles Lawn Bowls

2649 Steven Hooker - Pole Vault

2652 Mens Basketball

AUSTRALIAN CHAMPIONS - FRIDAY 24 MARCH 2006
Printed in Sheetlet Format No. 13 (180mx200m) Only

NO.	DESCRIPTION	MUH	FU
2646	.50c Nathan Deakes - 50km Walk	1.00☐	1.00☐
2647	.50c Bronwyn Thompson - Long Jump	1.00☐	1.00☐
2568	.50c Equality – Humanity - Destiny	1.00☐	1.00☐
2648	.50c Robert Newbery & Mathew Helm	1.00☐	1.00☐
	- Synchronised 10m Platform		
2649	.50c Steven Hooker - Pole Vault	1.00☐	1.00☐
2570	.50c Destiny – Equality – Humanity	1.00☐	1.00☐
2592	.50c Humanity – Destiny – Equality	1.00☐	1.00☐
2650	.50c Stuart Rendell – Hammer Throw	1.00☐	1.00☐
2651	.50c Kelvin Kerkow - Singles Lawn Bowls	1.00☐	1.00☐
2652	.50c Mens Basketball	1.00☐	1.00☐
2653	$5.00 Sheetlet No. 13 only	15.00☐	
	First Day Covers AP stamps only (7) each		2.50☐

2654 Womens 4x100m Relay

2655 Kym Howe - Pole Vault

2568 Equalty – Humanity – Destiny

2656 Womens Hockey

2657 Matthew Helm
   - 10m Platform Diving

2570 Destiny – Equality – Humanity

2592 Humanity – Destiny – Equality

2658 Mens 4x400m Athletics Relay

2659 Bradley Pitt - Boxing 91kg

2660 Jarrod Fletcher - Boxing 75kg

AUSTRALIAN CHAMPIONS - SATURDAY 25 MARCH 2006
Printed in Sheetlet Format No. 14 (180mx200m) Only

No.	Description	MUH	FU
2654	.50c Womens 4x100m Relay	1.00☐	1.00☐
2655	.50c Kym Howe - Pole Vault	1.00☐	1.00☐
2568	.50c Equalty – Humanity – Destiny	1.00☐	1.00☐
2656	.50c Womens Hockey	1.00☐	1.00☐
2657	.50c Matthew Helm - 10m Platform Diving	1.00☐	1.00☐
2570	.50c Destiny – Equality – Humanity	1.00☐	1.00☐
2592	.50c Humanity – Destiny – Equality	1.00☐	1.00☐
2658	.50c Mens 4x400m Athletics Relay	1.00☐	1.00☐
2659	.50c Bradley Pitt - Boxing 91kg	1.00☐	1.00☐
2660	.50c Jarrod Fletcher - Boxing 75kg	1.00☐	1.00☐
2661	$5.00 Sheetlet No. 14 only	15.00☐	

	First Day Covers AP stamps only (7) each	2.50☐

2662 Natalie Bates
- Womens Road Race

2663 Natalie Grinham & Joe Kneipp
- Squash Mixed Doubles

2664 Mens Hockey

2665 Rachael Grinham &
Natalie Grinham
- Squash Doubles

2666 Matthew Hayman
- Cycling Road Race

2668 Trapeze

2669 Dancers

2670 Indian Dancers

2671 Hand over to Delhi

2672 Fireworks

AUSTRALIAN CHAMPIONS - SUNDAY 26 MARCH 2006
Printed in Sheetlet Format No. 15 (180mx200m) Only

		MUH	FU
2662	.50c Natalie Bates - Womens Road Race	1.00☐	1.00☐
2663	.50c Natalie Grinham & Joe Kneipp		
	- Squash Mixed Doubles	1.00☐	1.00☐
2664	.50c Mens Hockey	1.00☐	1.00☐
2665	.50c Rachael Grinham & Natalie Grinham		
	- Squash Doubles	1.00☐	1.00☐
2666	.50c Matthew Hayman - Cycling Road Race	1.00☐	1.00☐
2667	$2.50 Sheetlet No 15 only	6.00☐	
	First Day Covers AP stamps only (5) each		2.50☐

CLOSING CEREMONY SUNDAY 26 MARCH 2006
Printed in Sheetlet Format No. 16 (180mx200m) Only

		MUH	FU
2668	.50c Trapeze	1.00☐	1.00☐
2669	.50c Dancers	1.00☐	1.00☐
2670	.50c Indian Dancers	1.00☐	1.00☐
2671	.50c Hand over to Delhi	1.00☐	1.00☐
2672	.50c Fireworks	1.00☐	1.00☐
2673	$2.50 Sheetlet No 16 only	6.00☐	
	First Day Covers AP stamps only (5) each		2.50☐

2674
2675
2676
2677
2678

2679
2680
2681
2682
2683

MEMORABLE MOMENTS OF XV111 COMMONWEALTH GAMES
Printed in Sheetled Format No. 17 (180mx200m) Only

Kerryn McCann – On Sunday 19 March Kerryn McCann, a 38 year old mother of two, triumphed in one of the closest marathon victories in history. Lifted by the ecstatic roar of the MCG crowd, McCann crossed the finishing line two seconds ahead of her nearest rival. It was truly a memorable moment that captured the imagination of all who witnessed it.

2674	.50c	1.00☐	1.00☐
2675	.50c	1.00☐	1.00☐
2676	.50c	1.00☐	1.00☐
2677	.50c	1.00☐	1.00☐
2678	50c	1.00☐	1.00☐
2679	.50c	1.00☐	1.00☐
2680	.50c	1.00☐	1.00☐
2681	.50c	1.00☐	1.00☐
2682	.50c	1.00☐	1.00☐
2683	.50c	1.00☐	1.00☐
2684	$5.00 Sheetlet No. 17 only	15.00☐	

First Day Covers AP stamps only (10) each 2.50☐

MELBOURNE 2006 COMMONWEALTH GAMES – SPORTS OF THE GAMES
2685 $24.95 Prestige booklet containing Imperforate block 4 of 2532, self adhesive types and gummed similar to 2532. Also 4 uncirculated x .50c coins included in booklet. 50.00☐

2688 Miniature Sheet

2686 Portrait by Pietro Annigoni   2687 Photographic Portrait by Cecil Beaton

The Queens 80th Birthday — 2006 19 April

2686	.50c Portrait by Pietro Annigoni	1.00	0.60
2687	$2.45 Photographic Portrait by Cecil Beaton	5.00	4.00
2688	$2.95 Miniature Sheet	6.00	5.00
2689	$10.95 Prestige booklet (20 x 50c) self adhesive	20.00	

First Day Cover AP stamps (2) alone		7.00
First Day Cover Miniature Sheet AP		7.00
PNC018 $14.95 Stamp & Coin Cover - Queen Elizabeth II 80th Birthday		25.00

2690 Koala   2691 Royal Exhibition Melbourne

2555 Platypus   2656 Short-beaked Echidna

2657 Common Wombat   2658 Tasmanian Devil

2659 Greater Bilby   2660 Dingo

International Post – Australian Native Wildlife — 2006 6 March

2555	.05c Platypus	0.20	0.20
2656	.25c Short-beaked Echidna	0.50	0.50
2657	$1.25 Common Wombat	2.50	2.50
2658	$1.85 Tasmanian Devil	4.00	4.00
2659	$2.50 Greater Bilby	5.00	5.00
2660	$3.70 Dingo	7.00	6.00

| First Day Cover (6) AP | | 20.00 |

International Post – Greetings from Australia — 2006 2 May

2690	$1.25 Koala	2.00	2.00
2691	$1.85 Royal Exhibition Melbourne	3.50	3.50
2692	$12.95 Booklet – Greetings from Aust.	25.00	
2693	$14.95 Booklet – Heritage Buildings	30.00	

| First Day Cover (2) AP | | 7.00 |

2694 Point Lonsdale Vic   2695 Cape Don NT   2696 Wollongong Head NSW   2697 Casuarina Point WA   2698 Point Cartwright QLD

Lighthouses of the 20th Century — 2006 2 May

2694	.50c Point Lonsdale Vic (1902)	1.00	0.70
2695	.50c Cape Don NT (1916)	1.00	0.70
2696	.50c Wollongong Head NSW (1937)	1.00	0.70
2697	.50c Casuarina Point WA (1971)	1.00	0.70
2698	.50c Point Cartwright QLD (1979)	1.00	0.70
2699	Se-tenant strip (2694/2698)	5.50	5.00
2700	$10.95 Prestige Booklet (20x.50c) self adhesive	20.00	
	Also issued roll 100x.50c self adhesive		
	First Day Cover (5) AP		5.00

NO.	DESCRIPTION	MUH	FU	NO.	DESCRIPTION	MUH	FU

2701 Soccer Player – balancing ball   2702 Soccer Player – kicking ball

2703 International Post-Soccer Player   2704 International Post-Soccer Player

Soccer in Australia   **2006 9 May**

		MUH	FU
2701	.50c Soccer Player – balancing ball	1.00☐	0.70☐
2702	.50c Soccer Player – kicking ball	1.00☐	0.70☐
2703	$1.25 International Post-Soccer Player	2.00☐	1.60☐
2704	$1.85 International Post-Soccer Player	3.50☐	1.50☐
2705	$4.10 Circular Miniature Sheet (4) - Large oval	8.00☐	8.00☐
2706	$5.00 Booklet (10x0.50c) self adhesive	8.50☐	
	First Day Cover (4) AP		9.00☐
	First Day Cover – Circular Miniature Sheet AP		9.00☐
	Diameter 180mm		

| 2707 Postie Kate – Sorting Mail | 2708 Postie Kate – Delivering by bike | 2709 Postie Kate – Delivering by post | 2710 Postie Kate - Special delivery | 2711 Postie Kate - Parcel deliver |

Postie Kate – Childrens Stamp Issue 2006 1 June

2707	.50c Postie Kate – Sorting Mail	0.90☐	0.70☐
2708	.50c Postie Kate - Delivering by bike	0.90☐	0.70☐
2709	.50c Postie Kate - Delivering by post	0.90☐	0.70☐
2710	.50c Postie Kate - Special delivery	0.90☐	0.70☐
2711	.50c Postie Kate - Parcel deliver	0.90☐	0.70☐
2712	Se-tenant strip (2707/2711)	5.00☐	4.00☐
2713	$2.50 Miniature Sheet (5) self adhesive	5.00☐	5.00☐
2714	$10.00 Booklet 20x.50c self adhesive	20.00☐	
2715	$5.00 Booklet (10x.50c) self adhesive	10.00☐	
	First Day Cover (5) AP		4.50☐

2720 Miniature Sheet

2716 Humpback Whale

2717 Blue Whale

2718 Fin Whale

2719 Southern Bottlenose Whale

Whales Down Under 2006 6 June

2716	.50c Humpback Whale	0.90☐	0.70☐
2717	.50c Blue Whale	0.90☐	0.70☐
2718	$1.25 International Post-Fin Whale	2.00☐	2.00☐
2719	$1.85 Inernational Post-Southern Bottlenose Whale	3.50☐	3.50☐
2720	$4.10 Miniature Sheet	7.50☐	
	Also issued in roll 100x.50c self adhesive stamps		
	First Day Cover (4) or Miniature Sheet AP		8.00☐

2721   2722   2723   2724

Extreme Sports   **2006 18 July**

2721	0.50 Surfing	0.90 ☐	0.70 ☐
2722	$1.00 Snowboards	1.80 ☐	1.20 ☐
2723	$1.45 Skateboarding	2.50 ☐	1.80 ☐
2724	$2.00 Freestyle Motox	3.50 ☐	2.00 ☐
	First Day Cover (4) AP		10.00 ☐

2725   2726   2727   2728   2729

Driving Through the Years   **2006 15 August**

2725	0.50 Ford Model Truck 1917	0.90 ☐	0.70 ☐
2726	0.50 Holden FE sedan 1956	0.90 ☐	0.70 ☐
2727	0.50 Morris Mini 1961	0.90 ☐	0.70 ☐
2728	0.50 Holden Sandman 1976	0.90 ☐	0.70 ☐
2729	0.50 Toyota Landcruiser 1985	0.90 ☐	0.70 ☐
2730	Se-tenant strip (2725/2729)	5.00 ☐	4.00 ☐
2731	$5.00 Booklet (10x0.50c x 5 types) self adhesive, each	9.00 ☐	
	First Day Cover (5) AP		6.00 ☐

2732   2733   2734   2735   2736

2737   2738   2739   2740   2741

Australian Rock Posters   **2006 12 September**

2732	0.50 Sunbury Rock Festival 1972	0.90 ☐	0.70 ☐
2733	0.50 Magic Dirt 2002	0.90 ☐	0.70 ☐
2734	0.50 Master Apprentices 1969	0.90 ☐	0.70 ☐
2735	0.50 Goanna – Spirit of Place 1983	0.90 ☐	0.70 ☐
2736	0.50 Angels – Sports 1979	0.90 ☐	0.70 ☐
2737	0.50 Midnight Oil 1979	0.90 ☐	0.70 ☐
2738	0.50 Big Day Out 2003	0.90 ☐	0.70 ☐
2739	0.50 Apollo Bay Festival 1999	0.90 ☐	0.70 ☐
2740	0.50 Rolling Stones Aust. Tour 1973	0.90 ☐	0.70 ☐
2741	0.50 Mental As Anything 1990	0.90 ☐	0.70 ☐
2742	$5.00 Booklet (10x50c) self adhesive	9.00 ☐	
2743	$5.00 Sheetlet (10x50c) all different	9.00 ☐	
	First Day Cover (10) AP		10.00 ☐

RENNIKS

NO.	DESCRIPTION	MUH	FU	NO.	DESCRIPTION	MUH	FU

2744   2745   2746   2747   2748

2744

Dangerous Australians   2006   3   October

			MUH	FU
2744	0.50	Great White Shark	0.90 □	0.70 □
2745	0.50	Eastern Brown Snake	0.90 □	0.70 □
2746	0.50	Box Jellyfish	0.90 □	0.70 □
2747	0.50	Saltwater Crocodile	0.90 □	0.70 □
2748	0.50	Blue Ringed Octopus	0.90 □	0.70 □
2749		Se-tenant strip (2744/2748)	5.00 □	4.00 □
2750	$1.00	Yellow Bellied Sea Snake	1.90 □	1.90 □
2751	$5.00	Booklet (10x50c) self adhesive		9.00 □
2752	$3.50	Miniature sheet	6.50 □	6.50 □
2753	$3.50	Miniature sheet-special edition	30.00 □	30.00 □
		with spider		
		First Day Cover (6) AP		7.00 □

Stamp & Coin Expo–China   26-29 October

2x different miniature sheets which included the $1.25 koala (Cat No 2690) featuring the Great Wall of China and the Sydney Opera House, were issued during the course of this Expo. It is not the policy of this catalogue to provide a value of miniature sheets etc issued for stamp and coin expos.

2754   2755   2756   2757   2758

Australia – 50 Years of Television   2006   24   October

			MUH	FU				MUH	FU
2754	0.50	In Melbourne Tonight Channel 9	0.90 □	0.70 □	2758	0.50	Kath & Kim Channel 2	0.90 □	0.70 □
2755	0.50	Homicide Channel 7	0.90 □	0.70 □	2759	$2.50	Se-tenant strip (2754/2758)	5.00 □	4.00 □
2756	0.50	Dateline SBS	0.90 □	0.70 □	2760	$5.00	Booklet (10x50c) 3 types, each self adhesive	9.00 □	
2757	0.50	Neighbours Channel 10	0.90 □	0.70 □			First Day Cover (5) AP		6.00 □

2761   2762

2764   2765

50 Years on - The Melbourne Olympics   2006   1   November

			MUH	FU
2761	0.50	1956 Melbourne Skyline (2/-design)	0.90 □	0.90 □
2762	0.50	2006 Melbourne Skyline	0.90 □	0.90 □
2763	$1.00	Se-tenant pair (2761/2762)	2.00 □	2.00 □

			MUH	FU
2764	$1.00	1956 Collins Street (1/-design)	1.80 □	1.50
2765	$1.00	2006 Collins Street	1.80 □	1.50
2766	$2.00	Se-tenant pair (2764/2765)	4.00 □	4.00
		First Day Cover (4) AP	7.00 □	

2767   2768   2769

Christmas 2006 Issue   2006   1   November

2767	0.45 Virgin Mary and Jesus	0.80 □	0.50 □
2768	0.50 Wise Man	0.90 □	0.60 □
2769	$1.05 International Post - Young shepherd boy	2.00 □	2.00 □
2770	$9.00 Booklet (20x45c) self adhesive	16.00 □	
2771	$5.25 Booklet (5x$1.05) self adhesive	9.00 □	
2772	$5.25 Sheetlet (5x$1.05)	9.00 □	
	First Day Cover (3) AP	5.00 □	
	First Day Cover Sheetlet (5) AP	8.00 □	

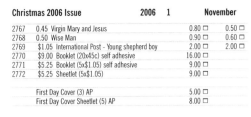

2773   2774

Australia Wins the Ashes 2006-2007   2007   16 January

2773	0.50 The Ashes reclaimed	0.90 □	0.50 □
2774	$1.85 International Post - Players with replica Ashes Urn	2.80 □	2.00 □
2775	$2.35 Miniature sheet	4.00 □	4.00 □

	First Day Cover (2) AP	3.50 □
	First Day Cover Miniature sheet only AP	4.00 □
PNC20	$19.95 Stamp & Coin cover 2007 Ashes Victory	150.00 □

2776   2777   2778   2779   2780   2781

2782   2783   2784   2785   2786   2787

Legends of Australian Horse Racing   2007   24   January
Issued in Se-tenant pairs

2776	0.50 Scobie Beasley 1936	0.90 □	0.80 □
2777	0.50 Beasley on Santa Clause 1964	0.90 □	0.80 □
2778	0.50 Bart Cummings 1966	0.90 □	0.80 □
2779	0.50 Cummings with Melbourne Cup 2001	0.90 □	0.80 □
2780	0.50 Roy Higgins 1965	0.90 □	0.80 □
2781	0.50 Higgins on Light Fingers 1965	0.90 □	0.80 □
2782	0.50 Bob Ingham 1970	0.90 □	0.80 □
2783	0.50 Ingham with Lonhro 2004	0.90 □	0.80 □
2784	0.50 George Moore 1957	0.90 □	0.80 □
2785	0.50 Moore on Tulloch 1960	0.90 □	0.80 □
2786	0.50 John Tapp 1972	0.90 □	0.80 □
2787	0.50 Tapp as a race caller 1998	0.90 □	0.80 □
2788	$5.00 Booklets (10x50c) self adhesive -3 x types	9.00 □	
2789	$22.95 Prestige booklet self adhesive	35.00 □	
	First Day Covers (2 x covers) AP	10.00 □	

RENNIKS

NO.	DESCRIPTION	MUH	FU	NO.	DESCRIPTION	MUH	FU

2790   2791   2792   2793

2797

Australian Wildflowers – Definitives   2007   13 February

2790	0.50 Tasmanian Christmas Bell	0.80 ☐	0.60 ☐
2791	0.50 Green Spider Flower	0.80 ☐	0.60 ☐
2792	0.50 Shorts Desert Rose	0.80 ☐	0.60 ☐
2793	0.50 Phebalium White	0.80 ☐	0.60 ☐
2794	Se-tenant strip (2790/2793)	4.00 ☐	3.50 ☐
2795	$5.00 Booklet (10x50c) self adhesive	9.00 ☐	
2796	$10.00 Booklet (20x50c) self adhesive	18.00 ☐	
	First Day Cover (4) AP		5.00 ☐

12TH FINA World Championships   2007   20 February

2797	0.50 Melbourne 2007 logo	0.90 ☐	0.70 ☐
	Also issued in self adhesive format		
	First Day Cover (1) AP		2.00 ☐

2798   2799   2800

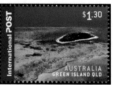

2801   2802   2803

nternational Stamps – Island Jewels   2007   5 March

2798	0.10 Maria Island Tasmania	0.20 ☐	0.20 ☐
2799	0.30 Rottnest Island, West Australia	0.50 ☐	0.50 ☐
2800	$1.30 Green Island, Queensland	2.50 ☐	2.50 ☐
2801	$1.95 Fraser Island, Queensland	3.50 ☐	3.50 ☐
2802	$2.60 Kangaroo Island, South Australian	5.00 ☐	5.00 ☐
2803	$3.85 Lord Howe Island, NSW	7.00 ☐	7.00 ☐
	First Day Cover (6) AP		19.00 ☐

2804   2805

![Year of the Surf Lifesaver 50c stamps]

2807   2808

Year of the Surf Lifesaver   **2007**   **6 March**

No.	Description	MUH	FU
2804	0.50 Female Lifesaver	0.90 □	0.70 □
2805	0.50 Male Lifesaver	0.70 □	
2806	$1.00 Sc-tenant pair (2804/2805)	2.00 □	1.80 □
2807	$1.00 Surf boat crew	1.80 □	1.30 □
2808	$2.00 Nippers	3.60 □	3.00 □
2809	$4.90 Miniature sheet	10.00 □	10.00 □
	Featuring 2x$2.45 lenticular stamps		

No.	Description	MUH	FU
2810	$12.95 Prestige booklet	25.00 □	
	Also issued in roll self adhesive format		
	First Day cover (includes lenticular issues) AP		9.00□
	First Day Cover – Miniature sheet only		9.00 □
PNC021	$14.95 Stamp & Coin cover	25.00 □	
	Year of the surf lifesaver		

CRENNIKS

NO.	DESCRIPTION	MUH	FU	NO.	DESCRIPTION	MUH	FU

2811   2812   2813   2814   2815   2816

2817   2818   2819   2820   2821   2822

Signs of the Zodiac   2007   3 April

No.		Description	MUH	FU
2811	0.50	Aries	0.80 □	0.40 □
2812	0.50	Taurus	0.80 □	0.40 □
2813	0.50	Gemini	0.80 □	0.40 □
2814	0.50	Cancer	0.80 □	0.40 □
2815	0.50	Leo	0.80 □	0.40 □
2816	0.50	Virgo	0.80 □	0.40 □
2817	0.50	Libra	0.80 □	0.40 □
2818	0.50	Scorpio	0.80 □	0.40 □
2819	0.50	Sagittarius	0.80 □	0.40 □
2820	0.50	Capricorn	0.80 □	0.40 □
2821	0.50	Aquarius	0.80 □	0.40 □
2822	0.50	Pisces	0.80 □	0.40 □
2823	$60.00	Complete set of 12xbooklets		
		(each 10x50c self adhesive) issued each star sign	110.00 □	
		First Day Cover (12) AP		10.00 □

2824   2825   2826   2827

Nostalgic Tourism   2007   10 April

No.	Description	MUH	FU
2824	0.50 At the Beach (Percy Trompf)	0.80 □	0.60 □
2825	$1.00 Fishing (John Vickery)	1.60 □	1.20 □
2826	$2.00 Riding in the Country (Jas, Northfield)	3.00 □	2.00 □
2827	$2.45 Winter Sport (Jas, Northfield)	4.00 □	2.60 □
2828	$10.95 Prestige booklet	18.00 □	
	First Day Cover (4) AP		11.00 □

2829

Queen's Birthday   2007   18 April

No.	Description	MUH	FU
2829	0.50 Queen Elizabeth in Australia	0.80 □	0.60 □
	First Day Cover (AP)		2.00 □

2830   2831   2832

Historic Shipwrecks   2007   1 May

			MUH	FU
2830	0.50 Steamship "Admella"		0.90 ☐	0.70 ☐
2831	$1.00 Iron clipper "Loch Ard"		1.80 ☐	1.20 ☐
2832	$2.00 Wooden clipper "Dunbar"		3.50 ☐	2.80 ☐
	First Day Cover (3) AP			6.50 ☐

International Stamps – Country to Coast   2007   8 May

		MUH	FU
2833	$1.30 Yellow footed Rock Wallaby	2.30 ☐	1.80 ☐
2834	$1.95 Sydney Harbour Bridge	3.00 ☐	2.50 ☐
2835	$13.95 Prestige booklet	22.00 ☐	
	First Day Cover (2) AP		6.00 ☐

2833   2834

2836   2837   2838   2839   2840

Circus Under the Big Top   2007   15 May

		MUH	FU				MUH	FU
2836	0.50 Firewalker on cycle	0.90 ☐	0.70 ☐	2841	0.50 Se-tenant strip (2836/2840)		5.00 ☐	4.00 ☐
2837	0.50 Contortionists	0.90 ☐	0.70 ☐	2842	$5.00 Booklet (10x50c) self adhsive		9.00 ☐	
2838	0.50 Trapeze artists	0.90 ☐	0.70 ☐	2843	$12.95 Prestige booklet with special features		22.00 ☐	
2839	0.50 Banana Lady	0.90 ☐	0.70 ☐					
2840	0.50 Male canon flyer	0.90 ☐	0.70 ☐		First Day Cover (5) AP			6.00 ☐

2844   2845   2846   2847   2848

Big Things   2007   5 June

		MUH	FU
2844	0.50 Big Guitar – Tamworth NSW	0.90 ☐	0.70 ☐
2845	0.50 Big Lobster – Kingston SA	0.90 ☐	0.70 ☐
2846	0.50 Big Banana – Coffs Harbour NSW	0.90 ☐	0.70 ☐
2847	0.50 Big Merino Ewe – Goulburn NSW	0.90 ☐	0.70 ☐
2848	0.50 Big Pineapple – Nambour QLD	0.90 ☐	0.70 ☐
2849	$2.50 Se-tenant strip (2844/2848)	5.00 ☐	4.00 ☐
2850	$5.00 Booklet (10x50c) self adhesive	9.00 ☐	
	First Day Cover (5) AP		5.00 ☐

75TH Anniversary of Sydney Harbour Bridge 2007 — 15 June

2851	$3.90 Miniature Sheet (2x$1.95 international stamps)	8.00 ☐	8.00 ☐
2852	$3.90 Miniature Sheet but with National Philatelic Exhibition overstamp	8.00 ☐	8.00 ☐
	First Day Cover		9.00 ☐
PNC22	$14.95 Stamp & Coin cover Sydney Harbour Bridge		25.00 ☐

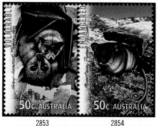

2853   2854

2856

2857

Threatened Wildlife 2007 — 26 June

2853	0.50 Grey headed flying fox	0.90 ☐	0.70 ☐
2854	0.50 Mountain Pygmy-possum	0.90 ☐	0.70 ☐
2855	$1.00 Se-tenant pair (2853/2854)	2.00 ☐	1.70 ☐
2856	$1.25 International Post-Flatback Turtle	2.00 ☐	1.50 ☐
2857	$1.30 International Post-Wandering Albatross	2.20 ☐	1.70 ☐
2858	$10.95 Prestige Booklet	20.00 ☐	
	First Day Cover (4) AP		7.00 ☐

2859   2860

2862   2863

Landmarks: Australian Modern Architecture 2007 — 10 July

2859	0.50 ICI House – Melbourne	0.90 ☐	0.70 ☐
2860	0.50 Academy of Science – Canberra	0.90 ☐	0.70 ☐
2861	$1.00 Se-tenant pair (2859/2860)	2.00 ☐	1.70 ☐
2862	$1.00 Council House – Perth	1.80 ☐	1.20 ☐
2863	$2.45 Opera House – Sydney	4.00 ☐	3.00 ☐
2864	$4.45 Miniature Sheet	10.00 ☐	9.00 ☐
	First Day Cover (4) AP		8.00 ☐

| 2865 | 2866 | 2867 | 2868 | 2869 |

Market Feast 2007 24 July

No.	Description	MUH	FU
2865	0.50 Queen Victoria Markets – Melbourne	0.90 ☐	0.70 ☐
2866	0.50 Rusty's Market - Cairns	0.90 ☐	0.70 ☐
2867	0.50 Sydney Fish Markets	0.90 ☐	0.70 ☐
2868	0.50 Adelaide Central Market	0.90 ☐	0.70 ☐
2869	0.50 Hume Murray Farmers Markets – Albury	0.90 ☐	0.70 ☐
2870	$2.50 Se-tenant strip (2865/2870)	5.00 ☐	4.00 ☐
2871	$5.00 Booklets (10x50c) self adhesive	9.00 ☐	
	First Day Cover (5) AP		6.00 ☐

| 2872 |

APEC FORUM 2007 28 August

No.	Description	MUH	FU
2872	0.50 Forum logo	0.90 ☐	0.70 ☐
	Also issued in self adhesive format		
	First Day Cover AP		2.00 ☐

50th Anniversary of the Special Air Service 2007 4 September

No.	Description	MUH	FU
2873	0.50 SAS Logo & motto	0.90 ☐	0.70 ☐
	First Day Cover AP		2.00 ☐
PNC23	$14.95 Stamp & Coin Cover - 50th Anniversary of SAS	45.00 ☐	

| 2873 |

| 2874 | 2875 | 2876 | 2877 | 2878 |

Australian Botanic Gardens 2007 12 September

No.	Description	MUH	FU
2874	0.50 Brisbane Botanic Gardens	0.90 ☐	0.70 ☐
2875	0.50 Kings Park Botanic Gardens – Perth	0.90 ☐	0.70 ☐
2876	0.50 Royal Botanic Gardens – Sydney	0.90 ☐	0.70 ☐
2877	0.50 Royal Botanic Gardens – Melbourne	0.90 ☐	0.70 ☐
2878	0.50 Botanic Gardens of Adelaide	0.90 ☐	0.70 ☐
2879	$2.50 Se-tenant strip (2874/2878)	5.00 ☐	4.00 ☐
2880	$10.00 Booklet (20x50c) self adhesive	17.00 ☐	
2881	$10.95 Prestige booklet	20.00 ☐	

NO.	DESCRIPTION	MUH	FU	NO.	DESCRIPTION	MUH	FU

2882	2883	2884	2885	2886	2888

First Day Cover (5) AP 4.00□

BLAST OFF! 50 Years in Space 2007 2 October

2882	0.50	Sputnik 1957	0.90 □	0.70 □
2883	0.50	First Space Walk 1965	0.90 □	0.70 □
2884	0.50	First Moon Walk 1969	0.90 □	0.70 □
2885	0.50	Voyager 1977	0.90 □	0.70 □
2886	0.50	International Space Station 1998-90	0.90 □	0.70 □

2887	$2.50	Se-tenant strip (2882/2886)	5.00 □	5.00 □
2888	$1.00	Hubble Space Telescope	1.80 □	1.20 □
2889	$3.50	Miniature sheet	6.00 □	6.00 □
2890	$5.00	Booklet (10x50c) self adhesive	9.00 □	
2891	$10.95	Prestige booklet	20.00 □	
		First Day Cover (6) AP		7.00 □
PNC024	$99.00	Stamp & Coin Cover - Fifty Years in Space	135.00□	

2892	2893	2894	2895	2896

Caravanning Through the Years 2007 16 October

2892	0.50	Caravanning 1950's	0.90 □	0.70 □
2893	0.50	Caravanning 1960's	0.90 □	0.70 □
2894	0.50	Caravanning 1970's	0.90 □	0.70 □
2895	0.50	Caravanning 1980's	0.90 □	0.70 □

2896	0.50	Caravanning today	0.90 □	0.70 □
2897	$2.50	Se-tenant strip (2892/2896)	5.00 □	4.00 □
2898	$5.00	Booklet (10x50c) (5xtypes) self adhesive	9.00 □	
2899	$10.95	Prestige booklet	20.00 □	
		First Day Cover (5) AP		4.00 □

2900

2901

2902

2903 2904

50 Years of Australian Christmas Stamps   2007   1 November

No.	Description	MUH	FU
2900	0.50 Infant Samuel 1957	0.90 ☐	0.40 ☐
2901	0.45 Surfing Santa 1977	0.80 ☐	0.40 ☐
2902	$1.10 International Stamp Stained Glass 1984	1.60 ☐	1.20 ☐
2903	0.45 Bush Nativity 1990	0.80 ☐	0.40 ☐
2904	0.45 Madonna & Child 1996	0.80 ☐	0.40 ☐
2905	0.90 Se-tenant pair (2903/2904)	2.00 ☐	1.30 ☐
2906	$2.95 Miniature Sheet – self adhesive	4.50 ☐	4.50 ☐
2907	$9.00 Booklet (20x45c) self adhesive	16.00 ☐	
2908	$10.95 Prestige Booklet	20.00 ☐	
	First Day Cover (4) AP		3.00 ☐
	First Day Cover Internat. Stamp (1) AP		2.50 ☐
PNC025	$19.95 Stamp & Coin Cover - Bouncing Kangaroo	30.00 ☐	
	Note: Stamp Cat. 2453 appears on this cover		
	Issued 03/12/2007		

Signs of the Zodiac   2008   8 January

A series of 12 x New 2008 Zodiac Booklets were Issued providing relevant information about the sun sign, predictions on love, career, money and health for 2008. Each booklet contains 20 x 0.50c self adhesive format.

Due to their near exact resemblance to those Zodiac Booklets issued 03.04.07 we have not listed individually, the 2008 series. Values would be similar.

2909

Special Occasions – Love Bloom   2008   15 January

2909	0.50 Red Rose	0.80 ☐	0.40 ☐
2910	$10.95 Prestige booklet	16.00 ☐	
	First Day Cover AP		2.50 ☐

2911   2912   2913   2914

Australian Legends of Philanthropy   2008   23 January

2911	0.50 Dame Edith Murdoch AC OBE	0.80 ☐	0.40 ☐
2912	0.50 Victor Smorgan AC & Loti Smorgon AO	0.80 ☐	0.40 ☐
2913	0.50 Lady (Mary) Fairfax AC OBE	0.80 ☐	0.40 ☐
2914	0.50 Frank Lowy AC	0.80 ☐	0.40 ☐

2915	$2.00 Se-tenant strip (2911/2914)	4.00 ☐	4.00 ☐
	Also issued in roll (100x50c) self adhesive		
	First Day Cover (4) AP		3.50 ☐

Organ and Tissue Donation   2008   5 February

2916	0.50 Organ & Tissue Donation	0.80 ☐	0.40 ☐
2917	$5.00 Booklet (10x50c) self adhesive	9.00 ☐	
	First Day Cover AP		2.50 ☐

2916

2918   2919   2920

Centenary of Scouting in Australia   2008   19 February

2918	0.50 Contemporary scouts	0.80 ☐	0.50 ☐
2919	$1.35 International Post – International scouts	2.00 ☐	1.50 ☐
2920	$2.00 International Post – Lord Robert Baden-Powell	3.50 ☐	3.00 ☐
	Also issued in roll (20x50c) self adhesive format		
	First Day Cover (3) AP		7.00 ☐
PNC026	$14.95 Stamp & Coin Cover	20.00 ☐	
	Centenary of Scouting in Australian		

2921

2922

2925

2926

2927

World Youth Day   2008   4 March

2925	0.50 Greeting During Mass	0.80 ☐	0.50 ☐
2926	$1.35 Pastoral Staff	2.00 ☐	1.40 ☐
2927	$2.00 A Blessing	3.00 ☐	2.00 ☐
	First Day Cover (3) AP		6.00 ☐
PNC027	$14.95 Stamp & Coin Cover featuring Pope Benedict	25.00 ☐	
	Stamp and Medallion cover also issued		

2923

2924

International Post Series – Gorgeous Australia   2008   3 March

2921	$1.35 Grose River Gorge – NSW	2.00 ☐	1.40 ☐
2922	$2.00 Walpa Gorge – NT	3.00 ☐	2.00 ☐
2923	$2.70 Katherine Gorge – NT	4.00 ☐	2.50 ☐
2924	$4.00 Geikie Gorge – WA	6.00 ☐	4.00 ☐
	2921 and 2922 both issued in sheetlets of 5 in self adhesive format		
	First Day Cover (4) AP		15.00 ☐

Centenary of Rugby League   2008   24 March

2928	0.50 Broncos/Brisbane	0.80 ☐	0.40 ☐
2929	0.50 Bulldogs/Canterbury Bankstown	0.80 ☐	0.40 ☐
2930	0.50 Cowboys/Townsville	0.80 ☐	0.40 ☐
2931	0.50 Dragons/St George	0.80 ☐	0.40 ☐
2932	0.50 Eels/Parramatta	0.80 ☐	0.40 ☐
2933	0.50 Knights/Newcastle	0.80 ☐	0.40 ☐
2934	0.50 Panthers/Penrith	0.80 ☐	0.40 ☐
2935	0.50 Rabbitohs/Sth Sydney	0.80 ☐	0.40 ☐
2936	0.50 Raiders/Canberra	0.80 ☐	0.40 ☐
2937	0.50 Roosters/Eastern Suburbs	0.80 ☐	0.40 ☐
2938	0.50 Sea Eagles/Manly	0.80 ☐	0.40 ☐
2939	0.50 Sharks/Cronulla	0.80 ☐	0.40 ☐
2940	0.50 Storm/Melbourne	0.80 ☐	0.40 ☐
2941	0.50 Titans/Gold Coast	0.80 ☐	0.40 ☐
2942	0.50 West Tigers/Western Suburbs	0.80 ☐	0.40 ☐
2943	0.50 Warriors/Auckland NZ	0.80 ☐	0.40 ☐
2944	$5.00 Booklets 17 x diff types (each 10x50c) all self adhesive	8.00 ☐	
2945	$15.95 Prestige Stamp & Coin booklet	20.00 ☐	
	First Day Cover (Set x 2) AP		12.00 ☐

⦿RENNIKS

NO.	DESCRIPTION	MUH	FU	NO.	DESCRIPTION	MUH	FU

| 2946 | 2947 | 2948 | 2949 | 2950 |

Heavy Haulers — 2008 — 1 April

2946	0.50 Face Shovel	0.80 ☐	0.40 ☐
2947	0.50 Haul Truck	0.80 ☐	0.40 ☐
2948	0.50 Road Train	0.80 ☐	0.40 ☐
2949	0.50 Ore Train	0.80 ☐	0.40 ☐

2950	0.50 MS Berge Stahl	0.80 ☐	0.40 ☐
2951	$2.50 Se-tenant strip (2946/2950)	5.00 ☐	3.00 ☐
2952	$10.00 Booklet (20x50c) self adhesive	16.00 ☐	
	First Day Cover (5) AP		4.50 ☐

| 2953 | 2954 | 2955 | 2956 | 2957 |

Lest We Forget – Anzac Day — 2008 — 16 April

2953	0.50 Veterans Marching	0.80 ☐	0.40 ☐
2954	0.50 Laying of Wreaths	0.80 ☐	0.40 ☐
2955	0.50 Playing Last Post	0.80 ☐	0.40 ☐
2956	0.50 War Veteran & Child	0.80 ☐	0.40 ☐
2957	0.50 Young People at Gallipoli	0.80 ☐	0.40 ☐

2958	$2.50 Se-tenant strip (2953/2957)	5.00 ☐	4.00 ☐
2959	$2.50 Miniature Sheet	5.00 ☐	5.00 ☐
2960	$10.95 Prestige Booklet	18.00 ☐	
	Also issued in self adhesive format		
	First Day Cover (5) AP		4.50 ☐

2961   2962

Queens Birthday   2008   18 April

No.	Description	MUH	FU
2961	0.50 HRH Queen Elizabeth II	0.80 ☐	.40 ☐
2962	$2.00 Order of Australia badge	2.90 ☐	2.00 ☐
2963	$2.50 Miniature Sheet	4.00 ☐	2.60 ☐
	First Day Cover (2) AP		4.50 ☐
	First Day Cover Miniature Sheet		4.50 ☐

2964   2965   2966   2967

Up Up and Away   2008   6 May

No.	Description	MUH	FU
2964	0.50 Balloons over Sydney	0.80 ☐	0.40 ☐
2965	0.50 Balloons over Mt Feathertop (Vic)	0.80 ☐	0.40 ☐
2966	0.50 Balloons over the Western MacDonnell Ranges (NT)	0.80 ☐	0.40 ☐
2967	0.50 Balloons over Canberra (Act)	0.80 ☐	0.40 ☐

No.	Description	MUH	FU
2968	Se-tenant strip (2964/2967) ☐	4.00 ☐	3.00
2969	$5.00 Booklet (10x50c) self adhesive	8.00 ☐	
2970	$10.95 Prestige booklet	16.50 ☐	
	First Day Cover (4) AP	4.00 ☐	

2977

Beijing Olympic Games   2008   4 June

No.	Description	MUH	FU
2971	0.50 Dragon design Also issued in self adhesive format	0.80 ☐	0.50 ☐
	First Day Cover (1) AP		2.50 ☐
PNC028	$14.95 Stamp & Coin cover - featuring dragon artwork	25.00 ☐	

2972   2973   2974   2975   2976

Australian Working Dogs   2008   10 June

No.	Description	MUH	FU
2972	0.50 German Shepherd	0.80 ☐	0.40 ☐
2973	0.50 Australian Cattle Dog	0.80 ☐	0.40 ☐
2974	0.50 Beagle hound	0.80 ☐	0.40 ☐
2975	0.50 Border Collie	0.80 ☐	0.40 ☐
2976	0.50 Labrador	0.80 ☐	0.40 ☐
2977	Se-tenant strip (2970/2974)	5.00 ☐	4.00 ☐
2978	$5.00 Booklet (10x50c) self adhesive booklets (10x50c) issued for each stamp	8.00 ☐	
2979	$10.95 Prestige booklet	16.50 ☐	
	First Day Cover (5) AP		4.50 ☐

'Frama' Vending Machine Labels

On the 22nd of February 1984, seven "Frama" vending machines sold on a trial basis, labels, imperforate and gummed. The initial trial was considered to be a success and quantities of machines were placed at general post offices, major post offices and various locations throughout Australia. There are believed to be more than 150 Frama machines in current use. Labels are usually referred to by name Framas but they are actual postage stamps and fully collectable. They are only available from vending machines and are not sold over the post office counter.

F001. Barred Edge

F006. Multiple Platypuses

Frama Vending Machine Label FVML: - Barred Edge

1984 22 Feb

| F001 | 30c (with postcode) | 2.00☐ | 2.00☐ |
| F002 | 33c (with & without postcode) | 3.00☐ | 3.00☐ |

FVML: Special Americas Cup CUPEX Overprint

1987 30 Jan

Multiple Platypuses

| F006 | 50c | 2.00☐ | 2.00☐ |

F003. Multiple Kangaroo

F007. Multiple Echidnas

FVML: Multiple Kangaroos

1985 22 Oct

| F003 | 33c (with & without postcode) | 1.00☐ | 1.00☐ |

FVML: Multiple Echidnas

1987 02 Sep

| F007 | 37c (with & without postcodes) | 1.00☐ | 1.00☐ |

F004. Multiple Platypuses

F008. Aeropex Overprint

FVML: Multiple Platypuses

1986 26 Aug

| F004 | 36c (with & without postcode) | 1.00☐ | 1.00☐ |
| F005 | 37c (with & without postcode) | 1.00☐ | 1.00☐ |

FVML: AEROPEX 88

1988 08 Apr

overprint on Multiple Echidnas

| F008 | $1 Aeropex Overprint | 3.00☐ | 3.00☐ |

NO.	DESCRIPTION	MUH	FU	NO.	DESCRIPTION	MUH	FU

F009. Sydpex 88 overprint

FVML: Sydpex 88 overprint   **1988 29 Jul**
Multiple Echidnas
F009   50c   2.00☐   2.00☐

F010. Multiple Possums

Frama Vending Machine Labels   **1988 30 Sep**
Multiple Possums
F010   39c   1.00☐   1.00☐

F011. Multiple Frill Necked Lizards

FVML: Multiple Frill Necked Lizards   **1989 01 Sep**
F011   41c   1.00☐   0.90☐
F012 $1   5.00☐   5.00☐

F012. Multiple Frill Necked Lizards

FVML: Essen Stamp Fair Logo   **1990 19 Apr**
Overprint on Multiple Frilled Necked LizardsAustralia Post was represented at the Essen Stamp Fair. A Frama machine was in use from 19-24 April with a further limited stock being available in Australia

F013. Multiple Koalas

F014. NORPEX '91 Overprint

FVML: Special NORPEX '91   **1991 05 Oct**
Overprint on Koalas.FVML: Multiple Koalas   1990 01 Sep
F013   43c (with postcode or machine number)   1.10☐   0.90☐
     Available at Norpex in Newcastle, on 5-6 Oct 91.
     Also on sale through AustraliaPost by mail order for a limited period.
F014   50c   4.00☐   4.00☐

F015. Multiple Emus

FVML: Multiple Emus   **1992 02 Jan**
F015   45c (with postcode or machine number)   1.00☐   0.90☐

F016. National Stamp Show Overprint

FVML: National Stamp Show   **1992 04 Jun**
Multiple Emus
F016   45c   1.10☐   1.00☐
F017   70c   1.75☐   1.60☐
F018 $1.20   2.60☐   2.50☐

NO.	DESCRIPTION	MUH	FU	NO.	DESCRIPTION	MUH	FU

F019. PEELPEX

FVML: Special PEELPEX Cliche   **1992 19 Sep**
Multiple Emus

F019	50c	2.50⬜	2.50⬜

F020. QLD '93 Cliche

FVML: Special QLD '93 Cliche   **1993 12 Jun**
Multiple Emus

F020	45c	3.00⬜	3.00⬜
F021	70c	4.00⬜	4.00⬜
F022	$1.20	5.00⬜	5.00⬜

F023. WAPEX '93 Cliche

FVML: WAPEX '93 Cliche   **1993 22 Sep**
Multiple Emus

F023	50c 2.50	2.50 ⬜	2.50⬜

F024. DINO '93 Cliche

FVML: Special DINO '93 Cliche   **1993 22 Oct**
Multiple Emus

F024	45c	3.00⬜	3.00 1
F025	70c	4.00⬜	4.00⬜
F026	$1.20	5.00⬜	5.00⬜

F027. FAMILY 94 Cliche

FVML: Special FAMILY 94 Cliche   **1994 11 Jun**
Multiple Emus

F027	50c	3.00⬜	3.00⬜
F028	70c	4.00⬜	4.00⬜
F029	$1.20	5.00⬜	5.00⬜

F030. Waratah

FVML: Waratah   **1994 08 Sep**

F030	45c Waratah	1.20⬜	1.20⬜

F031. ZOOS '94 Cliche

FVML: Special ZOOS '94 Cliche   **1994 21 Oct**

F031	45c	3.00⬜	3.00⬜
F032	70c	4.00⬜	4.00⬜
F033	$1.20	5.00⬜	5.00⬜

F034. AEROPEX '94 Cliche

FVML: Special AEROPEX '94 Cliche   **1994 18 Nov**

F034	$1.00	2.50⬜	2.50⬜

F035. Festive Design

FVML: New Festive design printed over 3 labels   **1996 06 Jun**
F035   45c festive design   1.20☐   1.20☐

F036. Aboriginal Design

1999 19 Mar   Aboriginal design
F03645c 1.00☐0.50☐

F037. GPO Postcode

F038. No Postcode

Farewell Frama Vending Machine Stamp
F037   50c GPO Postcode   1.20☐   1.20☐
F038   50c No Postcode   1.20☐   1.20☐

A selection of Frama labels

British Commonwealth Occupation Force

103-BCOF. Kangaroo

119-BCOF. Elizabeth

101-BCOF. KGVI

106-BCOF. Kookaburra

108-BCOF. Lyre Bird

013-BCOF. Kangaroo

109-BCOF. Elizabeth

British Commonwealth Forces Overseas   1947 08 May

For use by Australian Forces in Japan,   withdrawn from sale 12 Feb 1949
Number in brackets ( ) is the standard issue stamp

NO.	DESCRIPTION	MUH	FU	FU
01-BCOF	½d Orange Kangaroo (103)	3.00 ☐	2.00 ☐	5.00 ☐
02-BCOF	1d Purple Elizabeth II (119)	3.00 ☐	2.00 ☐	3.00 ☐
03-BCOF	3d Brown KGV1 (101)	5.00 ☐	3.00 ☐	4.00 ☐
04-BCOF	6d Brown Kookaburra (106)	12.00 ☐	8.00 ☐	12.00 ☐
05-BCOF	1/- Green Lyre Bird (108)	15.00 ☐	10.00 ☐	20.00 ☐
06-BCOF	2/- Maroon Kangaroo (13)	45.00 ☐	30.00 ☐	60.00 ☐
07-BCOF	5/- Claret 'Robes' (109)	200.00 ☐	130.00 ☐	200.00 ☐

AUSTRALIAN ANTARCTIC TERRITORY

Australian Antarctic Territory stamps are on sale for a limited period from the date of issue at all official Australian Post Offices. After this, they are only available from philatelic sales centres and from Post Offices within 'A.A.T'. All decimal issues from Australian Antarctic Territory remain valid for use within the Territory and Australia indefinitely, therefore, for all intents and purposes, they should be considered to be an 'Australian Issue'.

AAT-001. Map of Antarctica

AAT-007. Sir Douglas Mawson

50th Anniversary of 1911 Antarctic Expedition   **1961 18 Oct**
AAT-007 5d Grey Green Sir Douglas Mawson   0.60☐   0.50☐

AAT-002. Explorers at South Magnetic Pole

AAT-003. Explorers at South Magnetic Pole

AAT-008. Golden Aurora

AAT-009. Banding Penguins

AAT-004. ANARE Weasel Tractor

AAT-010. Ship & Iceberg

AAT-011. Branding Elephant Seals

AAT-005. Dog Sled & Team

AAT-006. Emperor Penguins

AAT-012. Measuring Snow Strata

AAT-013. Wind Gauges

AUSTRALIAN ANTARCTIC TERRITORIES   **1957 27 Mar**
AAT-001 2/- Blue Map of Antarctica   4.00☐   1.80☐

Definitives   **195916 Dec**
(5d Brown, 8d, 1/-, 2/3), (5d Blue)   05-Jul-61
AAT-002 5d Brown Explorers   0.60☐   0.50 1
AAT-003 5d Blue Explorers   0.60☐   0.50 1
AAT-004 8d Blue ANARE Weasel Tractor   3.00☐   1.00☐
AAT-005 1/- Blue Green Dog Sled & Team   4.00☐   1.80☐
AAT-006 2/3 Green Emperor Penguins   10.00☐   5.00☐

AAT-014. Weather Balloon

AAT-015. Helicopter

AAT-019. Ice - Sastrugi

AAT-016. Radio Operator

AAT-020. Pancake ice

10th Anniversary of the Antarctic Treaty — 1971 23 Jul

| AAT-019 | 6c Ice - Sastrugi | 0.80☐ | 0.60☐ |
| AAT-020 | 30c Pancake ice | 4.00☐ | 2.50☐ |

AAT-017. Ice Compression Tests

AAT-021. James Cook/Sextant & Compass

AAT-018. Parahelion (Mock Sun)

AAT-022. Resolution
& Map of Antarctic

Definitive Issue — 1966 28 Sep

AAT-008	1c Golden Aurora	0.50☐	0.30☐
AAT-009	2c Banding Penguins	0.50☐	1.00☐
AAT-010	4c Ship & Iceberg	0.60☐	0.40☐
AAT-011	5c branding Elephant Seals	1.00☐	0.50☐
AAT-012	7c Measuring Snow Strata	1.00☐	0.50☐
AAT-013	10c Wind Gauges	1.50☐	0.60☐
AAT-014	15c Weather Balloon	4.00☐	4.00☐
AAT-015	20c Helicopter	5.00☐	4.00☐
AAT-016	25c Radio Operator	5.00☐	5.00☐
AAT-017	50c Ice Compression Tests	20.00☐	15.00☐
AAT-018	$1 Parahelion (Mock Sun)	30.00☐	20.00☐

200th Anniversary Circumnavigation of the Antarctic by Captain James Cook — 1972 13 Sep

| AAT-021 | 7c James Cook/Sextant & Compass | 1.00☐ | 0.60☐ |
| AAT-022 | 35c Ship & Map of Antarctic | 4.00☐ | 3.00☐ |

AAT-023. Plankton - Red Shrimp

AAT-024. Mawso's D H Gypsy Moth

AAT-025. Adelie Penguins

AAT-026. Rymill's DH Fox Moth

AAI-027. Leopard Seal

AAI-028. Killer Whale

AAI-029. Albatross in flight

AAT-030. Wilkin's Lockhead Vega

AAT-031. Ellsworth's Northrop Gamma

AAT-032. Christensen's Avro Avian

AAT-033. Byrd's Ford Tri Motor

AAT-034. Sperm Whale & Squid

Definitives: Food Chain & Explorers' Aircraft   1973 15 Aug

		MUH	FU
AAT-023	1c Plankton - Red Shrimp	0.30☐	0.30☐
AAT-024	5c Mawso's D H Gypsy Moth	0.50☐	0.60☐
AAT 025	7c Adelie Penguins	0.80☐	0.60☐
AAT-026	8c Rymill's DH Fox Moth	0.50☐	0.40☐
AAT-027	9c Leopard Seal	0.50☐	0.40☐
AAT-028	10c Killer Whale	3.00☐	0.90☐
AAT-029	20c Albatross in flight	0.50☐	0.40☐
AAT-030	25c Wilkin's Lockhead Vega	0.80☐	0.60☐
AAT-031	30c Ellsworth's Northrop Gamma	0.80☐	0.60☐
AAT-032	35c Christensen's Avro Avian	0.80☐	0.60☐
AAT-033	50c Byrd's Ford Tri Motor	1.00☐	0.60☐
AAT-034	$1 Sperm Whale & Squid	2.00☐	1.00☐

AAT-035. Byrd, Plane & Map

AAT-036. Byrd, Plane & Mountain

50th Anniversary First Flight over the South Pole   1979 20 Jun

		MUH	FU
AAT-035	20c Byrd, Plane & Map	0.50 ☐	0.40☐
AAT-036	55c Byrd, Plane & Mountain	1.00 ☐	0.60☐

AAT-037. SY Aurora

AAT-038. RY Penola

AAT-039. MV Thala Dan

AAT-040. HMS Challenger

AAT-041. Morning

AAT-042. SY Nimrod

AAT-043. RRS Discovery II

AAT-044. RYS Terra Nova

AAT-045. SS Endurance

AAT-046. SS Fram

AAT-047. MS Nella Dan

AAT-048. MS Kista Dan

AAT-049. L'Astrolabe

AAT-050. SS Norvegio

AAT-051. SY Discovery

Definitives - Antarctic Ships — 1979-82

NO.	DESCRIPTION	MUH	FU
AAT-037	1c SY Aurora	0.30	0.30
AAT-038	2c RY Penola	0.30	0.30
AAT-039	5c MV Thala Dan	0.30	0.30
AAT-040	10c H M S Challenger	0.50	0.30
AAT-041	15c Morning	0.50	0.30
AAT-042	15c SY Nimrod	0.40	0.30
AAT-043	20c RRS Discovery II	0.50	0.30
AAT-044	22c RYS Terra Nova	0.50	0.30
AAT-045	25c SS Endurance	0.60	0.40
AAT-046	30c SS Fram	0.70	0.40
AAT-047	35c MS Nella Dan	0.70	0.40
AAT-048	40c MS Kista Dan	0.80	0.40
AAT-049	45c L'Astrolabe	0.90	0.40
AAT-050	50c SS Norvegio	0.90	0.50
AAT-051	55c SY Discovery	1.00	0.60
AAT-052	$1 HMS Resolution	1.50	0.90

AAT-052. HMS Resolution

AAT-053. Mawson & view

AAT-054. Mawson & map

Sir Douglas Mawson Centenary — 1982 05 May

		MUH	FU
AAT-053	27c Mawson	0.50	0.25
AAT-054	75c Mawson	1.00	0.40

AAT-060. Se-tenant strip (5 values)

AAT-055. Light-mantled Sooty Albatross AAT-056. Macquarie Island Shags AAT-057. Elephant Seals AAT-058. Royal Penguins AAT-059. Antarctic Prion

Regional Wildlife — 1983 06 Apr

		MUH	FU
AAT-055	27c Lightmantled Sooty Albatross	0.70	0.50
AAT-056	27c Macquarie Island Shags	0.70	0.50
AAT-057	27c Elephant Seals	0.70	0.50
AAT-058	27c Royal Penguins	0.70	0.50
AAT-059	27c Antarctic Prion	0.70	0.50
AAT-060	Se-tenant strip (5 values)	3.00	3.00

AAT-061. List of Scientific Disciplines & Expedition Member

12th Antarctic Treaty Consultative Meeting, Canberra — 1983 07 Sep

		MUH	FU
AAT-061	27c Expedition Member	0.50	0.30

AAT-062. Compass & Dip Circle

AAT-063. Aneroid Barometer Theodolite

75th Anniversary, Expedition to the South Magnetic Pole — 1984 16 Jan

Definitives,(Antarctic Scenes)

		MUH	FU
AAT-062	30c Compass & Dip Circle	0.60	0.40
AAT-063	85c Aneroid Barometer Theodolite	1.50	0.90

AAT-064. Summer Afternoon

AAT-065. Dog Team

AAT-066. Late Summer's Evening

AAT-067. Prince Charles Mountain

AAT-068. Summer Morning

AAT-069. Sea Ice & Iceberg

AAT-070. Mount Coates

AAT-071. Iceberg Alley Mawson

AAT-072. Evening, Early Winter

AAT-073. Brash Ice

AAT-074. Midwinter Shadows

AAT-075. Coastline

AAT-076. Landing Field

AAT-077. Ice

AAT-078. Emperor Penguins

Definitives (Antarctic Scenes) 1984-87

NO.	DESCRIPTION	MUH	FU
AAT-064	2c Summer Afternoon	0.30 ▢	0.30 ▢
AAT-065	5c Dog Team	0.30 ▢	0.30 ▢
AAT-066	10c Late Summer's Evening	0.30 ▢	0.30 ▢
AAT-067	15c Prince Charles Mountain	0.40 ▢	0.30 ▢
AAT-068	20c Summer Morning	0.50 ▢	0.40 ▢
AAT-069	25c Sea Ice & Iceberg	0.60 ▢	0.40 ▢
AAT-070	30c Mount Coates	0.60 ▢	0.40 ▢
AAT-071	33c Iceberg Alley Mawson	0.70 ▢	0.40 ▢
AAT-072	36c Evening, Early Winter	0.75 ▢	0.40 ▢
AAT-073	45c Brash Ice	0.90 ▢	0.40 ▢
AAT-074	60c Midwinter Shadows	1.20 ▢	0.90 ▢
AAT-075	75c Coastline	1.30 ▢	1.00 ▢
AAT-076	85c Landing Field	1.40 ▢	1.00 ▢
AAT-077	90c Ice	1.40 ▢	1.00 ▢
AAT-078	$1 Emperor Penguins	1.50 ▢	1.00 ▢

AAT-079. Antarctic Landscape

25th Anniversary of the Antarctic Treaty   **1986 17 Sep**
AAT-079 36c Antarctic Landscape   0.50☐   0.40☐

AAT-085. Joined strip (5)

AAT-080. Nella Dan & Dolphins   AAT-081. Davis Station & Penguins   AAT-082. Helicopter & Seal   AAT-083. Tracked Vehicle & Penguins   AAT-084. Photographer & Albatross

Environment, Conservation & Technology   **1988 20 Jul**

AAT-080	37c Nella Dan & Dolphins	1.00☐	0.70☐
AAT-081	37c Davis Station & Penguins	1.00☐	0.70☐
AAT-082	37c Helicopter & Seal	1.00☐	0.70☐
AAT-083	37c TrackedVehicle & Penguins	1.00☐	0.70☐
AAT-084	37c Photographer & Albatross	1.00☐	0.70☐
AAT-085	Joined strip (5)	6.00☐	4.50☐

AAT-086. Antarctica

AAT-087. Iceberg Alley

AAT-088. Glacial Flow

AAT-089. Frozen Sea

Landscapes - Paintings by Sydney Nolan   **1989 14 Jun**

AAT-086	39c Antarctica	0.80☐	0.40☐
AAT-087	39c Iceberg Alley	0.80☐	0.40☐
AAT-088	60c Glacial Flow	1.20☐	1.00☐
AAT-089	80c Frozen Sea	1.80☐	1.20☐

AAT-090. Southern Lights

AAT-091. RSV Aurora Australis

Anniversaries   **1991 20 Jun**

AAT-090	30th Anniversary Antarctic Treaty		
	43c Southern Lights	0.80☐	0.30☐
AAT-091	Maiden Voyage Aurora Australis		
	$1.20 RSV Aurora Australis	2.20☐	1.50☐

AAT-092. Adelie Penguin

AAT-093. Elephant Seal

AAT-094. Northern Giant Petrel

AAT-095. Weddell Seal

AAT-096. Emperor Penguin

Antarctic Regional Wildlife   1992 14 May

NO.	DESCRIPTION	MUH	FU
AAT-092	45c Adelie Penguin	0.70☐	0.40☐
AAT-093	75c Elephant Seal	1.30☐	0.90☐
AAT-094	85c Northern Giant Petrel	1.50☐	0.90☐
AAT-095	95c Weddell Seal	1.80☐	1.30☐
AAT-096	$1.20 Emperor Penguin	2.40☐	1.80☐

AAT-098. Fur Seal

AAT-097. Royal Penguin

AAT-099. King Penguin

Antarctic Regional Wildlife - Series II   1993 14 Jan

NO.	DESCRIPTION	MUH	FU
AAT-097	$1 Royal Penguin	1.50☐	1.30☐
AAT-098	$1.40 Fur Seal	2.00☐	1.50☐
AAT-099	$1.50 King Penguin	2.50☐	2.00☐

AAT-100. Husky

AAT-101. Dog Team

AAT-104. Hourglass   AAT-105. Minke Whale
Dolphins

AAT-102. Husky

AAT-103. Husky Team

AAT-107. Humpback Whale

The Last Huskies   **1994 13 Jan**
AAT-100   45c Husky   0.70☐   0.30☐
AAT-101   75c Dog Team   1.00☐   0.70☐
AAT-102   85c Husky   1.30☐   0.90☐
AAT-103 $1.05 Husky Team   2.00☐   2.00☐
          First Day Cover (4) AP   6.50☐

AAT-108. Killer Whale

Whales & Dolphins   **1995 15 Jun**
AAT-104   45c Hourglass Dolphins   0.90☐   0.80☐
AAT-105   45c Minke Whale   0.90☐   0.80☐
AAT-106   Se-tenant pair (AAT-104/AAT-105) 2.00☐   2.00☐
AAT-107   45c Humpback Whale   1.00☐   0.90☐
AAT-108 $1.00 Killer Whale   2.00☐   1.50☐
AAT-109   Miniature Sheet (4)   6.00☐   6.00☐
          First Day Cover (stamps) AP   6.00☐
          First Day Cover (Miniature Sheet) AP   6.00☐

AAT-109. Miniature Sheet (4)

AAT-110. Rafting Sea Ice   AAT-111. Shadows on Plateau

AAT-113. Ice Cave

AAT-114. Twelve Lakes

Antarctic Landscapes   1996 16 May

AAT-110	45c Rafting Sea Ice	0.90	0.80
AAT-111	45c Shadows on Plateau	0.90	0.80
AAT-112	Se-tenant pair (110/111)	2.20	1.80
AAT-113	$1 Ice Cave	2.20	2.00
AAT-114	$1.20 Twelve Lakes	2.50	2.40
	First Day Cover AP		6.00

AAT-116. Apple Huts   AAT-115. Interior of Hut

AAT-118. Surveying

AAT-119. Measuring Light

AAT-120. Geologists leaving Camp

50th Anniversary of ANARE   1997 15 May
Australian National Antarctic Research Expedition

AAT-115	45c Interior of Hut	1.00	0.80
AAT-116	45c Apple Huts	1.00	0.80
AAT-117	45c Se-tenant pair (115/116)	2.00	2.00
AAT-118	95c Surveying	2.20	2.00
AAT-119	$1.05 Measuring Light	2.50	1.90
AAT-120	$1.20 Geologists leaving Camp	2.50	2.00
	First Day Cover (4) AP		8.00

AAT-121. RSV Aurora Australis   AAT-122. Skidoos - Motorised Toboggans

AAT-124. Helicopter lifting a Quad

AAT-125. Antarctic Hagglunds

Antarctic Territory Transport   1998 5 Mar

AAT-121	45c RSV Aurora Australis	0.90	0.80
AAT-122	45c Skidoos - Motorised Toboggans	0.90	0.80
AAT-123	Se-tenant pair (AAT-121/AAT-122)	2.00	2.00
AAT-124	$1 Helicopter lifting a Quad	2.00	1.60
AAT-125	$2 Antarctic Hagglunds	3.50	3.00
	First Day Cover (6) AP		8.00

NO.	DESCRIPTION	MUH	FU	NO.	DESCRIPTION	MUH	FU

AAT-126. Mawson   AAT-127. Cape Denison

AAT-131 Adelie Penguin   AAT-132 Emperor Penguin

Antarctic Penguins   2000 24 Jul

AAT-131	45c Adelie Penguin	1.00☐	0.70☐
AAT-132	45c Emperor Penguin	1.00☐	0.70☐
AAT-133	Se-tenant pair (131/132)	2.00☐	1.80☐
	First Day Cover (2) AP		3.00☐

AAT-129. Huskies   AAT-130. Mawson's Hut

Mawson   1999 13 May

AAT-126	45c Mawson as a young man	1.00☐	0.50☐
AAT-127	45c Cape Denison Home of the Blizzard	1.00☐	0.50☐
AAT-128	Se-tenant pair AAT-126/AAT-127	2.00☐	1.50☐
AAT-129	90c Huskies	2.00☐	1.80☐
AAT-130	$1.35 Mawson's Hut under repair	3.00☐	2.20☐
	First Day Cover (4) AP		8.00☐

AAT- 134. Discovery - Antartica
AAT- 135. Discovery - Louis Bernacchi
AAT- 136. Discovery - Nimrod
AAT- 137. Discovery - Sth Magnetic Pole
AAT- 138. Discovery - Taylor & Debenham

AAT- 139. Exploration - First Radio
AAT- 140. Exploration - First Flight
AAT- 141. Exploration - Sir Douglas Mawson
AAT- 142. Exploration - BANZARE
AAT- 143. Exploration - Australia's Claim

AAT- 144. Settlement & Science - ANARE establishment
AAT- 145. Settlement & Science - Transport
AAT- 146. Settlement & Science - Aurora
AAT- 147. Settlement & Science - Climate
AAT- 148. Settlement & Science - Clothing

AAT- 149. Technology & Communication- Nella Dan
AAT- 150. Technology & Communication- First Women
AAT- 151. Technology & Communication- Communications
AAT- 152. Technology & Communication- Tourism
AAT- 153. Technology & Communication- Satellite

NO.	DESCRIPTION	MUH	FU

Australians in the Antarctic — 2001 17 May

NO.	DESCRIPTION	MUH	FU
AAT-134	5c Discovery - Antartica	0.30	0.30
AAT-135	5c Discovery - Louis Bernacchi	0.30	0.30
AAT-136	5c Discovery - Nimrod	0.30	0.30
AAT-137	5c Discovery - Sth Magnetic Pole	0.30	0.30
AAT-138	5c Discovery - Taylor & Debenham	0.30	0.30
AAT-139	10c Exploration - First Radio	0.30	0.30
AAT-140	10c Exploration - First Flight	0.30	0.30
AAT-141	10c Exploration - Sir Douglas Mawson	0.30	0.30
AAT-142	10c Exploration - BANZARE	0.30	0.30
AAT-143	10c Exploration - Australia's Claim	0.30	0.30
AAT-144	25c Settlement & Science - ANARE Establishment	0.40	0.40
AAT-145	25c Settlement & Science - Transport	0.40	0.40
AAT-146	25c Settlement & Science - Aurora	0.40	0.40
AAT-147	25c Settlement & Science - Climate	0.40	0.40
AAT-148	25c Settlement & Science - Clothing	0.40	0.40
AAT-149	45c Technology & Communication - Nella Dan	0.70	0.50
AAT-150	45c Technology & Communication - First Women	0.70	0.70
AAT-151	45c Technology & Communication - Communications	0.70	0.70
AAT-152	45c Technology & Communication - Tourism	0.70	0.70
AAT-153	45c Technology & Communication - Satellite	0.70	0.70
AAT-154	$4.25 Sheetlet of 20	10.00	8.50
	First Day Cover (Set x 2) AP		12.00

AAT-160. Davis Station   AAT-161. Casey Station

AAT-162. Macquarie Island Staton   AAT-163. Mawson Station

Australian Antarctic Territory Research — 2002 02 Jul

		MUH	FU
AAT-160	45c Davis Station	0.80	0.60
AAT-161	45c Casey Station	0.80	0.60
AAT-162	45c Macquarie Island Staton	0.80	0.60
AAT-163	45c Mawson Station	0.80	0.60
AAT-164	Se-tenant block x 4 (160/164)	4.00	3.00
	First Day Cover (Block x 4) AP		7.00

AAT-165. Kista Dan (1953-1957)   AAT-166. Magga Dan (1953-1961)

AAT- 155. Mother & Pup on Ice   AAT- 156. Bull on Ice

AAT- 157. Mother & Pup Underwater   AAT- 158. Adult Underwater

Leopard Seals — 2001 11 Sep

		MUH	FU
AAT-155	45c Mother & Pup on Ice	0.80	0.80
AAT-156	45c Bull on Ice	0.80	0.80
AAT-157	45c Mother & Pup Underwater	0.80	0.80
AAT-158	Adult Underwater	0.80	0.80
AAT-159	Block of Four (155-158)	4.00	4.00
	First Day Cover (Block x 4)		5.00

AAT-168. Thala Dan (1957-1982)

AAT-169. Nella Dan (1962-1987)

Antartic Ships — 2003 15 Apr

		MUH	FU
AAT-165	50c Kista Dan (1953-1957)	0.80	0.60
AAT-166	50c Magga Dan (1953-1961)	0.80	0.60
AAT-167	Se-tenant pair (165/166)	2.00	2.00
AAT-168	$1.00 Thala Dan (1957-1982)	1.80	1.20
AAT-169	$1.45 Nella Dan (1962-1987)	2.80	1.50
	First Day Cover (4) AP		8.00

AAT-170. Naming Ceremony   AAT-171. View of Mawson Station

AAT-173. Floating Caravan

AAT-174. Auster Penguin Rookery

AAT Mawson Station 1954-2004

2004 13 Feb

NO.	Description	MUH	FU
AAT-170	50c Naming Ceremony	0.80 ▢	0.60 ▢
AAT-171	50c View of Mawson Station	0.80 ▢	0.60 ▢
AAT-172	$1.00 Se-tenant pair (170/171)	2.00 ▢	1.60 ▢
AAT-173	$1.00 Floating Caravan	1.80 ▢	1.80 ▢
AAT-174	$1.45 Auster Penguin Rookery	2.80 ▢	2.50 ▢
	First Day Cover (4) AP		6.50 ▢

AAT-175 Helicopter   AAT-176 DHC-2 Beaver

AAT-178 Pilatus PC-6

AAT-179 Douglas DC-3

AVIATION IN THE AAT

2005 Sept 6

NO.	Description	MUH	FU
AAT-175	50c Helicopter	.80 ▢	0.60 ▢
AAT-176	50c DHC-2 Beaver	.80 ▢	0.60 ▢
AAT-177	Se-tenant pair (175/176)	1.70 ▢	1.30 ▢
AAT-178	$1.00 Pilatus PC-6	2.00 ▢	1.30 ▢
AAT-179	$1.45 Douglas DC-3	2.50 ▢	2.20 ▢
	First Day Cover (4) AP		6.50 ▢

AAT – 181 Adult with egg   AAT – 180
                                 Marching to nesting sites

AAT – 183 Male and female

AAT – 182 Birds sparring

ROYAL PENGUINS

2007 7 August

NO.	Description	MUH	FU
AAT – 180	0.50 Marching to nesting sites	0.90 ▢	0.70 ▢
AAT – 181	0.50 Adult with egg	0.90 ▢	0.70 ▢
AAT – 182	$1.00 Birds sparring	1.60 ▢	1.20 ▢
AAT – 183	$1.00 Male and female	1.60 ▢	1.20 ▢
	First Day Cover (4) AP		6.50 ▢

Australasian Philatelic Wholesalers Pty Ltd

Exciting NEW Australian Packets

Higher Values Only

Following hundreds of requests over the years, we have finally produced packs of all different higher values only.

The only stamps included are those with a face value over the basic postage rate at the time of issue.

All packs contain issues from Pre-Decimal to recent issues and both definitive and commemorative issues.

Order Form

PER PACK	DESCRIPTION	PRICE	QTY	TOTAL
	Australian Higher Values			
200	Different	12.00		
250	Different	30.00		
300	Different	55.00		
350	Different	87.50		
400	Different	120.00		
450	Different	230.00		
500	Different	350.00		
	Postage & Packing	3.00	—	
	Total Amount			

Please send this order to:

Name ....

Address ....

Postcode ....

I am Paying by: Cheque/Money Order (made payable to Australasian Philatelic Wholesalers Pty Ltd)

or Bankcard/ Visacard/ Mastercard/Amex/DinersClub (circle one) Expiry date on card: . . . .

|_|_|_| |_|_|_| |_|_|_| |_|_|_| |_|_|_|

Signature : ....

Stanley Gibbons

2008 Australia Colour Catalogue

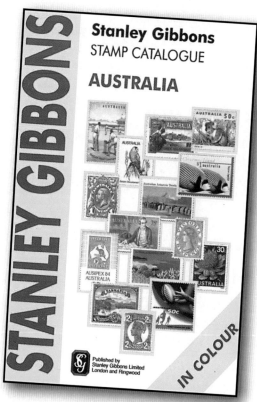

Stanley Gibbons
STAMP CATALOGUE

AUSTRALIA

Published by
Stanley Gibbons Limited
London and Ringwood

IN COLOUR

$67.50

*This **NEW 4th Edition (2008)** in **FULL COLOUR** and with the unique and sought after Stanley Gibbons numbering system includes:*

- AUSTRALIAN COLONIES all comprehensively listed
- AUSTRALIA PRE-DECIMAL – Specialised listing including flaws/varieties in KGV and KGV1 periods
- AUSTRALIA – DECIMAL PERIOD (1967 – 2008) – Including all booklets in full colour
- AUSTRALIA O.S. ISSUES
- NEW GUINEA (1914 – 1932)
- NORFOLK ISLAND (1947 – 2008)
- PAPUA & NEW GUINEA (1952-1975)
- CHRISTMAS ISLAND (1958 – 2008)
- AUSTRALIAN ANTARCTIC TERRITORY (1958 – 2008)
- COCOS ISLAND (1963 – 2008)
- BRITISH COMMONWEALTH OCCUPATION FORCES - 1946 Issues
- NAURU (1916 – 1965)
- INTERNATIONAL PHILATELIC GLOSSARY

Bound in a NEW STYLE A4 format this new 2008 catalogue caters for both the new and specialized collectors seeking more detailed and advanced information.

This NEW 2008 edition, and latest, is a welcome addition to the highly popular Stanley Gibbons range.

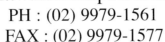

The Premier Guide for Australian Coin and Banknote Values

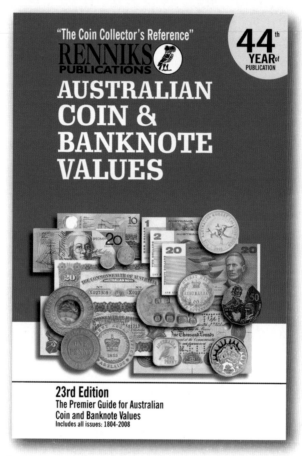

"The Coin Collector's Reference"

RENNIKS PUBLICATIONS

44th YEAR of PUBLICATION

AUSTRALIAN COIN & BANKNOTE VALUES

23rd Edition
The Premier Guide for Australian
Coin and Banknote Values
Includes all issues: 1804-2008

This comprehensive guide to Australian Coin & Banknote Values contains over 1,900 photographs, and thousands of valuations. This book is a must for all collectors, whether you are just beginning or an advanced collector. Latest information compiled on computer databases ensures up to date accuracy of pricing. Quality reproduction of photos makes it easy to identify items. Plus NEW Royal Australian Mint, Note Printing Australia & GoldCorp products. Softcover and hardcover editons available.

A perfect gift for any collector.
Softcover or Hardcover

RENNIKS PUBLICATIONS

Available from your your favourite stamp or coin dealer, as well as from bookstores & newsagents.

Illuminated Magnifiers

LU 5 LED M
Stainless steel LED illuminated magnifier
First class acrylic lens and ergonomic modern design metal handle. Excellent optical quality. Lens diameter: 9 cm. Magnification: 2X. Battery operated, 3 x button cell SR 54 to IEC standard (included), 2 very bright LEDs. Soft material cover to protect lens.

$49.95

LU 24 LED
Pocket magnifier with LED
Magnification: 10X, glass lens
1 LED. Foldaway.
Lens diameter: 18mm.
Battery operated (battery incl. /2 x 3AG12).

$16.50

LU 190 LED
LED illuminated magnifier
Lens diameter: 37mm,
magnification 3.2X, glass lens,
casing: aluminium.
Battery operated (battery incl. /2 x AA 1.5V).
Total length: 173mm. 6X LED's.

$49.95

LU 170
Illuminated magnifier
With light, 5-X magnification, lens size 40 x 36mm, aspherical, retractable. Requres 2 x AAA/UM4 batteries (not included).

$13.75

LU 4 LED
Frameless LED illuminated magnifier
With high-quality acrylic lens and modern ergonomically designed handle. Excellent optical quality. Lens diameter 7.5cm. Magnification: 2.5X. 2 LED's. Battery operated, 3x coin cell SR54 (IEC standard/battery incl.). Comes in a soft protective pouch.

$27.50

LU 150
LED illuminated magnifier -
extra bright light, now with LED's, battery operated, adjustable focus ring, 10X magnification with ultra-illumination of the object. Runs on 2 x 1.5V C/LR14 batteries. 2 bright LED's.

$27.50

RENNIKS PUBLICATIONS PTY LTD
Incorporating: **Brooklands Books Australia • LighthousePhilatelics**
Unit 3 37-39 Green Street Banksmeadow NSW 2019 Australia
Tel: (02) 9695 7055 Fax: (02) 9695 7355 Email: info@renniks.com
Website: www.renniks.com

PETERSHAM STAMP & COIN SUPER FAIR

AUSTRALASIA   AUSTRALASIA

**Proudly organised by the Stamp & Coin Dealers'
Association of Australasia Inc.
(SCDAA)**

Twenty-seven local & interstate dealers buying & selling
stamps, coins, banknotes, postal history, postcards,
phonecards, pins, medals, ephemera & other collectables.

2009

2009 - 2010 SHOW DATES

2010

29th March, 2009 – 31st May, 2009
30th August, 2009 – 29th November, 2009
31st January, 2010– 30th May, 2010
29th August, 2010 – 31st October, 2010

& thereafter every fifth Sunday of those months which have five Sundays

Petersham Town Hall

107 Crystal Street, Petersham (Sydney)

Close to Petersham railway station

9.30am till 4pm
Admission Only $1
Cafeteria
FREE VALUATIONS

Bring that old collection along & find out what it is worth.

Trade with confidence in
SCDAA Members
www.scdaa.com

AUSTRALASIA   AUSTRALASIA

 **Lighthouse**
>> Symbol of Quality <<

Insist on the best...

STOCK BOOKS WITH WHITE PAGES - MORE POPULAR TYPES

THE BASIC REQUIREMENT FOR EVERY COLLECTOR...
White cardboard pages with glassine pockets. All stock books have double glassine interleaving. A choice of five colours. Stock books with 48 or more pages are double linen hinged.

LIGHTHOUSE STOCK BOOKS - HARD COVERS

Ref No	Size in mm	Pages	Interleaving	Binding	Price
L 4/8	230 x 305	16	double	rigid	$15.00
L 4/16	230 x 305	32	double	rigid	$25.00
L 4/24	230 x 305	48	double	DLH*	$42.50
L 4/24T	230 x 305	48 (divided)	double	DLH*	$49.95
L 4/32	230 x 305	64	double	DLH*	$49.95
L 4/32T	230 x 305	64 (divided)	double	DLH*	$59.95

*Double Linen Hinged

LIGHTHOUSE STOCK BOOKS WITH BLACK PAGES - MORE POPULAR TYPES

The premier choice of the discriminating philatelist, and for many collectors who prefer stock books with black pages for the presentation of their stamps. Stock books are distinguished by many special features including:
- ✔ Crystal clear pockets
- ✔ Double glassine interleaving
- ✔ Available 5 x colours

LIGHTHOUSE STOCK BOOKS - HARD COVERS

Ref No	Size in mm	Pages	Interleaving	Binding	Price
LS 4/8	230 x 305	16	double	rigid	$23.50
LS 4/16	230 x 305	32	double	rigid	$29.50
LS 4/24	230 x 305	48	double	DLH*	$49.95
LS 4/32	230 x 305	64	double	DLH*	$55.90

*Double Linen Hinged

LEATHER STOCK BOOKS WITH CRYSTAL CLEAR POCKETS AND INTERLEAVING - MORE POPULAR TYPES

These are Lighthouse's most sophisticated books. All have crystal clear pockets and double interleaving. Nothing to spoil the viewing of your stamps. Available in a choice of five colours.
✔ double interleaving ✔ black or white pages (see listing) ✔ padded cover made of deluxe leather ✔ in protective cardboard box

LIGHTHOUSE STOCK BOOKS - CRYSTAL CLEAR

Ref No	Size in mm	Pages	Binding	Price
LZS 4/16 N	230 x 305	32 black	DLH*	$62.50
LZS 4/24 N	230 x 305	48 black	DLH*	$88.90
LZS 4/32 N	230 x 305	64 black	DLH*	$115.00

*Double Linen Hinged

STOCKBOOK SPECIALS

✔ padded covers ✔ double linen hinged ✔ black or white pages (see listing) ✔ interleaving

Ref No	Size in mm	Pages	Binding	Price
LP 4/30	230 x 305	60 white	DLH*	$39.95
LSP 4/30	230 x 305	60 black	DLH*	$49.95

*double linen hinged

Also refer to the Lighthouse Product Guide for the complete range.

Available from all good stamp shops, or direct from Renniks Publications

Shop
where you see this sign!

You can buy with confidence from members of the
Australasian Philatelic Traders' Association Inc.

APTA is a professional organisation with members
throughout Australia, New Zealand and overseas.

**For the nearest APTA member to you
visit our website www.apta.com.au**

**You can also email us at admin@apta.com.au or phone
or write to us for a complete up-to-date list of APTA dealers.**

APTA members can also issue **Warranty Certificates**
for more substantial purchases.

APTA Gift Vouchers are the ideal present for any collector.
They are available on-line from our website, by email or phone,
or you can write to us at the address below.

Serving Philately since 1948
**APTA, P.O. Box 415, BLACKBURN VIC. 3130
Tel 0409 123 393 or email: admin@apta.com.au**

Vario Stocksheet System

LIGHTHOUSE VARIO STOCK SHEETS

This versatile collection system has been developed for the discriminating collector who desires flexibility and wants to give his collection his special, personal touch and creativity.

Lighthouse offers the VARIO sheets in double-sided black and one-sided clear sheets. The two-sided black sheets have crystal clear pockets. Please refer to the diagram shown regarding the various pocket sizes and formats.

The outside dimensions are 216x280mm. Free of acids and chemical softeners.

★ Double Sided - Sealed On 3 Sides
★ Clear Heat Sealed Pockets (Black Or Clear)
★ Fit Standard 3-ring & 4-ring Binders

PACK OF 5 $7.00

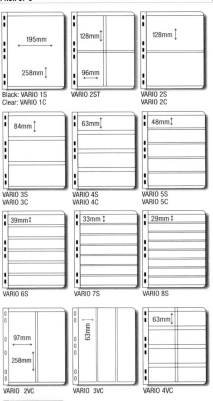

Black: VARIO 1S
Clear: VARIO 1C — 195mm / 258mm

VARIO 2ST — 128mm / 96mm

VARIO 2S
VARIO 2C — 128mm

VARIO 3S
VARIO 3C — 84mm

VARIO 4S
VARIO 4C — 63mm

VARIO 5S
VARIO 5C — 48mm

VARIO 6S — 39mm

VARIO 7S — 33mm

VARIO 8S — 29mm

VARIO 2VC — 97mm / 258mm

VARIO 3VC — 63mm

VARIO 4VC — 63mm

VARIO ZWL
interleaves

VARIO BINDERS AND SLIPCASES

VARIO F	VARIO 4-ring Binder & Slipcase (capacity 30 vario sheets)	$49.95
VARIO G	VARIO D-ring Binder & Slipcase (capacity 60 vario sheets)	$69.50
CLVABIN	Vario "Classic" Binder	$34.95
BLATTW	Page lifters for VARIO binders (2)	$6.50

VARIO INTERLEAVING

VARIOZWL	Acid-free plastic interleaving (pack 5)	$4.25

VARIO album. For collecting and sorting

Ideal for storing, re-arranging or keeping all those extras. Expand the album by adding more VARIO or VARIO PLUS pages.

- Padded 4-ring binder with matching slipcase. Colours: red, blue, green, brown and black
- Black double-sided VARIO 6S pages with 180 strips + 2 sheet-lifters
- 2 black fly-leaves
- Total capacity 30 pages.

VARIO F6S
Vario 4-ring Binder & Slipcase with 15 x Vario 6

$57.95

Australasian Philatelic Wholesalers Pty Ltd
Packets and Mixtures Order Form

PER PACK	DESCRIPTION	PRICE	QTY	TOTAL
	Australia			
100	Different	1.30		
200	Different	2.60		
300	Different	4.00		
400	Different	6.00		
500	Different	10.00		
600	Different	15.00		
800	Different	30.00		
1,000	Different	70.00		
1,200	Different	160.00		
	Large Size Only, Australia			
100	Different	1.80		
200	Different	3.60		
300	Different	6.00		
400	Different	10.00		
500	Different	17.00		
600	Different	32.00		
800	Different	120.00		
1,000	Different	200.00		
	Mint Unhinged, Australia			
100	Different	15.00		
200	Different	35.00		
300	Different	60.00		
400	Different	100.00		
	Australian Imprint Blocks of 4			
20	Different	35.00		
30	Different	55.00		
40	Different	75.00		
50	Different	100.00		
	Total Column 1			

PER PACK	DESCRIPTION	PRICE	QTY	TOTAL
	Australian On Paper Mixtures			
1 Kilo	Australian Charity Grade	20.00		
10 Kilo	Australian Charity Grade	150.00		
1 Kilo	Australian Comms. Only	34.00		
10 Kilo	Australian Comms. Only	260.00		
	British Pacific Islands (No Aust or NZ)			
100	Different	10.00		
200	Different	35.00		
300	Different	65.00		
500	Different	120.00		
800	Different	300.00		
1,000	Different	400.00		
1,500	Different	650.00		
	Great Britain			
100	Different	3.00		
200	Different	6.00		
300	Different	10.50		
400	Different	18.00		
500	Different	26.00		
600	Different	37.00		
800	Different	68.00		
1,000	Different	110.00		
1,500	Different	350.00		
	New Zealand			
100	Different	2.50		
200	Different	5.00		
300	Different	8.50		
400	Different	13.00		
500	Different	20.00		
600	Different	30.00		
700	Different	55.00		
800	Different	80.00		
1,000	Different	175.00		
1,250	Different	350.00		
1,500	Different	995.00		
	Total Column 2			

Total Both Columns $

Postage & Packing $3.00

Total $

Please send this order to:

Name ....

Address ....

.... Postcode ....

I am Paying by: Cheque/Money Order (made payable to Australasian Philatelic Wholesalers Pty Ltd)

or Bankcard/ Visacard/ Mastercard/Amex/DinersClub (circle one) Expiry date on card: . . . .

Signature : ....

Mail or Fax this order form to:

APW P/L
10a Atherton Road,
Oakleigh V 3166

Phone 03 9568 6441
Fax 03 9568 5169